Drag

Berkeley Series in British Studies

EDITED BY JAMES VERNON

Drag

A BRITISH HISTORY

Jacob Bloomfield

UNIVERSITY OF CALIFORNIA PRESS

University of California Press
Oakland, California

© 2023 by Jacob Bloomfield

Library of Congress Cataloging-in-Publication Data
First paperback printing 2024
Names: Bloomfield, Jacob, 1990- author.
Title: Drag : a British history / Jacob Bloomfield.
Other titles: Berkeley series in British studies ; 23.
Description: Oakland, California : University of California Press,
[2023] | Series: Berkeley series in British Studies ; 23 | Includes
bibliographical references and index.
Identifiers: LCCN 2022053629 (print) | LCCN 2022053630 (ebook) |
ISBN 9780520409651 (pb) | ISBN 9780520393332 (ebook) Subjects:
LCSH: Drag queens—Great Britain—History. Classification: LCC
HQ77.2.G7 .B566 2023 (print) | LCC HQ77.2.G7 (ebook) | DDC
306.760941—dc23/eng/20230111
LC record available at https://lccn.loc.gov/2022053629
LC ebook record available at https://lccn.loc.gov/2022053630

Manufactured in the United States of America

32 31 30 29 28 27 26 25 24
10 9 8 7 6 5 4 3 2 1

The publisher and the University of California Press Foundation gratefully acknowledge the generous support of the Ahmanson Foundation Endowment Fund in Humanities.

To Jack

Contents

Illustrations

Acknowledgments

I first wish to thank the team at the University of California Press for their kind support of this project. James Vernon has been the ideal editor. I will be forever grateful for his rigor, advice, and patience. I am grateful to my diligent copy editor, Sharron Wood.

The Zukunftskolleg at the University of Konstanz has provided a wonderful environment for me in which to complete this book. I am grateful for the fantastic support the Zukunftskolleg provided, and for the support of the University of Kent School of History, which generously gave me an Honorary Research Fellowship.

I have been fortunate to receive support, financial and otherwise, from several generous institutions. This publication has been made possible by the Jones Travelling Grant administered by the University of Manchester, the Social History Society 2018 Keele Conference Bursary administered by the Keele University School of Humanities, a research grant from the Society for Theatre Research, the Scouloudi Foundation in association with the Institute of Historical Research, the University of East Anglia Archives and Collections Visiting Fellowship, and the Zukunftskolleg. I am also grateful to the Royal Historical Society for making me an Early Career Member.

Portions of this book have previously appeared as Jacob Bloomfield, "Male Cross-Dressing Performance in Britain, 1918–1970,"

PhD thesis (University of Manchester, 2018); Jacob Bloomfield, "*Splinters*: Cross-Dressing Ex-Servicemen on the Interwar Stage," *Twentieth Century British History* 30:1 (2019): 1–28; and Jacob Bloomfield, "*Soldiers in Skirts*: Cross-Dressing Ex-Servicemen, Sexuality and Censorship in Post-War Britain," in *Drag Histories, Herstories and Hairstories: Drag in a Changing Scene, Volume* 2, ed. Mark Edward and Stephen Farrier.

Portions of this book have been presented for the following academic conferences, events, and organizations: the Social History Society Annual Conference (2015, 2018); the South East Hub for History Conference (2015); the Historicising Trans* Conference (2015); DUCKIE: Lady Malcolm's Servants' Ball (2016); the International Federation for Theatre Research Conference (2016, 2021); the Manchester Drag Symposium (2017); Masculinities in Twentieth-Century Britain (2018); the Centre for the History of Medicine, Ethics and Medical Humanities and the Centre for the History of War, Media and Society, University of Kent (2019); Queer Research Network Manchester (2019); and the Queer History Conference (2019).

I have been gratified by the generosity of the academic community who have lent edits, advice, and pastoral care. There are too many charitable, kind, and sagacious academic mentors to name here, but they include: Laura Doan and Frank Mort (my PhD supervisors who made me a proper historian), the thoughtful peer reviewers for this book, Paul R. Deslandes and Charlotte Wildman (my extraordinarily supportive viva examiners), Christina Wald and Martin Rempe (my wonderful local hosts at the University of Konstanz), Michael Bronski, Dan Edmonds, David Gilbert, Matt Houlbrook, Louise Jackson, Dominic Janes, Michelle Johansen, Claire Jones, Amane Kasai, Robert V. Kenny, Eric Lott, Neil McKenna, Ben Mechen, Steve Nicholson, Edward Owens, Lisa Z. Sigel, Bertrand Taithe, Charles Upchurch, Emma Vickers, and Chris Waters. I am also indebted to the many archivists who have helped me immeasurably, including Steven Dryden, Justine Mann, and Simon Sladen. My students throughout the years have been consistently curious, canny, and creative; I am a better scholar thanks to them. Thanks to Focusmate for helping to keep me on task.

I have been blessed by the support of lovely friends who have kindly housed me on my many archival ventures. Endless thanks to Sam and Leo, Verity and Alex, McAsh and Aunt Jane, Oli, Jon, Jo, Sol, Kirsty, Reem and Beth, Tuppie, and Urte for their love and charity. Thanks also to my New York friends, including Jonah who has provided laughter and challenging debates. Moses Berner, Sylvia, Camilla, Kasumi, Sophie (and Annie), and Jack McGinn have kept me safe. Tai and her mother Ren kept my spirits up.

I owe so much to the numerous great teachers in my life. Ed Herzman, Rebecca Morrissey, Michael Kabot, Ms. Lasalle, Ms. Steffen, Doc, Esther, Kirsten, Franny, Wendell, and Karen—I don't know where I would be without your brilliance. Thanks to Dave Arroyo for always telling me to "go for it." The wisdom, encouragement, and loving toughness of David Vadim has always spurred me on.

My family has supported me in every way throughout this process. I am so fortunate to have them by my side. All my love to Mom, Dad, Caleb, and our beloved family dogs. Thanks also to Lynette, who has played no small part in raising me and continues to provide love, kindness, and delicious food.

Introduction

On the evening of 6 February 1958, Ronald John Hill entered the Twentieth Century Theatre in Notting Hill and took his seat seven rows from the stage. Hill attended the theater that evening not as a patron, but in his capacity as secretary to the Lord Chamberlain's Office, Britain's state theater censor.[1] Hill's task that night—not an unusual one for those under the employ of the Lord Chamberlain—was to observe the "all-male revue" *We're No Ladies* (1958), which starred an ensemble of men dressed as women.[2] The secretary was to judge whether the content featured in that night's program constituted indecent material and to report his findings back to the Office.

Seated around him in the filled stalls of the theater, as he noted later, was an audience of "most respectable" people with "many accompanied by wives and girl-friends."[3] After the orchestra had struck up the overture and the curtain was raised, Hill must have made himself somewhat conspicuous to his neighbors in the seats close by as he anxiously struggled to take diligent notes in the darkness of theater. The studiousness with which Hill carried out this task belied the frivolous content of his transcriptions.

Some of the gags the secretary observed were relatively wholesome:

CORAL: Well, it wasn't me who was appearing in that notorious
   Seaweed Nightclub last Saturday.
MIRANDA: Well, as a matter of fact, I did a wonderful dance there,
   wearing only twelve beads.
CORAL: Yes, and ten of those were perspiration.[4]

Yet Hill noted that, on this night, the cast of female impersonators uttered some raunchier gags that were not in the version of the script approved by the Lord Chamberlain's Office.[5] Such dialogue included references to sex work:

[PERFORMER 1:] I [w]as standing on the corner of Bond Street
   minding me own business.
[PERFORMER 2:] How's business?
[PERFORMER 1:] Dreadful[6]

References to homosexual subculture:

MAN: Is this the Gypsy Encampment
HAG: *It's Camp all right*[7]

And allusions to cruising for sex while cross-dressed:

She went out with a Pole and came back with a Czech [cheque][8]

Hill was stubbornly unmoved by humor of this type, and he was surprised that the "large" and "most respectable" audience around him reacted to the jokes with great enthusiasm. "The introductory remark 'This is Camp all right' which is specialised actors' slang for a homosexual gathering was greeted with a roar of laughter from the whole audience," he recalled, "who must thus be more familiar with the phraseology of the perverted than appeared."[9] Another source of bemusement for Hill was the glamour on show that evening. "The show was very well dressed—how do they find the money," the secretary wondered, adding that "some of the actors were so good they might have been thought to be women."[10]

Hill left the theater concluding that the producers of *We're No Ladies* were not only guilty of providing "mediocre revue/variety entertainment" but that they had also violated theater censorship laws by going off-script that night.[11] Nonetheless, Hill magnanimously suggested to his superiors in the Lord Chamberlain's Office that the producers of the show be let off with a "stern warning" rather than being prosecuted.[12] As far as the act of female impersonation was concerned, Hill expressed discomfort but ultimate acquiescence. While he admitted euphemistically that "my impression as to the habits of some of the actors, whilst not given here, is pretty firmly formed in my own mind," he surmised that he could find "no concrete evidence of the Twentieth Century Theatre becoming a focal point for pederasts."[13] Hill further conceded that drag performance enjoyed a privileged position within Britain's theatrical heritage and he was thus resigned to the practice continuing unabated in general, despite its potentially immoral connotations. "There is no law which prevents female impersonation on the stage; it is in fact as old as the stage," he noted.[14]

Others, however, saw the female impersonation in *We're No Ladies* as a matter of much graver concern. One letter the Lord Chamberlain's Office received regarding the show contended that the performance was "in fact a vehicle for the basest perversion—a smutty badly performed homosexual orgy, in which the 'converted' audience joins—it is not even funny."[15] The correspondent, H.C.R.A. Bennett, took particular exception to the singing of "God Save the Queen" at the show's closing—a common practice in the contemporary theater—which some of the female impersonators had warbled in soprano voices. "That these men exist and that they work their evil on each other we all know," Bennett opined, "but to stand and sing the 'National Anthem' in both 'soprano' and normal male voices . . . is an insult to a gracious lady and a great position, and an affront to English people."[16] Other letters followed along similar lines. "I was appalled and amazed," announced one Brian Boss, "that such a production as 'We are no Ladies' [sic] . . . should be allowed to take place publicly and even more that it should be open to youths and children. . . . [The Lord Chamberlain] should certainly pay a visit to this 'show' and see for himself the blatant and undisguised perversion which is displayed."[17] A. P. J. Rydekker, another complainant, surmised that "the entire performance was openly suggestive of homosexuality."[18] What constituted an evening of pleasurable light entertainment to the audience described in Hill's report was clearly a profoundly distressing experience for others.

We're No Ladies was a lowbrow drag show, cobbled together by dame comedians Phil Starr and Terry Dennis, which experienced a short run of only five nights in February 1958.[19] Yet looking at the Lord Chamberlain's file on this revue provides us with an edifying glimpse into what mid-twentieth-century British society made of men wearing women's clothes onstage. That file records numerous examples of what drag represented in the minds of contemporary spectators: airy popular entertainment, a source of humor, second-rate comedy, tackiness, glamour, timeworn theatrical heritage, pederasty, perversity, homosexuality, evil, and a threat to the nation and national institutions.

Given that so many meanings have been, and continue to be, attached to drag, an objective sense of what constitutes drag can be elusive. Drag is readily defined, in the past and in the present, as a kind of performance that comments on gender, even if gender is not always a central theme. Historically and presently, drag has also been invoked as a synonym for cross-dressing, but, as this book is concerned with drag on stage, screen, radio, and record, I will use drag to mean drag performance unless otherwise stated. During the century under consideration in this book, 1870 to 1970, drag artists were commonly referred to as "female impersonators"—men who wore women's clothes in the context of a performance—with the act of performing drag referred to as "female impersonation." Female impersonation and drag fall under the wider umbrella of cross-dressing (the wearing of clothes, in public or private, not typically associated with one's sex) and of gender variance (gender presentations or gendered understandings of oneself, expressed through comportment, clothes, and other means, that are unconventional in a given cultural context). Drag performance has historically been linked to, though is not synonymous with, the phenomenon of transvestism, cross-dressing that is suggested to be habitual, compulsive, or generally done repeatedly.

It is not unusual for scholarly and popular analyses of drag to essentialize the medium as being a "homosexual" or queer art form.[20] Literary critic Marjorie Garber has acknowledged drag's important place in queer culture while opining that a tendency among commentators to essentialize drag as a queer art form has obscured the medium's broader cultural significance.[21] *Drag: A British History* can be read in part as a queer history but, in focusing on the period from 1870 to 1970, when drag could comfortably lay claim to being a mass cultural form, the book asserts drag's important place in the history of British popular culture more generally. Further, owing to its status as a mass cultural form, drag during this period offered a space for British people from all sorts of backgrounds—not just same-sex-desiring and gender-nonconforming people—to consider and discuss gender and sexuality.

Drag: A British History deals specifically with male drag performance. The histories of male and female cross-dressing performance are distinct, with different cultural meanings having been being attached to each. Thus, I feel that male and female drag histories are not equatable enough to warrant a combined study in this case. Historical analyses of female drag have tended to focus on performers of the Victorian era and the early twentieth century like Vesta Tilley, Annie Hindle, and Sarah Bernhardt.[22] Other examples have included an investigation of the phenomenon of women playing Peter Pan in Garber's *Vested Interests: Cross-Dressing and Cultural Anxiety* (1992) and historian Jim Davis's research on women in the role of the principal boy in pantomime.[23] Yet the limited historiography on the subject leaves significant avenues of inquiry yet to be explored.[24] This book is not intended to be encyclopedic. The book will not provide a comprehensive account of all drag performers and performances. Instead, it focuses on representative case studies to reveal the varied renderings of drag and the manifold meanings associated with the art form between 1870 and 1970.

Drag: A British History will uncover how performances and meanings of drag emerged, developed, and changed, all while the art form aroused controversy. The controversies surrounding drag were culturally and historically specific, defying categorizations that mark prominent present-day cultural understandings of sexuality and gender expression, such as hetero/homosexuality and "homophobia." For all the anxieties it provoked, however, drag endured as an intrinsic part of British popular culture between 1870 and 1970, valued and enjoyed by audiences from all walks of life. Drag has not only persisted as a national cultural institution but has, in many ways, been at the forefront of new developments in nineteenth- and twentieth-century popular culture.

In illuminating drag's important place in British culture, this book unsettles narratives of repression that so often preoccupy the history of sexuality. Drag performances created positive experiences for practitioners and observers, such as fun, kinship, fulfillment, and career success, that could operate alongside sexual and gender-based repression.[25] Moreover, perceptions of drag, and male gender variance more widely, did not proceed linearly from a state of Victorian vilification to gradual acceptance. In studying the history of drag performance, we see that attitudes toward gender and sexuality do not fit neatly into a teleological narrative leading from subjugation to liberation. Culturally conservative Victorian attitudes did not seriously hinder the growth of drag as a theatrical form in the nineteenth century, nor did the liberalization of social and cultural attitudes in the 1950s and 1960s, usually associated with "permissiveness," prompt a newfound acceptance of the art form.

It is tempting, from a present-day standpoint, to understand historical objections to gender-variant men as evidence that female impersonators, and cross-dressers more generally, were part of a long-oppressed group resisting and challenging heteronormative understandings of gender and sexuality.[26] It is true that the state sometimes arrested, charged, and prosecuted men who wore women's clothes on the street, in venues such as public houses, and at parties, though there was no law that specifically illegalized cross-dressing.[27] It is also true that drag performance faced varying degrees of criticism from cultural observers. However, there was never a pronounced effort to eradicate male cross-dressing generally, and certainly no such effort to eradicate female impersonation from the stage. In that sense, negative historical assessments of drag performance by the press, the courts, the police, and other agents cannot be solely read as signs of authoritarian censure and closure. As we saw in the case of Secretary Hill, for example, if an observer critiqued or expressed discomfort regarding a certain drag performance, those negative sentiments did not necessarily extend to the art form as a whole, nor did such opinions always lead an observer to argue that the offending performance should be stamped out entirely. Negative, as well as positive, reactions to drag existed on a spectrum.

Nonetheless, it was the case that sometimes when men performed as women onstage, and when men wore women's clothes in general, it was read as a statement on their sexuality. Early public discussions surrounding male gender variance and its connection to sexual immorality demonstrate that the link between the two concepts was, historically, not always straightforward or particularly pronounced. From the early eighteenth century, if not earlier, groups of men were cultivating visible social networks oriented around a shared identification with feminine gender presentation and same-sex desire.[28] The members of this "molly" subculture would refer to each other using feminine "maiden names," exhibit effete behaviors, and engage in homosexual acts.[29] Contemporary observers were made aware of this subculture through firsthand experiences, court cases following raids on "molly houses" (public houses, inns, private residences, or other venues where mollies congregated), and published accounts.[30] For example, a 1709 pamphlet reported on groups of men who "are so far degenerated from all Masculine Deportment that they rather fancy themselves Women ... affecting to speak, walk, talk, curtsy, cry, scold & mimic all manner of Effeminacy."[31] By the mid-nineteenth century, the London guidebook *Yokel's Preceptor* (ca. 1855) was forcefully warning readers to beware of "the increase of these monsters in the shape of men, commonly called Margeries, Pooffs &c."[32] Other, less extreme expressions of unconventional masculinity were also increasingly deemed to be problematic by the eighteenth and nineteenth centuries. Ostentatiously fashionable men, known popularly as "macaronis" in the eighteenth century and "dandies" by the early nineteenth century, were regular subjects of mockery in the contemporary press due to their perceived effeminacy.[33]

Despite the growing prevalence of the association between male gender variance and sexual immorality in the eighteenth and nineteenth centuries, gender-variant men were not ubiquitously or straightforwardly perceived as a societal threat. While contemporary press treatments of macaronis and dandies might have appeared hostile on the surface, these critiques were more likely to express playful mockery, or even fascination, rather than serious censure.[34] Reports of outright cross-dressing, such as coverage of molly house raids or the arrests of individual cross-dressed men in public spaces, helped to dredge up a spectacle, but press attention on cases like these was often fleeting.[35] Some quarters of the press struck a hostile tone toward male cross-dressers ensnared by police, as in the case of the 1725/26 raid on Mother Clap's molly house, but the press was also prone to portraying cases involving male cross-dressing as amusing diversions, not unlike the drag performances that would increasingly populate nineteenth-century light entertainment.[36] Courtroom spectators, too, often saw trials involving male cross-dressing as a pleasurable amusement. Members of the public were known to flock to courtrooms where cross-dressed men could be seen in the dock. These trials were sometimes punctuated at regular increments with laughter or other open expressions of delight from the crowd, even as the court tried to cast gender-variant men as menacing.[37]

In a fashion similar to that of the press, eighteenth- to mid-nineteenth-century law enforcement was also inconsistent in its attitude toward male cross-dressing. The rate of arrests and convictions relating to the practice fluctuated throughout this period. Eighteenth-century molly house raids were purposefully presented as dramatic spectacles, often leading to the arrests of large groups of people, some of whom experienced penalties as severe as execution for homosexual offenses.[38] However, the raids were infrequent, and by the 1820s and 1830s they had mostly fallen out of favor as a law enforcement tactic.[39] The "drag ball" scene, extant in cities and suburbs across Britain, was lively, quotidian, and mostly uninterrupted by police action aside from some outstanding incidents.[40] Raids of drag balls only tended to occur if the events caused significant local social disturbance.[41] The policing of male cross-dressing from the 1820s and 1830s, in line with wider reforms of police tactics in the period, tended to place less of an emphasis on irregular spectacles. Arrests became more mundane, consistent, and more often targeted toward individual offenders.[42] Men who wore women's clothes in public could be charged with a variety of offenses, such as vagrancy or outraging public decency. The practice was increasingly linked to prostitution or seen more generally as a means to induce other men into committing vice.[43] However, during the nineteenth century law enforcement did not specifically target male cross-dressers when it came to arrests for homosexual offenses. Men wearing women's clothes represented only a small portion of those charged with homosexual offenses in the period.[44] Further, men wearing women's clothes were largely spared from arrest and, when arrests centering on cross-dressed men did occur, many of the subsequent legal proceedings ended in acquittal or a lenient sentence.[45]

Even as men in women's clothes were subjected to arrest in the streets, female impersonation on the stage remained relatively untarnished. Take the 1870–71 case of two London-based female impersonators, Ernest Boulton and Frederick William Park, who were arrested outside the Strand Theatre in London while cross-dressed and charged with conspiracy to commit sodomy. During the pair's trial the defense successfully argued that Boulton and Park's propensity for offstage cross-dressing was not indicative of sexual immorality but was the result of excessive identification with their theatrical drag.[46] The court heard that Boulton's female impersonations had recently played to rave reviews in areas such as Scarborough and Essex, where his onstage antics had been enjoyed by local clergymen and nobility. Commercial photographs of a cross-dressed Boulton sold briskly wherever he performed, and he was even invited to appear in women's clothes at private events and in people's homes.[47] The trial, at times, resembled an extension of Boulton and Park's theatrical drag act. Throngs of spectators vied to see the defendants wearing women's clothes in the dock; witness testimony describing the pair's larks elicited audible delight in the courtroom; and Boulton and Park's ultimate acquittal was reportedly met with loud cheers and exclamations of "Bravo!"[48]

Indeed, female impersonation onstage became ever more popular during the decade of Boulton and Park's trial. This coincided with the surging popularity of the music hall, new understandings of sexuality and gender, and new ways of performing drag—in addition to the popularization of the term *drag* itself. As the theater in general became the dominant cultural form by the late nineteenth century, facilitated in large part by the mass popularity of the music hall, drag performance reached a greater number of spectators than ever before.[49] Some of the most popular theatrical attractions of the age involved drag. Music hall star Dan Leno, arguably the most famous British entertainer during his heyday in the mid-1880s until his death in 1904, lent a newfound complexity to the characterization of the dame (a theatrical role typically involving a comic depiction of an older woman played by a man) in his celebrated Drury Lane theater pantomimes, where he imbued roles like Mother Goose with a combination of physically robust slapstick and moving pathos.[50] The play *Charley's Aunt* (1892), originally starring William Sydney Penley (figure 1) as Oxford undergraduate Lord Fancourt Babberley, who spends much of the play in disguise as an old dowager, emerged as a singular theatrical sensation in its native Britain and abroad, breaking records with its initial four-year, 1,469-show run in London.[51]

Concurrent with the preponderance of theatrical drag in the late Victorian period, there came a greater scrutiny of cross-dressing in general. A critical development in this area was the advent of works in the late 1860s and 1870s that would become foundational to the field of sexology. The significance of protosexology and sexology to a study of drag does not necessarily lie in the disciplines' influence on or popularity among laypeople, which was limited.[52] Drag on the stage was making more of an impact on wider cultural discussions

FIGURE 1. William Sydney Penley in *Charley's Aunt*, 1892. Credit: © National Portrait Gallery, London.

around female impersonation, cross-dressing, and gender variance than scholarship by sexologists and sexual theorists. The rise of sexology is mainly significant here because it marked the first time that gender variance and related phenomena such as transvestism came under serious scientific inquiry. More than that, the development of sexology represented the strongest, clearest, most intellectually grounded arguments to date that the act of cross-dressing indicated something about the cross-dresser's psyche and persona.

Early sexology is today arguably most associated with the conceptual "birth" of "homosexuality" as argued by philosopher Michel Foucault, but gender variance and transvestism were also central concerns of the field.[53] Foundational theorists in the discipline, like lawyer Karl Heinrich Ulrichs and psychiatrist Carl Friedrich Otto Westphal, tended to conflate the concepts of sexual and gender subjectivity. For these theorists, same-sex desire and transvestism were two possible symptoms of an individual's psychic identification with the opposite sex. Ulrichs argued that the *Urning*'s—his term for men who experienced same-sex desire—affection for other men was not merely predicated on their amorous or sexual object choice but was rooted in a deep-seated feminine persona. "The Urning is not a man but a type of feminine being who is female not only in the realm of sexual feelings," Ulrichs argued. "His entire spiritual organism, his entire spiritual temperament and character is feminine."[54] In the 1869 article, whose publication date Foucault demarcated as the "date of birth" of homosexuality, Westphal recalled the cases of a transvestic male patient, as well as a female patient who desired to be a man.[55] In his book *Psychopathia Sexualis* (1886), sexologist Richard von Krafft-Ebing bound up same-sex desire with gender variance when he referred to "degrees" of "antipathic sexual instinct," the symptoms of which could range from individuals expressing character traits associated with the other sex, to same-sex desire, to physical hermaphroditism in more extreme cases.[56] In subsequent decades, gender variance and transvestism continued to be a core focus of sexology, with landmark studies in the field including Magnus Hirschfeld's *Transvestites: The Erotic Drive to Cross-Dress* (1910) and Havelock Ellis's *Eonism* (1928).

On transvestism, medical practitioners Hirschfeld and Ellis argued that although the practice could be an expression of one's sexuality or cross-gender identification, this was not always the case. Nor did same-sex desire or gender nonconformity always manifest themselves through cross-dressing. Hirschfeld theorized that around 50 to 60 percent of same-sex desiring men were "virile" masculine types.[57] Even within the demographic of effeminate same-sex desiring men, "hardly 10 percent" of them cross-dressed, and "still fewer" had the urge to live full time as women—a trait Hirschfeld seemed to define as a particularly potent case of transvestism.[58] Furthermore, most of the male transvestites analyzed by Hirschfeld pursued relationships with women, with many of these relationships being described as "happy."[59] Hirschfeld also considered whether theatrical female impersonators tended to be same-sex desiring men. On this issue he differentiated between actors who occasionally dabbled in female impersonation for the sake of taking on a more diverse range of roles or who cross-dressed for "comic effect" versus "professional female and male impersonators," among whom there existed "surely a great number of intermediary types."[60] Ellis agreed with Hirschfeld that transvestism could be associated with a range of sexual proclivities and identities. Ellis identified five main categories of male "eonists" (Ellis's term for transvestites): those who were attracted to women, those who were attracted to men, those who were attracted to both men and women, narcissists for whom transvestism facilitated a love of self, and those who wanted to adopt feminine occupations and/or personae.[61]

Psychoanalyst Sigmund Freud, who forcefully argued that gender variance and same-sex desire were not essentially linked, did not study transvestism specifically, though from his work on other forms of stigmatized sexual behavior it can be assumed that Freud considered transvestism a fetish that could be experienced by individuals of all sexualities, borne out of "the shock of threatened castration at the sight of female genitals" in men and penis envy in women.[62] Freud's adherents subsequently drew upon the psychoanalyst's theories to analyze transvestism. In the 1920s, psychoanalysts Wilhelm Stekel and Emil Gutheil argued that, though transvestism resembled fetishism, it was in fact a "special form of a compulsion neurosis in which the patient's desire for the genitals of the other sex is displaced to the clothing." The transvestite ultimately aspires to "sexual metamorphosis," Stekel and Gutheil posited.[63] This understanding of a transvestite as an individual who wants to change their sex was reflected in mid-twentieth-century popular discussions of individuals whom we would refer to as transgender today. For example, media sensation Christine Jorgensen, who underwent gender-affirming surgeries in the early 1950s, was often referred to as a "transvestite" in the media.[64] Female impersonators and those who cross-dressed in private who did not experience cross-gender identification were also called transvestites by the mid-twentieth-century media.[65] Stekel and Gutheil further identified "the importance of latent homosexuality as an important casual factor in transvestism."[66] The pair retrospectively criticized Hirschfeld for overlooking what they saw as the latent homosexuality of transvestites whom he had identified as nonhomosexual. By the mid-twentieth century, theories about the motivations behind transvestism were manifold. These included the beliefs that transvestism created relief from castration anxiety through the imagining of a "phallic woman"; that transvestism was caused by overbearing mothers; that, for men, dressing as women allowed them to express emotion better; and that transvestism could be a form of obsessive-compulsive disorder.[67] A lively debate also continued regarding the extent to which transvestism was linked to homosexuality.

The link between gender variance and same-sex desire was debated not only among medical experts but also among same-sex desiring laypeople, some of whom rejected any association with gender variance. For example, prominent British homosexual law reform advocates of the 1950s and 1960s, such as journalist Peter Wildeblood, publicly emphasized a clear delineation between homosexual object choice and gender presentation. "Everyone has seen the pathetically flambouyant pansy with the flapping wrists," Wildeblood wrote in his memoir *Against the Law* (1955), "[but] most of us are not like that. We do our best to look like everyone else and we usually succeed."[68] Historian David Halperin has observed that similarly, by the 1970s, Foucault and other gay men were predicting that effeminate homosexuals were "the last remnants of a soon-to-be extinct species" as masculine gay identities appeared to be ascendant within Western gay culture.[69]

Some of the nineteenth- and twentieth-century lay observers who perceived gender variance, cross-dressing, and sexuality as being linked saw this association as a reason for viewing manifestations of gender variance, like drag, in a negative light. Others, however, were attracted to cross-dressing and female impersonation because of their perceived relationship to sexuality. Letters that featured lush descriptions of observers' engagement with female impersonation, published in newspapers such as *Society* and *London Life*, often suggested that correspondents' fascination with the performers went beyond mere appreciation for female impersonators' technical skill and was sexual in nature. Some of these letters read as partial or entire sexual fantasy rather than truthful descriptions of letter writers' experiences. Regardless of the factual accuracy of the letters, they demonstrate that male cross-dressing and female impersonation were sexually tantalizing to a portion of observers. Writing to the Victorian newspaper *Society* in 1893, a correspondent, implied to be male, retrospectively pored over the body of a female impersonator he had allegedly seen: "The bust and hips were accentuated by the marvellous slimness of the waist, whilst the shapely limbs, clad in pink tights and gauzy skirts, terminated in a pair of ankles and feet that would have put to shame many a fashionable dame."[70] "Dublin," as the correspondent called himself, went on to allege that he was invited to the female impersonator's dressing room where he saw the performer partially undressed in "a cream satin corset, laced painfully tight . . . the demurest of black stockings and white lace underwear." Dublin was then purportedly invited to inspect the female impersonator's wardrobe, which included "every article of feminine underwear of the most diaphanous nature," while the performer took off his cloak, allowing Dublin to ogle more of his body.[71] Along similar lines, a 1939 letter to the paper *London Life* went into great detail recalling the body of a female impersonator seen by the writer. Describing the female impersonator as having "wonderful ££10,000 legs," the writer gushed over the performer's "daintily manicured hand," "those inviting Cupid lips," and "chic little high-heeled one-strap shoes [that] were on the darting feet, the shining black silk sheath of the tights, with their perfectly straight, thin seam right up the back, showing off delightfully the slim, rounded and quickly moving legs."[72] Some women, or correspondents claiming to be women, also found male cross-dressing to be a turn-on. "Cine Enthusiast" wrote to *London Life* in 1935 describing a sexually charged experience dressing her husband up as a woman for a party. "I made him take a hot bath with plenty of bath salts, and then led him to our bedroom, where I had laid out some of my daintiest clothes for him," she recalled. Cine Enthusiast went on to describe her husband's cross-dressed body in admiring terms: "It was surprising to see how his slim figure responded to the tight-lacing I subjected him to, and when I had placed a padded brassiere in position, pulled on and tautly suspended his long silk stockings, and slipped him into a pair of figure-fitting satin and lace cami-knickers, I was still more surprised to see how completely feminine his contours were." She added that her husband made "a really pretty girl."[73]

Some individuals associated male cross-dressing with titillating sexual humiliation and masochism. A person who wrote in to *Society* in 1894, for example, alleged that his wife forced him to wear tight corsets as well as "a complete female outfit for morning and evening wear, including under-clothing, etc." The writer claimed that his wife locked a "steel belt" around his corsets to prevent him from loosening them and employed an especially tight "'punishment' corset . . . which at once is produced at any sign of rebellion."[74] Although this letter is framed as an airing of frustrations, it was likely written to sexually gratify the correspondent and *Society*'s readers. A 1941 letter to the paper *London Life* insisted that "When a husband is definitely the weaker partner of a marriage, and is content to accept domestic life, it seems only reasonable that his wife should have the privilege of dressing him as she wishes to . . . complete 'petticoat servitude' is not an unfair price for escape from the real responsibilities."[75] Others wrote into these and other publications on the topic of subjugating young male domestic servants by dressing them up in a maid's uniform.[76]

Some male cross-dressers got a sexual thrill from wearing women's clothes for reasons that included an affinity for certain fabrics, a feeling of relaxation or self-confidence that came with wearing the clothes, and associations with childhood experiences involving cross-dressing.[77] For such individuals, theatrical female impersonation was a potential means to indulge their transvestism fetish. One retired theatrical female impersonator who wrote to *London Life* in 1941 reported that "I am getting on now (nearly sixty-one) and have long ago given up the stage, but I have kept my love of lingerie and corsets, and still make quite a good-looking matron."[78] Another correspondent to *London Life* that year suggested that his work as a female impersonator was an outgrowth of his "cissy" identity.[79]

Then there were observers who did not necessarily see drag as an outright turn-on but for whom drag represented a racy, sexually charged experience. Take, for example, the "pansy craze" of the early 1930s, when the fad among modish New York City club goers was to take in shows featuring the "camp antics" of effeminate male performers.[80] A chief appeal of the pansy craze was the thrill of engaging, in a limited way, with the contemporary pansy subculture. In particular, it was a sign of sophistication to be au fait with the colloquialisms of this subculture. Mainstream periodicals printed "homosexual glossar[ies]" with definitions of words and phrases like "camp" and "to go in drag" for the benefit of straight readers.[81] The knowing laughter elicited among the "most respectable" audience by lines like "It's camp all right" in *We're No Ladies* reflected this trend.[82]

From the early 1870s, new language and methods for scrutinizing, defining, and understanding male cross-dressing were also developing in the media. One of the most glaring examples of this process was the emergence of the term *drag* itself: the first published use of the word *drag* as relating to cross-dressing occurred in a 29 May 1870 issue of *Reynolds's Newspaper* in an article on the Boulton and Park case.[83] Readers became further acquainted with the term *drag* through subsequent articles on the case, such as a 31 May 1870 article in the *Times* that mused whether "in another year or two 'drag' might have become quite an institution, and open carriages might have displayed their disguised occupants without suspicion."[84] The term had been well known to those with insider knowledge prior to its first public appearance in print. In pretrial correspondence, Ernest Boulton and his associates referred to drag to mean cross-dressing.[85] Theater historian Laurence Senelick has traced the first use of drag in relation to cross-dressing to mid-nineteenth-century Britain, where it evolved from the expression "putting on the drag," a colloquialism for the act of putting the brake on a coach, or the act of slowing down. Putting on the drag then became associated with the drag of a gown's train, which then morphed into "to go on the drag" or "to flash the drag," meaning to don feminine attire for the purpose of soliciting sex from men.[86] From this, the definition of drag was adopted by theatrical circles to indicate petticoats or skirts worn by cross-dressing male actors and the "feminine clothing" worn by "eccentric youths when dressing up in skirts."[87]

As new ways of talking about cross-dressing were emerging, the nature of drag performance was also undergoing a process of change in the final decades of the nineteenth century. This phenomenon was most evident in the growing ubiquity of the dame role and the rise of "glamour drag." Male cross-dressing performance was famously an institution on the Elizabethan and Jacobean stage, where adolescent boys and young men, usually no older than twenty-one or twenty-two years old, tended to play all women's roles.[88] However, once actresses became more common in Britain from the 1660s, the tradition of the boy player dissipated quickly.[89] After the use of boy players fell out of fashion, the dominant form of male cross-dressing performance became the dame role.[90] It was not until the end of the nineteenth century, though, that the dame became the theatrical fixture that we know her as today, due in large part to the growth of pantomime, in which the dame became a staple element.[91] Theatergoers' appetite for dame acts continued into the twentieth century, with dame comedians like Douglas Byng and Arthur Lucan emerging as some of the most successful entertainers of the 1930s through the 1950s.[92] Lucan in particular took the dame role to new heights by parlaying his character Old Mother Riley into a stage, screen, and radio franchise. Though his work was sometimes dismissed by critics as "never considered to be 'West End,'" Lucan's resonance with working-class audiences in the suburbs, provinces, and industrial cities demonstrates that this demographic did not simply seek mindless escapism.[93] Instead, the enduring popularity of Old Mother Riley—always unapologetically working class, protective of community and family, and hostile toward elites—shows that working-class theater-goers were drawn to entertainment that, in addition to being pleasurable, emphasized themes of social consciousness and class solidarity.[94] The dame has retained her status as a cultural touchstone to the present day, where she is arguably most associated with the Christmas pantomime, frequently a child's earliest engagement with live theater.

In addition to the dame, a newer style of female impersonation was resonating with British theatergoers by the 1870s. This type of female impersonation, which would eventually be referred to as glamour drag, featured stylish, elegant, and deliberately alluring renderings of femininity that often drew from the images of contemporary female stars.[95] Some female impersonators who practiced glamour drag made a conscious effort to be sexually appealing, while others aimed to evoke fashionableness and grace rather than sensuality. Glamour drag artists were popular throughout Britain on a regional and nationwide level. Further, foreign female impersonators who practiced glamour drag made a strong impression in Britain, while some British glamour drag performers had successful careers abroad. During the nineteenth and twentieth centuries, fashion magazines, internationally popular plays, Hollywood, and other media helped to shape a more globally homogenous view of feminine beauty, especially in the West.[96] This meant that practitioners of glamour drag throughout Britain and other parts of the world were increasingly drawing inspiration from the same or similar reference points, thus making it easier for such artists to become popular outside their home countries.

In a notable example of a British glamour drag practitioner making an impression abroad, Ernest Boulton, newly christened with the stage name Ernest Byne, successfully transferred his drag act to the American stage with little apparent alteration only three years after his and Frederick William Park's 1871 trial. Boulton's female impersonations, in which he played beautiful young women, were reportedly received just as rapturously in the United States as his pretrial performances were in Britain.[97] Another glamorous British female impersonator who found success abroad was Birmingham-born Bert Errol (figure 2). Errol, who was famed for his high-pitched feminine vocal range and lavish outfits, undertook successful tours in Australia, New Zealand, South Africa, Canada, and the United States, as well as his native Britain, from the 1900s through the 1940s.[98] Foreign glamour drag acts who achieved popularity in Britain included Mystery Gauze (figure 3). Described alternatingly as "Canadian Indian," "Indian," "coloured," or some combination of these, Gauze toured Britain throughout the mid-1900s and then appeared there again during the mid-1910s. In a typical description of Gauze's act, Norwich's *Eastern Daily Press* reported that "the audience were completely taken in by [the act] . . . in which a coloured person, dressed as a lady, and singing with a feminine voice, brought the turn to a conclusion by a decidedly manly utterance which undeceived the audience."[99] Other critics were apparently not "undeceived," however. A review in the *Leeds Mercury* called Gauze "an Indian *female* performer," while the *Dundee Evening Telegraph* referred to Gauze as "another lady artiste of the Canadian Indian type."[100] The Swedish female impersonator John Lind (figure 4) received positive reviews for his 1904 performances at the London Pavilion, with one critic enthusing, "Never was there such a waving of plump white arms, or such a lavish display of shoulders and back."[101] Julian Eltinge (figure 5), arguably the most famous American female impersonator of the early twentieth century, staged a command performance at Windsor Castle in 1906, where an appreciative King Edward VII gifted him a white bulldog.[102] In contrast to the above examples, female impersonator Billie Manders was more of a regional celebrity. Manders was indelibly associated with North Wales (specifically Rhyl), where he performed regularly with the Catlin's Royal Pierrots troupe throughout the 1910s, and then with his own troupe, the Quaintesques, from 1921 until his death in 1950.[103] In addition to his stage shows, Manders also made frequent BBC radio appearances between 1929 and 1949.[104] Other popular, glamorous early-twentieth-century drag artistes included Spanish female impersonator Derkas and the American acrobat Barbette (figure 6), both of whom made acclaimed appearances in British theaters in the 1920s and 1930s.[105] Demonstrating the dynamism of the art form, practitioners of glamour drag easily transitioned from the stage to early motion pictures and television soon after the establishment of those media. Drag entertainer Danny La Rue epitomized the cultural reach of glamour drag through the 1960s as he spun his act into a media empire that included his own eponymous club, the longest-running pantomime in modern history, a film vehicle, and multiple television specials.

By 1970, informed observers were remarking that "in Great Britain today female impersonators are enjoying a vogue unparalleled since the introduction into music hall and pantomime of the comic dame," an appraisal that anticipates the heralding of drag's current cultural moment by today's critics.[106] The chronology of this book begins in 1870 with the growing cultural prominence of the dame and glamour drag, buttressed by the flourishing theater industry, and ends in 1970 with the art form having persisted as a staple of British popular culture. Of course, drag continued to be prevalent after 1970, but, as it had done a century earlier, the practice was undergoing a phase of significant transformation in terms of how it was performed, perceived, and discussed.

On the one hand, renderings of drag were becoming less straightforward. A number of popular musicians were now presenting themselves in drag or drag-adjacent modes, a phenomenon that has been credited, at least in part, to Rolling Stones lead singer Mick Jagger wearing a dress during a 1969 Rolling Stones concert in Hyde Park.[107]

FIGURE 2. Postcard depicting Bert Errol, 1925. Credit: Bert Errol, in character, wearing an elaborate white dress. Process print, 1925. Wellcome Collection.

FIGURE 3. Postcard depicting Mystery Gauze, ca. 1900s. Credit: Private collection of the author.

DOFF BROS.   ? LIND. ?   MANCHESTER

FIGURE 4. Postcard depicting John Lind, ca. 1900s. Credit: Mander and Mitchenson / University of Bristol / ArenaPAL.

IMPERSONATION EXTRAORDINARY: "THE WONDERFUL ELTINGE."

FROM AMATEUR TO PROFESSIONAL IMPERSONATOR OF WOMEN ON THE STAGE: MR. ELTINGE,
WHO IS APPEARING AT THE PALACE.

Mr. Julian Eltinge became known to the public while taking leading girl parts at Harvard College and playing leads in such well-known operas as "Baron Humbug," "Miss Simplicity," "Malady," and "Coreopsis," given by the Boston Cadets and the bankers of Boston, whose amateur performances are the most extraordinary and elaborate in the States. These plays are specially written for "all male" shows, half of the number (125 actors) playing girl parts. Eltinge created the leading lady part for four seasons with no thought of professional work; but when he finished his schooling the most prominent managers of America were bidding high for the services of this young artist (then 19 years old) until such a figure was reached that he accepted. Mr. Eltinge's make-up is the most elaborate in the profession, it taking him from 1½ to 2 hours for each performance.

FIGURE 5. Julian Eltinge in various outfits with accompanying news article, 1906. Credit: Mander and Mitchenson/University of Bristol/ArenaPAL.

A CHARMING "DECEIVER":
BABETTE, THE MYSTERY OF THE
OLYMPIA CIRCUS.

The Olympia Circus was due to open on
Monday last, Dec. 20. Babette, who is
pictured above, is the mystery of the
entertainment. She is a charming artist
whose rôle is to deceive spectators in a
startling manner.

FIGURE 6. Photograph of Barbette (credited incorrectly as "Babette") with accompanying news article, 1926. Credit: Mander and Mitchenson/University of Bristol/ArenaPAL.

In this way, the popularity of drag was maintained into the new millennium, not just by drag artists themselves, but also by performers who did not consider themselves drag artists. As more diluted forms of drag permeated media like popular music, drag in its purer form was being more overtly claimed by the gay community as a gay art form by 1970 and after, a process that disrupted drag's status as a mass cultural form. For example, the UK Gay Liberation Front (GLF), formed in 1970, employed "radical drag" in its activism. Perhaps the most famous example of this occurred during the GLF's protest against the evangelical Christian campaign group Nationwide Festival of Light's 1971 inaugural meeting, where drag performance was utilized to mock and derail the event.[108] Subsequent scholarly analyses of drag often fell under the purview of the discipline now known as queer studies, and this is still the case.[109]

This book is timely given the surge of popular interest in drag today. The drag queen competition television show *RuPaul's Drag Race* (2009–present) has become a global phenomenon, spawning British and other international editions in addition to the US-based original. The show's popularity has led to tours and conventions covering six continents that feature live appearances by the program's former contestants. The documentary *Paris Is Burning* (1990), which chronicles the subcultural drag ball scene in late-1980s New York City, mostly composed of working-class Black and Latine gender nonconforming people, has been subjected to renewed attention thanks to its exposure on *Drag Race*. Capitalizing on this, the American FX Network has produced a television series called *Pose* (2018–21), now syndicated globally, which dramatizes the subculture depicted in *Paris Is Burning*. Outside the UK version of *Drag Race* (2019–present), British drag has recently experienced prominent exposure in the West End (e.g., the musical *Everybody's Talking about Jamie* [2017–present]); in film (e.g., the 2021 film adaptation of *Jamie*); on television (e.g., *Drag SOS* [2019]); in art galleries and museums (e.g., the 2018 Hayward

Gallery exhibition *DRAG: Self-portraits and Body Politics*); in events for children in public libraries; in advertising (e.g., the 2019 "Drag Cleans" campaign by cleaning supply brand Method); on internet platforms such as Instagram and TikTok; and live in nightclubs, pubs, and performing arts spaces throughout the country.[110] Drag's current conspicuousness has faced a backlash, notably from right-wing politicians in the United States, some of whom have proposed regulations on drag performances.[111] Demonstrations against drag, which have in turn sparked pro-drag counterdemonstrations, have proliferated in the United Kingdom at the time of writing.[112] Drag has also faced criticism from within, with some in the drag community pushing back against what they perceive as the sanitized, generic nature of mainstream, commercial drag.[113]

The present-day visibility of drag has led some cultural observers to claim that drag has recently gone mainstream after a long time in the shadows.[114] This narrative is not completely unfounded considering the persistent historical controversies surrounding drag and given that there have been notable countercultural, "underground" strains of drag (just as scores of other art forms also possess underground strains). However, to essentialize drag as a subcultural art form is to ignore obvious evidence of the sustained mainstream popularity and quotidian nature of the medium over time. Further, it is tempting to focus on historical reactions to drag at the poles of the spectrum: the high praise and sheer venom these shows and performers received. But perhaps the most intriguing, and illuminating, reactions were the nonreactions, those that did not read into what drag "meant" or what female impersonators might have been up to offstage. Many—if not most—observers of drag appeared to simply take in the show, have a pleasurable time, and leave the theater untroubled.[115]

Drag: A British History does not reject the narrative of drag's current popular moment, but the book does situate the phenomenon within a deeper and more complex history. This is not intended to nostalgically revere drag as it existed in the past. I welcome the developments associated with present-day iterations of drag and the drag scene. One major credit to the current state of the art form is that it has become more inclusive, both in terms of the types of performers who identify as drag artists and the types of performance considered to be drag. What drag constitutes now is commonly based on an artist's own self-definition. Such diverse, sometimes abstract, renderings of gender expression have propagated on the present-day drag scene to the extent that consciously performing a readily identifiable form of femininity or masculinity, once a staple of drag, is arguably unessential—though even the most abstract forms of present-day drag, such as "tranimals," prod spectators to consider gender.[116] Drag, like all art forms, is mutable in terms of the intent of the performers and how it is received by viewers. It can be liberating and reactionary, trivial and serious, shocking and placative. *Drag: A British History* seeks to demythologize drag by stressing its ordinariness while affirming its centrality to modern popular culture.

1 Old Mother Riley and the Modern Dame

OLD MOTHER RILEY—67-year-old Arthur Lucan—was chuckling in the wings of a theatre last night, awaiting his cue. When the cue came he did not take it. In the comical clothes and make-up of Old Mother Riley he had collapsed—and was dead.

Thus the career of Arthur Lucan came to a sudden end on 17 May 1954. Born Arthur Towle in Lincolnshire in 1885, Lucan was one of the most commercially successful entertainers in 1930s and 1940s Britain.[1] The actor was best known for his dame character Old Mother Riley, a wiry, feisty, sharp-tongued, surprisingly agile elderly woman whose appearances on stage and screen and in several other media tended to see her in domestic episodes quarreling with her daughter, Kitty, or pitted against antagonists in positions of power. Together with his wife, Kitty McShane (figure 7), who played Riley's daughter in their double act, Lucan established a towering media franchise based on his dame character consisting of stage plays, a fifteen-entry film series, gramophone records, BBC radio programs, and a regular full-page comic strip—all bearing the *Old Mother Riley* title.[2] Earning between £500 and £1,000 per week at the height of their fame, Lucan and McShane were named the second-most popular film stars of

FIGURE 7. Signed publicity photograph of Arthur Lucan (left) and Kitty McShane in character as Old Mother Riley and her daughter Kitty, ca. 1930s. Credit: Mander and Mitchenson / University of Bristol / ArenaPAL.

1941 and the third-highest grossing film stars of 1942 by the *Motion Picture Herald*.[3] The renown of the Old Mother Riley character led to regular press appraisal citing her as the top dame in Britain from the mid-1930s through the early 1950s. "Arthur Lucan, the male partner of the duo [Lucan and McShane], is considered Britain's finest 'dame' comedian," read a typical declaration of this status.[4] The entertainer was a pioneer in the media of film and radio, becoming the first female impersonator in Britain to star in his own radio series and the first male actor to play a female leading role in a feature-length British sound film.[5]

Despite these remarkable achievements, the end of Lucan's life was tinged with tragedy. Though he continued to star in films and plays into the 1950s, by the time of his death he was separated from his wife, Kitty, and had just been declared bankrupt after amassing a considerable tax debt.[6] Lucan went on to suffer further indignities posthumously, including dismissive remarks from critics who pigeonholed him as a provincial children's entertainer and insults to his legacy from politicians during a debate over a blue plaque commemorating the star.

Old Mother Riley was particularly popular among working-class family audiences living in industrial towns and cities, the provinces, and suburbs. More than a decade after Lucan's death, Riley remained a ubiquitous cultural figure for this demographic. "The tradition of female impersonation," observed BBC producer John Fisher in 1968, "will still today, to the man in the street, be quite simply the pantomime dame, Charley's Aunt and Old Mother Riley."[7] Lucan's huge appeal with poorer, nonmetropolitan theatergoers catapulted him to the height of fame, but it also led to his marginalization among cultural cognoscenti during his lifetime and posthumously. Obituaries coldly noted that Riley's act was "never considered to be 'West End,'" while Lucan has often been ignored entirely, or given only passing attention, in scholarship on drag and damery.[8]

Lucan's performances and career provide the historian with an ideal, and heretofore undervalued, case study for analyzing the archetype of the dame. Through Lucan's characterization and marketization of Old Mother Riley, we see that the dame is not a static Victorian-era museum piece but a dynamic cultural form that has adapted to dramaturgical innovations, changing tastes, and new technologies.[9] Lucan built upon the dame studies of late nineteenth- to early twentieth-century music hall comedian Dan Leno (figure 8), whose model of the "believable dame" imbued the role with a new-found emotional complexity marked by elements of pathos intermingled with the traditional slapstick comedy, as well as a sense of realism.[10] Leno also took the dame out of pantomime and placed her

FIGURE 8. Dan Leno as four characters, including one of his dame studies (top right), 1903. Credit: Mander and Mitchenson / University of Bristol / ArenaPAL.

in original theatrical creations in which she was the star, an approach Lucan would build upon by establishing an entire entertainment franchise around Old Mother Riley. In Lucan's dame we see how the cultural figure retained a consciousness of the past yet simultaneously constituted a modern creation on the cutting edge of interwar and postwar entertainment. Lucan's modernity lay in the emotional complexity he brought to his characterization of the dame, his use of old as well as relatively new media to develop his character into a highly marketable brand, and his ability to speak to the pertinent interests and concerns of the working classes.

The genre of pantomime and the cultural form of the dame have separate pre-Victorian histories that had converged by the late nineteenth century. The genesis of the pantomime lay in the opening of the Regency-period harlequinade. These opening sequences consisted of a short set of scenes with a nursery rhyme or fairy tale narrative and tended to be unrelated to the main harlequinade section of the show.[11] Pantomime also drew from slightly later genres, the extravaganza and the burlesque, which emerged after the loosening of restrictions on scripted theater following the passage of the Theatres Act 1843.[12] The extravaganza tended to satirize contemporary politics and culture under the auspices of a fairy tale or mythical setting, whereas the burlesque parodied famous historical events, works of literature, and theater.[13] By the late nineteenth century, these theatrical forms had merged into pantomime, a whimsical comedic spectacle combining broad humor with cultural and political satire, often featuring narratives based on fairy tales or literature.

Historians have traced the origins of the dame back to the trope of the frightful old "hag" in the ancient mythology of various cultures.[14] Early incarnations of the type of dame characters most commonly seen in British pantomime today appeared in comedic plays such as *The Provoked Wife* (1697) and *The Funeral; Or Grief A-La-Mode* (1701).[15] These plays featured popular scenes in which male characters disguise themselves as women in an absurd, ungainly fashion. The dame as a man masquerading as a woman within the context of a play's plot continued to be seen in comedies such as *Charley's Aunt* (1892), but dames increasingly tended to be comic older female characters played by men. Although the dame predates pantomime and has experienced a long history outside the genre, the figure had become so closely associated with pantomime by the late nineteenth and early twentieth centuries that by the time Old Mother Riley emerged, Lucan playing the dame outside of pantomime was seen as an innovative novelty. As one critic observed of the film *Old Mother Riley in Paris* (1938), "Those who like horseplay and would enjoy a full-length pantomime with the 'dame' as the star and no principal boy will enjoy this film from start to finish."[16] "It was as if Arthur Lucan took the Widow Twankey in Christmas Panto," another critic remarked, "and turned it into a lifelong year-round career."[17] Prior to Lucan, however, it was Dan Leno who confirmed the dame's place as star of the productions in which she appeared, pantomime and non-pantomime alike. Leno's innovative characterization of the dame, seen notably in his Surrey Theatre and Drury Lane pantomimes of the 1880s through 1900s, heralded a "golden era" of pantomime and elevated the dame figure to her "apotheosis."[18]

The British dame had contemporary counterparts in other countries' entertainment scenes. Despite pantomime not being the cultural touchstone in the United States that it is in Britain, dame-type characters played by men are woven into the fabric of American theatrical heritage. In blackface minstrelsy, the "funny ole gal," a comedic drag role "often performed by a large actor dressed in old and mismatched clothes," was a fixture of the nineteenth-century American stage, just as the British dame was becoming a theatrical fixture in her home country.[19] An 1879 description of minstrelsy's "funny ole gal" anticipates some observations that would be made of Lucan and Leno's dames, with their surprising athleticism and seemingly endless layers of dowdy, anachronistic dress: "Clad in some tawdry old gown of loud crude colours . . . display[ing] long frilled 'panties' and No. 13 valise shoes . . . the funny old gal is very often a gymnast of no mean amount of muscle."[20]

In the British context, Leno's dame portrayals retained some features of the figure's historical lineage while representing a departure from the past in other key areas, demonstrating the dame's transmutability even during the Victorian and early Edwardian periods. The entertainer's most celebrated roles were arguably Sister Anne in the 1901–2 Drury Lane pantomime *Bluebeard* and the title role in Drury Lane's *Mother Goose* the following Christmastime.[21] Leno also performed the dame character outside of pantomime, as in his highly popular song "I'll Marry Him," in which he played a gossipy, middle-aged, working-class woman who endeavors to forcibly marry the reluctant object of her quarter-century-long affections.[22] "I'll Marry Him" was one of several Leno routines to be immortalized on gramophone record. Leno as his dame character Mrs. Kelly, who is mentioned in "I'll Marry Him," and a small portion of his performance in *Bluebeard*, among other routines starring the entertainer, were captured in short films. The films were viewable in music halls, through Mutoscopes and Kinora viewers, and in flip-books.[23] In 1899, one of Leno's performances was broadcast via Electrophone to Queen Victoria in Windsor Castle in honor of the monarch's eightieth birthday.[24] Leno's embrace of then-new media anticipated similar moves by Lucan, as well as suggesting that drag, and the dame specifically, comfortably adapted to technological advances in the entertainment industry.

The earlier Victorian pantomime dame tended to be one-dimensional, more of a device for low comedy than a fully realized character, with much of the humor derived from an understanding that the audience was watching a male actor putting on a crude representation of a woman.[25] For Leno's believable dame, however, the humor lay in the context of the character and the play rather than his being a man playing a woman. The intricacies of Leno's portrayals implicitly encouraged the audience to separate the actor from his characters. As one contemporary observer remarked, "When we see Dan Leno as a woman and hear his delightful patter it never strikes us that he is a man imitating a woman."[26] It has been speculated that Leno's multidimensional dames were influenced by real women he had encountered during his working-class upbringing in London and Liverpool. "Homely, discursive, and confidential, not to say occasionally aggressive," is how Jay Hickory Wood, writer of several Drury Lane pantomimes, described the entertainer's studied dame characterizations, "not so much a picture of Dan Leno playing the part of a woman in a particular walk of life as the picture of what Dan Leno would have been if he had actually been that particular woman."[27] Leno's dame roles were just as emotionally demanding as any lead part in a serious drama, if not more so. As Mother Goose, for instance, Leno played three different iterations of the character (transformed in the play by way of magic): as a haughty, wealthy old woman, as a humble, poor old woman, and as a genuinely pretty, coquettish Mother Goose in her younger years (figure 9). Anticipating theater practitioner Konstantin Stanislavski's "system" approach to acting by decades, Leno consciously saw every performance as "a character study, his grasp of artistic and psychological detail adding depth to his depiction of both sexes alike," according to a recent biography.[28]

Leno's dames, with all their evident ingenuity, still remained grounded in some long-established precedents of damery and the genre of pantomime. This deference to tradition was most clearly seen in Leno's physicality, namely his reliance on slapstick comedy. Slapstick here is defined as a form of broad physical comedy often involving tripping, slipping, fighting, the throwing of objects such as food or crockery, and other such exaggerated actions and reactions. Injury and violence are frequently involved but not essential.[29] Leno's

MOTHER GOOSE Act II
DAN LENO AS MOTHER GOOSE

3056 PHOTO BASSANO.

ROTARY PHOTO.E.C.

FIGURE 9. Dan Leno as young Mother Goose, 1902. Credit: Mander and Mitch-enson / University of Bristol / ArenaPAL.

performances harkened back to the skillful athleticism and slapstick stylings employed by Regency-period clowns like Joseph Grimaldi, known for his challenging and sometimes dangerous physical stunts, in the protopantomime harlequinade.[30] Observers of Leno marveled at the actor's "driving urgency" that involved "arduous acrobatics, dancing and horseplay."[31] Describing Leno's uncannily cartoonish physicality, theater critic Richard Findlater has stated that "nobody could take their eyes off [Leno], as he darted about with staccato movements and furious energy."[32] This robust slapstick was elevated from mere tomfoolery when Leno married it with his rich character studies. "He had a hundred different ways of walking and dancing, each appropriate to the person he was representing," remarked the *Times*.[33] Some critics have speculated that this level of physical exertion, along with his tireless work ethic—it was not unusual for the entertainer to perform as many as four shows per night, each in a different venue—contributed to Leno's premature death in 1904, at the age of forty-three, from "general paralysis of the insane."[34]

Arthur Lucan, by the height of his career in the 1930s and 1940s, had inherited Leno's mantle as Britain's foremost dame comedian. His success lay in large part on taking aspects of the dame characterization Leno had devised or improved upon—believability, slapstick, and liberating the dame from the pantomime—while expanding on and recontextualizing these elements for twentieth-century audiences. A reliable component of Lucan's act that imbued it with believability and emotional complexity was the pathos that tempered Riley's manic slapstick comedy styles. Reviews of Riley stage and screen appearances often took notice of this feature. "[Lucan] subtly tempers his humour with sentiment—that the wild and extravagant gags not only promote an easy continuity of laughs, but contain no little human interest," read a typical assessment.[35] Take Lucan's "Old Match Seller" scene, praised by critics for its semi-tragic nature and regularly revived by Lucan throughout his career.[36] The scene sees Old

Mother Riley as a pitiable match seller who helps a bride (most frequently played by McShane) find her missing bridegroom on the day of her wedding. The scene begins melancholically as Riley encounters the desperate bride while the dame is peddling matches and balloons on the Thames Embankment. The tone quickly pivots to comedy though, as Riley responds to the bride's plight with feisty anti-male diatribes such as "[Men] will touch your heart on a Sunday night. Then they touch you for half a dollar till Friday," and "All men before wedlock should be padlocked!"[37] However, in the climax of the piece, Kitty's bridegroom is suddenly found; thus, she has not been jilted after all. Riley closes with a sentimental monologue: "Poor little kid. When she thought her romance had ended she found it had just begun. That's life. Sunshine and shadow, laughter and tears. Mistakes and regrets, and everything comes out right in the end."[38]

The sketch "Bridget's Night Out," famously performed before King George V and Queen Mary at the 1934 Royal Variety Performance, further advances this pleasurable mix of comedy and pathos.[39] It opens with Riley alone in the kitchen, fretting that her daughter still has not returned home from a night on the town (a "night" that has actually lasted from January to March, as is revealed in a later gag). Setting the tone for the sketch, Riley's monologue here oscillates between despair and angry feistiness, a series of conflicting emotions that parents who have been in similar situations might find relatable, even if her moods are exaggerated for comic effect in the scene:

Old Mother Riley: [Worried, manic] I wonder where she is, I wonder where she's gone, I wonder who she's with, I wonder what she's doing, I wonder what time it is; I hope she's *alriiight*. I wonder how long I slept. If I only knew what time it was, you know, I'd be more settled in my mind. I don't know how long I slept, I don't know how long she's been out, and I can't read the clock 'til it strikes. [A beat; then

Riley's grief transitions to anger] That's where she has me. *That's* where she has me *and* she knows it. She's *ooout* and here's me sitting pretty! Don't know whether it's daytime, nighttime, halftime, summertime, early closing or next Wednesday! . . . I've been sitting there since yesterday. *Sitting there since yesterday* waiting for her to come home tonight and now it's tomorrow! [Transitioning again into worriment] She's never done a thing like this before. THERE'S SOMETHING WRONG! THERE'S SOMETHING HAPPENED TO HER! ME LOVELY CHILD! SHE'S GONE FOREVER! SHE'S GO—[angry again; rolls up sleeves threateningly, as if preparing for a boxing match] When *she* comes home!⁴⁰

In this opening sequence, Riley's exaggerated gesticulations and agile body movements match the frenetic pace of the dialogue. Even while seated, Riley is rarely still, putting her head in her hands, shaking her arms with exasperation, and—in an action that constituted one of the character's trademarks—lifting herself up from her chair, supporting her full body weight with her arms, and twirling her legs around like a whirligig in a fit of nervous energy.⁴¹ When Kitty does finally come home, the ensuing row between the pair escalates into a cascade of crockery smashing. (Riley has saved months' worth of washing up for Kitty to do, practically all of which ends up smashed.) This sequence draws upon the trope of the pantomime "slosh" scene, commonly marked by two comedians dueling through the use of messy matter such as soapy water.⁴² The scene transcends one-note slapstick, however, in its modulation of the humor with sentimentality. After Riley injures her leg in the row, Kitty comes to her aid, making it appear as if the duo has reconciled. However, in a subversion of audience expectations, when Kitty remarks wistfully that "I've been wishing that me father was alive," Riley's calm shifts back to anger. "So you'd wish me bad luck, would you?!" Riley exclaims before leaping up (her leg has miraculously healed). With her rolling pin, Riley then proceeds to clear various shelves of crockery, leaving only a few cups and plates remaining in the cupboard.[43] Finally, though, after this chaotic climax, the scene ends on a note of pathos with Kitty tenderly singing a lullaby to Riley, seeing the dame off to bed, and dutifully agreeing to do the washing up. Just as "Bridget's Night Out" mixes comedy with earnest sentiment, the scene also represents an interplay between older and newer representations of the dame. For example, the extent to which the scene is steeped in domesticity—it is set entirely in a kitchen, with items like a rolling pin and crockery as the props—is an almost hyperbolic nod to the pre-Leno stock dames, who, when they were not housewives, were nearly always seen in some domestic role such as cook, governess, or in-home nurse.[44] "Bridget's Night Out" is also reliant on established comedic tropes from pantomime and its progenitors, such as the slosh sequence, the play of anticipation (e.g., the audience sees the crockery piled high and anticipates that this will lead to some comedic payoff) and relief (e.g., the release of anticipation after all the crockery has been smashed), and pleasurable incongruities like seeing an elderly woman perform feats of physical agility.[45] Yet the sketch also represents newer aspects of dame comedy: Lucan never draws attention to his maleness but remains in character; the scene's characters and relationships are emotionally nuanced; and audience expectations are confounded by surprising shifts in narrative tone.

Lucan's construction of the dame as a fully realized character existed amidst similar styles of damery. Lucan's contemporary Douglas Byng said of his dame performances, "I never took off my wig because I wanted the children to think I really was a dame. . . . You should play the character and be the character."[46] Following Lucan's successful forays into the film industry, comedian Norman Evans portrayed his famous dame characters Fanny Fairbottom and Fanny Lawton in the films *Demobbed* (1944) and *Over the Garden Wall* (1950), respectively. Though Evans also played male characters, he was perhaps best known as a believable dame in the "Over the Garden Wall" routine in which he gossiped with neighbors and admonished children—neither of whom were visible to the audience—via a lengthy, fast-paced monologue.[47] Lucan's level of dedication to Riley, practically the only character he played from the 1930s until his death, took the believable dame to unprecedented extremes.[48] Where Leno inhabited his roles while being a widely recognizable public figure in his own right, Lucan made himself practically invisible to audiences. As a testament to Lucan's skill as an actor, as well as the familiarity audiences formed with Riley across several decades, many theatergoers either willfully ignored Lucan as an entity or thought that Riley was actually played by an old woman.[49] "So complete is the caricature, so familiar the personality, that one tends to forget that Arthur Lucan—a mere male—is the artist behind the well-loved character," observed the *Portsmouth Evening News* of the revue *Going Gay* (1952), "Certainly there were many among last night's audience who spoke of 'her' and 'she' when commenting upon his part in this brand-new success."[50] One critic noted, after a screening of the film *Old Mother Riley in Paris* in Uppingham, "Arthur Lucan is the only male in British pictures to star in a female role, and so cleverly is the character portrayed that it is difficult to realise he is only playing the part."[51] A review of the first *Old Mother Riley* film (1937) read, "This is the first time that a screen actor has taken a leading woman role, and this brilliantly funny and convincing performance is certain of tremendous success."[52] Even recent commentators have overlooked the actor playing Riley. "In discussing the Mother Riley comedies," film scholar Marcia Landy has observed, "critics take Lucan's female impersonation for granted, referring to it only in passing."[53] Lucan's commitment to believability pushed the boundaries between admirable commitment to his craft and pathological fastidiousness. He had almost no public-facing persona outside of playing Riley, rarely granting interviews out of character.[54] In one notable example of his extreme dedication to the role, he attended recordings of episodes for the Old Mother Riley radio show, *Old Mother Riley Takes the Air* (1941), in full costume with the entire script committed to memory despite the nonvisual nature of the medium.[55] Another display of Lucan's fierce assiduity recalled how Dan Leno had allegedly worked himself to death decades earlier. During a show in 1936, Lucan fell from the stage, only to immediately get back up and continue his act. After finishing that night's program he was rushed to the hospital, where he was reportedly diagnosed with life-threatening internal injuries, leaving him bedridden for twelve weeks.[56]

Like Leno, Lucan too allegedly based his dame on real people in order to imbue his character with a greater sense of believability. In particular, Lucan appears to have drawn inspiration from his mother, Lucy Ann Towle. Some remembrances of Mrs. Towle certainly evoked similarities between her and the feisty Riley. One Boston resident diplomatically recalled Mrs. Towle as a "forthright figure who used to frequent the New Inn in Pen St, complete with rolling pin."[57] Arthur Lucan's nephew revealed that family members remembered Mrs. Towle as "a bit of a rum character. She enjoyed a drink, was often in the pub, and would frequently get so drunk that they would have to bring her home in a wheelbarrow."[58] Lucan's marriage likely provided him with artistic inspiration as well. Associates of Lucan and McShane observed that the arguments between Riley and her daughter Kitty mirrored the couple's real-life tempestuous relationship. However, unlike the pugnacious Riley, Lucan was reportedly "reticent to the point where it perhaps ceases to be a virtue."[59] Kitty, conversely, was widely deemed to be "by all accounts utterly egocentric, immature and unstable, much given to foul tempers and foul language, and whose talent was 'wafer-thin.'"[60]

It was a credit to Lucan's acting ability that critics and audiences found him to be so convincing despite the minimalistic nature of his makeup and costumes. All the actor needed to transform himself into Riley for the dame's film appearances was a wig, putty to exaggerate the shape of his nose, and basic stage makeup, though the makeup Lucan used for Riley's stage shows was slightly more elaborate.[61] Unlike many nineteenth-century stock pantomime dames, Lucan did not use stuffing to make himself appear more buxom, curvaceous, or rotund. Riley shared Lucan's slight frame, which he retained throughout his professional career.

Riley's clothes were arguably the character's most obvious reference to the nineteenth-century dame. Her conservative, darkly colored, well-worn clothing—often marked by a bonnet and shawl—did not differ greatly from that of her Victorian predecessors (figures 10 and 11). Riley's occupation as a washerwoman in many appearances harkened back to the Victorian dame as well.[62] The dame's antiquated fashions, still evident in present-day pantomimes, have rendered her superficially anachronistic, making it easy to overlook how subtler elements of the character have changed since the late nineteenth century. By the height of Lucan's career, the dame's aesthetic appeared so obviously superannuated that it was being played for laughs. In "Bridget's Night Out," for instance, Riley performs "a bizarre striptease as she prepares for bed," as one critic described. "Endless layers of underskirt are removed and folded, the final one placed in the oven and her corsets in the bread bin, all with a reverence appropriate to a ritual as old as time."[63] A script for the 1944 touring revue *Old Mother Riley and Her Daughter Kitty* describes Riley disrobing again, revealing "the most exaggerated long old fashioned coloured petticoats, striped stockings, and old fashioned Victorian long pantaloons reaching to her shoe tops."[64] In addition to providing amusing wordless character development—the sequence lends a supernaturally ancient quality to Riley—the mock striptease injects the dame with a deliberate lack of sex appeal, reassuring any audience member who might associate drag with sexual immorality.[65]

The interwar-through-postwar dame's shabby, old-fashioned look diverged from chic popular images of older women's fashions at the time. Standards of feminine beauty and glamour in this period were not rigidly defined by age. Until the mid-1960s it was common to see representations of fashionable older women who were comfortable looking their age featured prominently in popular media such as the magazines *Good Housekeeping*, *Woman's Weekly*, and British *Vogue*.[66] A typical interwar column venerating the older woman was "Middle Age Is Not a Thing to Dread" in *Woman's Weekly*, which argued that "the woman of forty-five, or even much older" was "amongst the most sought after and attractive" because she understood "how to dress, and how to be interesting."[67] For postwar readers of *Vogue*, the long-running fictional character Mrs. Exeter portrayed a woman who was unapologetic about "approaching sixty" and not looking "a day younger."[68] In "her" column, Mrs. Exeter argued that glamour went hand in hand with embracing one's age. She openly discussed issues pertaining to older readers, such as rheumatism. A likeness of the character even graced the cover of *Vogue* in 1950, and "she" appeared, played by various models, in fashion spreads inside the magazine throughout that decade.[69] The idealization of mature, dignified feminine beauty was likely aided in part by British culture's uneasy relationship with the concept of youthful feminine sexiness, which around the time of the Second World War was often portrayed as frivolous or sinister.[70] Although Old Mother Riley's drab clothes were out of touch with then-current fashions and the popular image of the chic older woman, many audience members likely found comfort in the old-fashioned values her clothing represented in addition to other nods to traditionalism, such as Riley's reining in of her wayward unmarried daughter, Kitty. Riley's fashions also emphasized her unapologetically working-class image—a key to the dame's immense popularity.

CHARLES MATHEWS AS "THE MAID OF ALL WORK."

FIGURE 10 (left). Charles James Mathews as "The Maid of All Work," 1863. Credit: Mander and Mitchenson/University of Bristol/ArenaPAL.

FIGURE 11 (right). Signed publicity photograph depicting Arthur Lucan, credited here as "Old Mother Hubbard" but dressed as he appeared as the titular character in the *Old Mother Riley* film series and reading an issue of British *Vogue*, ca. 1930s. Credit: From the private collection of Dr. Robert V. Kenny and David Tibet.

By the end of the 1940s, then, Arthur Lucan had excelled in theater, film, radio, and commercial recording. He had been named as one of the top three most popular and highest grossing film stars in Britain.[71] The first ten *Old Mother Riley* films earned £780,000 in total at the box office—nearly three times the combined budget of the films to that point.[72] In 1941 the BBC commissioned an *Old Mother Riley* radio series, *Old Mother Riley Takes the Air*. That same year also saw four 78 rpm gramophone records released by Columbia Records featuring Riley sketches.[73] This was all in addition to Lucan and McShane's ongoing stage shows that toured throughout Britain.

Despite this remarkable degree of national success, Lucan was often marginalized by critics as a niche performer: he was popular with working-class audiences in the provinces, suburbs, and industrial cities as well as with children, but he was spurned by cultural tastemakers in the West End and other bastions of high culture. A review of the second entry in the *Old Mother Riley* film series published in the distinctly high-cultural trade paper *Kinematograph Weekly* predicted that "it stands a first-rate chance of going over big with industrial and provincial audiences. . . . The picture represents a crazy but laughable caricature of low-class domesticity."[74] An appraisal of the film *Old Mother Riley's Circus* (1941) in the same periodical declared, "Mass industrial and family appeal is obvious."[75] Upon the release of Lucan's last film, *Mother Riley Meets the Vampire* (1952), costarring Bela Lugosi, the dame comedian had not shaken this perception of his fan base: "[It] will probably go extremely well on a line north of Coventry," observed the *Daily Film Renter* of the feature.[76] In contrast, Lucan's stage appearances in the West End were rare and produced mixed results. Instead, his theatrical tours visited areas such as Bangor, Birmingham, Bournemouth, New Cross, Hackney, Leicester, Swansea, Portsmouth, and Norwich.[77] None of the *Old Mother Riley* films were screened in the West End until 1949, twelve years after the first was produced.[78] The press reported on the dame's foray into the area with skepticism: "Old Mother Riley, darling of the provincial cinemas, took a London gamble last night by playing to her first West End audiences," reported the *Daily Mail* upon the release of *Old Mother Riley's New Venture* (1949).[79]

Lucan's posthumous reputation has similarly suffered. A 1975 proposal for a blue plaque commemorating Lucan generated a surprising amount of controversy in the Greater London Council, with Conservative councillors in particular responding with virulent negativity. Both sides in the ensuing debate framed the issue as one of elite high culture versus popular low culture. "Arthur Lucan[,] whose reputation as the creator of Old Mother Riley," argued the Tory councillor representing Chelsea, "in no way measures up to the criteria for a blue plaque and merely serves to lower the standards applicable in a misguided effort to curry popular favour."[80] Other Tory politicians dismissed Lucan as a "second-rate female impersonator."[81] Labour politicians rushed to the entertainer's defense, arguing that among their constituents he was a still-revered "figure in working-class folklore."[82] "A blue plaque is meant to be for the man in the street and not for just some snooty people opposite," contended the Labour councillor for Hackney South and Shoreditch.[83] Lucan's supporters won the debate, and a blue plaque dedicated to the actor was installed in 1978 at Lucan's former address, 11 Forty Lane, Wembley.

Rather than serving to marginalize his legacy, Lucan's resonance with working-class family audiences should be seen as an illuminating study of demographic taste in mid-twentieth-century Britain. In a period when high-minded cultural critics and left-wing commentators were bemoaning working-class entertainment for being low-brow escapism, Lucan's dame provided this audience with a sense of class solidarity and cultural affirmation as well as amusement.[84] The *Old Mother Riley* franchise showed Riley at perpetual war with those of higher status, whether they were the landlords she frequently outwitted in productions such as *Old Mother Riley in Paris* (1954), politicians and the capitalist establishment in *Old Mother Riley, MP* (1939), the powerful grocery store chain in *Old Mother Riley in Business* (1940; figure 12), or Lugosi's wicked baron in *Mother Riley Meets the Vampire*.[85] Sometimes Lucan's stage shows encouraged the audience to participate in these battles by prompting spectators to boo the landlord or to produce other such responses, provoking a sense of working-class agency against their "betters."[86]

Riley's sustained commitment to her working-class roots in each appearance stood in contrast to comparable contemporary British film stars such as George Formby and Gracie Fields, whose films went from

FIGURE 12. Old Mother Riley (far right) upsetting the establishment in a still from *Old Mother Riley in Business* (1940). Credit: Mander and Mitchenson / University of Bristol / ArenaPAL.

depicting the entertainers in working-class, communitarian regional settings reflecting their upbringings in Lancashire, to a detachment from place and community in favor of more economically liberal, individualist narratives. Film historian David Sutton has observed that Formby's first two films, *Boots! Boots!* (1934) and *Off the Dole* (1935), center Formby's working-class northern roots, with an emphasis on familial and communal ties. However, starting with *No Limit* (1937) Formby began to be depicted in "a generalized south," his aspirations shifted from the communal to the personal, and his characters could be interpreted as being middle class.[87] Where the earlier Fields film *Sing As We Go* (1935) sees her as a laid-off millworker traveling the north, a riposte to the supernaturally glamorous leading ladies of Hollywood, subsequent films such as *Queen of Hearts* (1936) and *The Show Goes On* (1937) depict Fields as a more glamorous social climber.[88] Riley, conversely, remained distinctly working class, provincial, unglamorous, and community minded in every appearance. To the extent that the character is ever seen achieving personal success and fame, she uses this power to uplift the collective. In *Old Mother Riley, MP*, for instance, the dame's ascendancy to "Minister for Strange Affairs" is not portrayed as a rags-to-riches story but as an excuse to upend the political establishment on behalf of working people. The film sees Riley beating her former boss (who is also a landlord) in an election and, once elected, fighting to conserve public parks ("poor people's gardens") and agitating for universal employment.[89] *Old Mother Riley in Business* also sees Riley in an uncharacteristically prosperous position, this time as an entrepreneur. Again, she exploits her success for the collective good, defending local shopkeepers against a greedy London-based grocery store chain using tactics such as pushing the chain's CEO into a river and barging in on a corporate board meeting.[90] Content of this nature endeared Lucan's dame to some politically minded left-wingers. *Love on the Dole* (1941) director John Baxter, who also helmed three *Old Mother Riley* films, praised Riley as "a great character for propaganda purposes."[91]

In Lucan's day popular culture and taste were often siloed based on demographic factors like geography and class. For example, whether films were seen in certain areas was highly dependent on the decisions of individual cinema managers, who prided themselves on their knowledge of local tastes, and therefore what films would play well with their patrons.[92] Lucan catered to this "localized nature of taste," but his success also lay in an understanding of motifs that would resonate broadly with working-class audiences around the country, regardless of where they lived.[93] Lucan regularly pandered to local audiences by referencing whatever locality he was appearing in.[94] A review of a show at the Nottingham Empire theater, for example, appreciated Riley's specific references to the area: "'She' attributes her 'snappy' appearance to the chic models 'she' picks up in Sneinton Market on Monday," the critic remarked.[95] A script from the 1944 revue *Old Mother Riley and Her Daughter Kitty* includes the lines "[It's] worth it just to see Brixton. Brixton. The sweetest spot this side of heaven and the other side of Clapham Common. Take no notice of that laughter. That's Streatham Hill jealousy." The script also has Riley claiming that she bought her "frock" from "(The local pawnbroker) in (local) street."[96] In lieu of explicit references to local areas, *Old Mother Riley* productions tended to be set in generalized villages or towns that her audiences could relate to. Scripts would often describe the settings as "a country village" or "a suburban home" without naming any specific, real-life locality.[97] The script for Lucan's last stage production, *Old Mother Riley in Paris*—which did not include Kitty at all and differed from the earlier film of the same name—featured references to the divisions between metropolitan and provincial life.[98] The show depicts Riley living in the fictional "Paradise Row," described as "a poor locality in a provincial town."[99] Conflict arises when Riley's son Pat (a completely new character) decides to run away with a vampy young woman from Kensington.[100] "Oh yes that is posh, isn't it? Very different to Paradise Row," confirms Old Mother Riley upon hearing of the young woman's origins. The vamp, who unkindly refers to Paradise Row as "a dump," whisks Pat away to Paris and fools him into becoming a stooge for an organized crime outfit. Riley initiates a rescue mission, ultimately taking Pat home, where he dutifully marries a "local girl."[101]

Aside from Riley's working-class nature, there were other elements that added to her apparent marginal status to high culture: her womanhood and her Irish ethnicity. Viewed today, Riley represents a regressive representation of womanhood in line with how older women have traditionally been depicted in comedy. Theater scholar Ruth Shade's definition of the typical comic older woman could almost be a description of Riley specifically, as well as countless other iterations of the pantomime dame: "The mature woman is often depicted in popular culture as formidable, dreadful, and frightening. . . . Almost all jokes about older women relate to one of three subjects—their controlling relationships with immediate family; their trivial interests (mostly gossiping, curtain-twitching or shopping); and, above all, a variety of negative manifestations of the menopause, including fluctuating moods and ill-temper, deteriorating physical appearance and diminishing sexual allure."[102] In this sense Lucan's act arguably constitutes a sexist caricature. Somewhat paradoxically though, Lucan's regressive gender politics serve to buttress the fairly pointed class politics evident in his performances. In her study of the "unruly woman," cultural studies scholar Kathleen Rowe has drawn upon the example of comedian Roseanne Barr in her eponymous sitcom. Barr, like Riley, is portrayed in the sitcom as working class, physically unattractive, loudmouthed, and ornery. Though Barr's broad humor is suggestive of sexist caricature, playing on the audience's "delight," "disgust," and "fear" in seeing a woman act in an unappealing fashion, her lack of investment in societal conventions frees her up to upend the restrictive social order.[103] Riley's marginality, as established by her sex as well as her age, class, and ethnicity, served the same purpose. Being played by a man gave Riley, and indeed the dame in general, further license to represent unruly womanhood.

Lucan's act certainly contained nods to a vague Irish heritage, though critics have debated the extent to which Riley was an Irish character and, if she was, whether the dame was meant to be from Ireland or representative of the diasporic community.[104] Examples of Lucan and McShane's references to Irish culture include the duo's brief appearance in the Irish-themed film *Kathleen Mavourneen* (1937), the inclusion of "Irish" ballads like "Danny Boy" and "When Irish Eyes Are Smiling" in some performances, and Dublin-born Kitty McShane's genuine Irish accent. Here lay a potential pitfall for Lucan. As an Englishman, he was susceptible to criticism for evoking the trope of the "stage Irishman," a then-centuries-old theatrical tradition that involved non-Irish performers enacting crude depictions of Irishmen that ranged from bestial and menacing to foolish and ridiculous, depending on contemporary views of the Irish at a given time.[105] During Lucan's lifetime, Irish immigrant communities were combating these stereotypes, figuratively and literally. In what could have been an ominous sign for Lucan, a 1907 performance of an "Irish Servant Girls" routine by cross-dressed stage Irishwomen the Russell Brothers in New York's Victoria Theatre was interrupted by a group calling itself the Society for the Prevention of Ridiculous and Pervasive Misrepresentation of the Irish Character, who heckled and hurled food at the performers.[106] Lucan received nothing approaching this level of venom; in fact, he was extolled several times by the Irish press, with some sources stating proudly—and incorrectly—that Lucan was from Ireland.[107] This suggests that Lucan's popularity drew from a milieu of working-class taste and solidarity that transcended ethnic barriers. Lucan's act echoed blackface minstrelsy in that his performance constituted a point of cross-ethnic white working-class unity, yet, unlike blackface minstrelsy, Lucan's stage Irishness did not represent a racialized other for the audience to construct their identities in opposition to.[108]

As well as transcending ethnic boundaries, Lucan's dame act also appealed to theatergoers of all ages. Riley's resonance with family audiences has led to Lucan being perceived as a children's performer, a descriptor that has likely encouraged the lack of serious analyses of the entertainer's career and legacy. This view is misleading but not unfounded. After the actor's death *Old Mother Riley* films became a fixture of cinema matinees for children. This phenomenon apparently motivated youngsters to visit Lucan's grave and "lay small bouquets of flowers, placed there by local children who had enjoyed watching his antics at their children's matinees."[109] There was also the original epitaph on Lucan's tombstone that read, "Arthur

Lucan. Better known and beloved by all children as Old Mother Riley. Don't cry as you pass by, just say a little prayer."[110] Yet to single out Lucan as a children's performer ignores that all variety and cinema entertainers of the 1930s and 1940s had strong motivations to appeal to families. While the core audience of the music hall and vaudeville was men, the variety theater and cinema relied on family audiences until the mid-1950s, when the industry shifted its focus toward appealing to the youth market.[111] Even single women were likely to bring along a male chaperone.[112] Thus it was incumbent upon practically all variety and cinema stars to have broad appeal across all age groups. Critics sometimes chided Lucan when they thought that his act was too risqué for children. As one reviewer complained, "[Lucan and McShane] certainly gave the children among the audience a good time. But why when it was to a large extent an entertainment staged for the benefit of children, did Arthur Lucan find it necessary to let his humor get near the 'border-line.'"[113] Critiques such as this were rare, however. Lucan's humor was sometimes referred to as "earthy" at worst, but the overwhelming majority of critics found it to be wholesome.[114]

Arthur Lucan exemplified how the twentieth-century dame harkened back to the cultural figure's past while at the same time being innovative and modern. Yet his legacy was, and continues to be, unfairly overlooked despite his status as one of the most successful British entertainers of his day. Still, there are clear signs that Lucan's legacy has lived on even if Riley is not as ubiquitous as she once was. Matronly dame duo Hinge and Bracket, who debuted at the 1974 Edinburgh Fringe, were praised for being "completely convincing characters" in their radio, television, and stage (including pantomime) act, which was heralded as a "new development in drag" but of course was not.[115] The dame creation of Rex Jameson, Mrs. Shufflewick, owed much to Lucan's characterization. Jameson, whose early theatrical experience can be traced to post–Second World War ex-servicemen's drag revues, famously performed as "Shuff" in venues such as the Windmill in Soho and the Black Cap gay pub in Camden from the 1950s until his death in 1983. Like Lucan, Jameson also demonstrated a commitment to making his dame believable, including attending radio appearances in full costume as Lucan did. Shuff harkened back to Riley's feistiness and slight frame too, but the humor of Jameson's dame was wryer and raunchier. Instead of directing her venom at family members or establishment figures, Shuff tended to deride the audience.[116] More recently, Lucan's presence has been felt in the hugely popular BBC sitcom *Mrs Brown's Boys* (2011–present). The show stars Brendan O'Carroll as the titular dame and his wife, Jennifer Gibney, as Mrs. Brown's daughter—a twenty-first century Lucan and McShane. The uncanny similarities do not end there: Mrs. Brown is Irish and has also appeared in her own film and stage show, O'Carroll's performances are known for broad humor interspersed with elements of pathos, and the show has also been widely dismissed by the cultural cognoscenti despite its immense popular success.[117] It is clear that the dame continues to occupy a privileged position in British entertainment, both inside and outside of pantomime. What is more, despite Arthur Lucan's oft-neglected legacy, Old Mother Riley's influence is still present in portrayals of the time-honored role.

2 Splinters

Cross-Dressing Ex-Servicemen on the Interwar Stage

One of the most conspicuous renderings of male gender variance in early twentieth-century Britain was a series of theatrical productions that starred casts of ex-servicemen in women's clothes. These shows all fell under the genre of the revue, a popular form of theatrical light entertainment introduced to Britain in the early 1910s and that featured a diverse set of scenes unified by a loose plot or theme.[1] Ex-servicemen's drag revues developed from female impersonation performed by and for British servicemen in concert parties on the front lines during the First World War.[2] This chapter will discuss what happened when ex-servicemen drag artistes transferred their act from the theater of war to the urban, suburban, and provincial theaters of the British variety circuit. Staging shows on the home front exposed ex-servicemen female impersonators to new forms of spectatorship that they did not encounter in wartime concert parties: the theatergoing public, arts criticism in the press, and state censorship.[3]

My focus here is the First World War troupe Les Rouges et Noirs, which first popularized the subgenre of ex-servicemen's drag revues with their debut production *Splinters* (1918) and continued to cultivate a successful career well into the 1930s.[4] The ensemble's productions tended to feature comedy sketches, dance, song, and similar revue fare under the auspices of giving audiences a taste of the wartime concert party experience. Though the tone of the shows was mostly light and comedic, the performers' drag was meant to be earnestly pretty, even alluring. For spectators, part of the fun of seeing Les Rouges was not to laugh at their female impersonations but to be taken in by their aesthetic appeal, perhaps forgetting momentarily that the cast was all male.

The members of Les Rouges were among the most celebrated performers of their day, whose accolades included an engagement at Windsor Castle and starring roles as the subjects of one of the very first motion picture "talkies" produced in Britain. The contemporary reception to the troupe's performances was multifaceted. The players of Les Rouges could, for instance, be seen at once as earnestly sensual and trivial fun, as troubling and reassuring, as comic and dramatic. The range of areas Les Rouges visited on their tours spoke to the ensemble's popularity throughout Britain. Their maiden tour from 1919 through 1924, for example, included engagements in every major English city, parts of Wales such as Swansea and Newport, Scottish cities like Glasgow and Edinburgh, seaside locales like Boscombe and Westcliff-on-Sea, and industrial areas such as Salford and Bradford.[5] As a whole, the response to Les Rouges by theatergoers and critics was overwhelmingly positive.

A significant source of the performers' appeal lay in their status as genuine discharged ex-servicemen, a feature of the productions that was regularly emphasized in promotional material, the content of the company's shows, and press coverage of Les Rouges. The artists' well-publicized participation in the war effort encouraged civilian audiences to view Les Rouges' shows as an authentic, informative, and entertaining way to engage with troops' wartime experiences during a period marked by uncertainties about how popular culture should engage with the war and its legacy.

Though the wartime service of Les Rouges' members was widely admired and remarked upon, the fundamental key to their popularity was ultimately simpler: the troupe's shows were highly entertaining and technically well produced. As one reviewer concluded in a typical assessment of the company, "The knowledge that the entertainment now being given at the Savoy has for years eased the monotony of life at the front for thousands of our fighting men would make us oblivious to any shortcomings. . . . But there are no shortcomings. The performers are good, many of them wonderfully good."[6] Particularly lauded by observers was the ensemble's skillful feminine mimicry. Critics unapologetically described the ex-servicemen artists as alluring beauties and the troupe's promotional material unselfconsciously boasted about "love letters" the performers received from male admirers.[7]

As Les Rouges were staging their widely acclaimed performances, male gender variance was becoming increasingly associated with transgressive cultural meanings by the state, the press, and other commentators. For example, men who wore makeup in public were held up as symbols of moral degradation in interwar London.[8] The "painted boy menace," as these individuals were referred to in an extended exposé by *John Bull* magazine in 1925, were regular targets of arrest for suspected homosexual offenses and were portrayed by the press as a dire threat to the nation's social fabric.[9] A 1932 raid on a ball conducted at Holland Park Avenue, London, where many of the attendees were cross-dressed men, led to the arrests of sixty patrons.[10] The organizers of Lady Malcolm's Servants' Ball, a fancy dress ball held annually for domestic servants at the Royal Albert Hall, announced in 1935 that the practice of male cross-dressing would no longer be allowed at the event, citing the association between male cross-dressing and sexual perversion as the reason for the new policy.[11] Some of the discourse regarding interwar ex-servicemen's drag revues reflected these contemporary anxieties about male gender variance. The Lord Chamberlain's Office, for example, voiced some wariness about the revues due to the perceived connection between male cross-dressing and sexual im-morality.[12] A small number of reviews for Les Rouges productions ex-pressed a belief that female impersonation was "distasteful" or associated with a "subtle unpleasantness," but such statements were often made to impress upon readers that the shows were *not* morally suspect, as one might have assumed.[13] Overall, any negative opinions communicated about the shows were in the minority and did not ap-pear to impede the success of the productions. In fact, Les Rouges' popularity inspired a surge in similar productions starring cross-dressed ex-servicemen immediately following the Second World War, such as *Soldiers in Skirts* (1945) and *Forces in Petticoats* (1952).

Scholarly accounts of gender variance in this period have focused on how the practice—whether rendered through female impersona-tion, unconventional gendered character traits, contemporary fash-ion trends that obfuscated aesthetic gender boundaries, or other ways—aroused controversies that revealed "anxiety about the blur-ring of gender lines [which] grew out of the experiences of the Great War" in particular.[14] And yet individuals presenting themselves in terms of gender variance were the objects of widespread, sustained, and unambiguous acclaim throughout the interwar period; female impersonation was intrinsic to the contemporary theatrical and popu-lar milieu.[15] Far from being a source of anxiety, the cross-dressing Les Rouges ensemble was lauded by commentators for providing the Brit-ish public with uncomplicated relief in uncertain times. In analyzing a markedly popular manifestation of female impersonation, this chapter both encourages historians of gender and sexuality to con-sider the diverse ways in which gender variance was interpreted and expressed and aims to contribute to existing historiographical discus-sions regarding the interwar popular culture of convalescence.[16]

Les Rouges et Noirs first developed their act in concert party the-atricals staged for their fellow servicemen during the First World War.[17] Concert parties were "practically universal" by the end of

1917, according to military historian J. G. Fuller, with at least 80 percent of divisions staging them over the course of the war.[18] Owing to high demand and the fact that entertainment for the forces was mostly organized by troops themselves, servicemen-performers were often given relatively light military duties so they could be "virtually full-time entertainers."[19] It was not unusual for divisional ensembles to stage hundreds of shows per year, with many companies traveling widely to perform for other divisions.[20] Individual concert party shows tended to consist of a series of unrelated turns, with female impersonation acts being a common feature. Concert party drag was manifold. Renderings of female impersonation included performances with erotic potential, comic dame portrayals, and earnest depictions of maternity.[21] The diverse femininities represented in First World War concert party drag reflected, to some extent, the types of female impersonation on the early twentieth-century British stage, where audiences could see men dressed as elderly comic dames or as glamorous, attractive women. What was unprecedented about Les Rouges, however, was the preeminent level of fame the ensemble achieved compared to their contemporary female impersonators.

Les Rouges was the first British troupe to turn a wartime female impersonation act into a successful touring revue on the home front.[22] The company originally starred Reg Stone, a.k.a. "Phil" (figure 13), the lead female impersonator; comedian Hal Jones as "Splinter," who played most of the leading male roles; and an all-male "beauty chorus."[23] The ensemble caught their big break in December 1918 when, at the War Office's behest, they performed a three-night public engagement of their show *Splinters* at the YMCA's Beaver Hut Theatre in The Strand.[24] These shows were an instant success, leading to a performance at Windsor Castle for King George V and Queen Mary and a UK-wide tour for general audiences from 1919 through 1924.[25] Les Rouges regularly toured British theaters into the late

THIS IS NOT A PAGE DEALING WITH A SOCIETY ENGAGEMENT!

IN TWO CHARACTERS: AS THE BEAUTY AND AS HIMSELF.

A casual glance at the photographs on the above page might suggest that it illustrated a society engagement—not a soldier-comedian in real life and on the stage! Mr. Reginald Stone, however, is the "leading lady" of the First Army Entertainers, "Les Rouges et Noirs," whose revue, "Splinters," is proving so great a success at the Savoy. The photographs need no comment, except that, if England succeeded in "carrying-on" at home by the substitution of women for men in certain trades, the B.E.F. were equally successful in their efforts to do the reverse.

Photographs by Foulsham and Banfield, Ltd.

FIGURE 13. Contrasting images depicting Reg Stone cross-dressed "as the beauty" and in military uniform "as himself," 1919. Credit: © British Library Board. All Rights Reserved / Bridgeman Images.

1930s and spawned three films under the *Splinters* moniker: *Splinters* (1930), *Splinters in the Navy* (1932), and *Splinters in the Air* (1937).[26]

A program from their August 1919 engagement at London's Savoy Theatre lends insight into how the troupe was promoted. Emphasizing Les Rouges' valor on the front, one notable anecdote in the program detailed how the company bravely returned to an evacuated camp under the cover of night to retrieve the frocks they left behind, with "shells screaming overhead and dropping sometimes sickeningly near."[27] This dramatic portrayal of the artists' dedication to their craft was tempered by the program's insistence that members of the troupe "regard their work in feminine garb as a huge joke, [but] there is no doubt they brought real and necessary entertainment and distraction to their soldier audiences in France."[28] While the program stressed that the performers considered cross-dressing a casual lark—"a huge joke"—rather than an act that held profound personal meaning, it was also noted unselfconsciously, and somewhat paradoxically, that this "joke" lasted after the performance had ended and that it could provoke potentially earnest emotions from spectators. "And, of course, they get love letters, treasured as souvenirs of a unique engagement," the program added.[29] This impassioned response to the shows was alleged to be a result of performers' ability to expertly imitate women, particularly British women. "What did the average Tommy long for . . . Just—GIRLS! But the genuine English-speaking variety was non est," insisted the program, "therefore a good colourable imitation was the next best thing."[30] Presumably this implied that servicemen preferred a congenial British femininity—even if it was performed by other men—over engaging with continental European women. Through promotional materials like the Savoy program, Les Rouges succinctly highlighted the main elements of their appeal: their commendable wartime service and their skillful female impersonation.

The content of the troupe's theatricals mostly involved usual revue-type offerings such as song and dance numbers and sketches featuring comedic patter. Some of the turns referred to life on the front, but this theme was not strictly adhered to. One particularly lauded scene from the debut *Splinters* production, "Tommy Buys a Souvenir," sees Hal Jones as a "Tommy" and Reg Stone as a lusty French souvenir shop assistant. Jones "dallies over long in her witching society," and much of the humor is derived from Jones's futile attempts at flirting with Stone's "saucy minx," who has a limited English vocabulary.[31] Another comic sketch called "The Tale of a Grandfather Clock" contrasts "bye-gone and present-day methods of lovemaking."[32] The scene features Stone as one half of an unsentimental "slangy Twentieth Century couple" who exchange crass contemporary insults, juxtaposed with a decorous Victorian couple.[33] In addition to comedic drag performances, the first publicly staged *Splinters* show also included more solemn turns. One critic wrote that a masculine-presenting cellist and singer, with a cross-dressed pianist, "brought a blur into my eyes."[34] A dance number performed by female impersonator Jack Hives reportedly made it appear "as though Maud Allan and her Salome dream were floating across the stage horizon again."[35]

Much of the original Les Rouges troupe disbanded in 1924, but subsequent iterations of the company continued to perform under the *Splinters* moniker into the late 1930s. For the most part, the format of the later productions did not differ greatly from that of the first *Splinters* show. One notable exception to this was the revue *Splinters 1914–1933* (1933), which boasted the radical novelty of "Real ladies introduced for the first time—in addition to the female impersonators."[36] Confusion as to the "true" sex of the performers, as implied by the alternative title of the show, *Which Is Which*, is the source of much comic business throughout. For instance, one scene revolves around "Hal greet[ing] the W.A.A.C. [Women's Army Auxiliary Corps] sergeant in familiar manner when he mistakes her for his pal in new guise."[37] By the end of their career in the 1930s, Les Rouges was clearly a well-established brand, with three *Splinters* films released—the first of which was one of the very first British motion picture "talkies"—and critics regularly attested to the troupe's ubiquitously cherished status in popular culture, as I will discuss later.

The critical reception to Les Rouges' initial public performances in Britain was almost universally positive. Reflecting the content of the ensemble's promotional material, critics tended to highlight the performers' wartime service while also marveling at the talent exhibited onstage. As the *Daily Telegraph* remarked of the troupe's Savoy debut, "It is quite easy to believe that those who made and performed that revue helped to win the war. How many tens of thousands of Tommies might have lost something of their indomitable British spirit and grit but for the stimulus at times of such jolly, honest fun as they got out of 'Splinters'!"[38] "[*Splinters*] gave last night's overflowing audience three hours of unmixed pleasure," raved the *Sussex Daily News*. "What it must have meant to troops undergoing all the horrors of the trenches one can only dimly speculate."[39] The *Times*, also emphasizing the ensemble's ability to authentically connect audiences with servicemen's experiences, concluded, "We are inclined to think [this was] the first time that the entertainment has been given in its entirety and as nearly as possible under the same conditions as prevailed during the war in France."[40] Les Rouges maintained their overwhelmingly favorable critical reputation into the 1930s, by which point they were widely viewed with nostalgic reverence. A 1934 article declared that "'Splinters' is now quite a household word. Mention of it conjures up something more than mere entertainment . . . romance."[41] A review of *Splinters* 1914–1933 (renamed *Splinters* 1914–1934 to take the New Year into account) indicated that the performers' efforts on the front lines still held cachet nearly sixteen years after the end of the Great War: "'Splinters,' the famous show which lightened the hearts of many in France during the war years . . . still retaining many long-remembered associations in the post-war period[,] makes a welcome return. . . . The show is rare fun from start to finish."[42] A significant part of Les Rouges' appeal lay in their ability to help audiences feel connected to servicemen's wartime experiences, specifically the phenomenon of the frontline concert party. The arts and visual culture played a critical role in shaping how the British public understood the First World War, both as it was occurring and in its aftermath.[43] Public consumption of war-related media was largely driven by a yearning for information about loved ones' experiences and those of British forces generally.[44] Artistic representations of the war were perceived to be more authentic and educational if Tommies themselves devised and took part in them. The ex-servicemen in the cast of the war play *Journey's End* (1929), for example, were praised for lending a sense of realism to the production, giving observers the impression that the actors were "re-enacting their past" onstage, thus enhancing the play's ability to inform and educate.[45] Seeing the recently discharged ex-servicemen artists of Les Rouges perform was both an entertaining and edifying exercise for the troupe's civilian audience members. Given the ubiquity of concert parties among British and Dominion forces, civilians likely would have heard about such entertainments from media reports or through contact with servicemen.[46] Evidence suggests that the common feature of drag in wartime concert parties was a source of particular fascination for the public on the home front. *Punch* magazine, for instance, reported on the phenomenon with playful bemusement several times over the course of the war.[47] Furthermore, some members of the public would have heard specifically of Les Rouges' concert parties by reputation through wartime reporting. This sparked an initial curiosity about the ensemble that could later be satiated by seeing their postwar public engagements. As one newspaper recalled, "During the war, occasionally by the London papers, and frequently through remarks made by men home on leave, people in England heard in a vague way of a concert party calling

themselves 'Les Rouges et Noirs,' who at rest camp and base la-
boured to amuse our men in their brief respites from the horrors of
the field."[48] Les Rouges revues informed civilians about an aspect of
the war that most of them would have been aware of, yet few had
seen firsthand. The fact that the shows were presented by a genuine
concert party ensemble—with their martial credentials detailed in
promotional materials like the August 1919 program—imbued the
productions with authenticity and strengthened their perceived educational potential in the eyes of a public whose hunger for information about troops' experiences lasted into the interwar period.

Les Rouges not only catered to the public's desire for authentic
representations of life on the front but also satisfied a demand for
light entertainment among war-weary theatergoers. Despite civilians' craving for information about the war, some methods of relay-
ing news from the front were deemed too frank and depressing. Roll
of Honour films, for example, were dropped from cinemas by 1917 as
patrons increasingly found them distressing.[49] Instead, many Britons
gravitated toward more reassuring ways of engaging with the war,
like viewing the latest sleek, modernized hospital trains that were
exhibited at railway stations yet were rarely used at the front.[50]
The early interwar period was marked by unease about the extent
to which society should dwell upon the subject of war. For ex-
servicemen who had experienced mental and physical trauma, an
emphasis was placed on the need to overcome their difficulties expe-
diently. Wounded troops were often encouraged to display inspiring
signs of recovery for the media and visitors to military hospitals.[51]
With respect to the arts, some commentators such as dramatist
St. John Greer Ervine argued that the nation was too "exhausted"
by war to "create a great drama or a great anything else until we have
recovered our health."[52] The British public's somewhat paradoxical
desire to learn more about the war and also to quickly overcome wartime trauma was demonstrated by the success of war-themed light

entertainment like the Charlie Chaplin comedy film *Shoulder Arms* (1918). Initially released days after the Armistice and rereleased several times during the interwar period owing to its popularity, *Shoulder Arms* was promoted as a film that addressed the war head-on while also helping cinemagoers move on emotionally. An advertisement for the film directed at cinema exhibitors proclaimed that it "has come at the right time. People can laugh at it without any guilty feeling now," while *Bioscope* magazine reported, "It is so lighthearted that every Tommy and Jack will roar themselves hoarse now it is past history."[53] Yet the film's broad humor did not obscure its perceived realism in the eyes of audiences. As film historian Michael Hammond has concluded, *Shoulder Arms* "depicts the stresses and discomforts of military life at the front, which resonated with soldiers and those at home imagining the conditions there."[54]

Like *Shoulder Arms*, Les Rouges' shows occupied a pleasurable middle ground between evoking servicemen's wartime experiences and providing light entertainment. Even the company's recreation of a battle and its aftermath in the first *Splinters* film, arguably the most dramatic performance of Les Rouges' career, was praised for its restraint. "The final sequence, which shows Hal Jones re-marshalling his complete company after the bombing attack that shattered their hard-won theatre[,] is rich with a comedy and pathos that cannot soon be forgotten," declared a glowing review in *Sketch* magazine: "In the handling of this episode Mr. Raymond [the director] shows the greatest artistic perception in avoiding the obvious temptation to condemn one or several of his valiant little band of actors to heroic deaths. . . . [T]he whole thing is merely a slice of make-believe set in the midst of a stern and terrible reality."[55] The battle scene depicts the artists quickly throwing khaki uniforms over their frocks after their concert party is disrupted by a bombing. The beauty chorus is then shown running outside to return fire, with frilly frocks still clearly peeking out underneath their uniforms. After shots are exchanged with the enemy, Les Rouges and their First Army comrades easily emerge victorious, with no casualties taken, before the end credits roll.[56] Ultimately, in addition to reinforcing the entertainers' ever-present masculinity (even while cross-dressed), this scene served to carefully connect audiences with the "stern and terrible reality" the Tommies faced without shattering the relatively light "slice of make-believe" that constitutes the film's true focal point. This low-stakes, pleasurable drama demonstrated by the battle scene echoes a trend evident in interwar popular culture that historian Alison Light has identified as "a literature of convalescence."[57] An example of this phenomenon was seen in contemporary "whodunit" mystery novels that took a mild, pleasurable approach to crime fiction rather than relying on melodrama or threat as earlier works in the genre had done.[58] Although the interwar whodunits and the *Splinters* film take place against the backdrop of perceivably lurid circumstances—crime and war, respectively—both approach their subjects in an "airy manner" that served to preoccupy rather than provoke pathos, even in the most serious scenes.[59] Through content like this in their stage and screen appearances, as well as their promotional material, Les Rouges cannily tapped into an interwar popular culture defined by audiences' desire for perceivably authentic, yet ultimately reassuring, war-themed media.

Les Rouges' status as ex-servicemen played upon pertinent contemporary patriotic motifs regarding the soldier's elevated place in interwar British culture. The patriotic ideal of the "soldier-hero" was often considered unassailable, even when there was evidence that servicemen had participated in sexual encounters with other men. By the early 1930s, the Brigade of Guards had experienced a number of recent scandals involving cases of guardsmen engaging in same-sex liaisons with older, wealthier men in London.[60] These were not isolated incidents but glimpses of a well-established commercial and social phenomenon where guardsmen exchanged sexual favors for money and luxuries.[61] When the guardsman's association with sexual availability was finally brought to light to the extent that it could no longer be ignored, the state defended the soldiers' conduct, thus jealously maintaining the guardsman's position as a totemic icon of masculinity and nationhood.[62] The War Office, setting the tone for the guardsmen's defense, blamed corrupting influences rather than moral failings on the part of soldiers. "The contamination of members of the armed forces stationed in London is a greater risk than that incurred in the provinces," argued the War Office, noting factors that might lead young guardsmen to be seduced into vice, including "an environment containing all shades of entertainment" and "[being] perpetually short of money."[63] The vulnerable guardsman was contrasted with the "evil" predatory "queer" who cravenly preyed upon young soldiers and represented an insidious threat to the health of the nation.[64] The presupposed masculine integrity of the guardsman and his indelible association with nationhood made it less likely for him to be labeled as a pervert or, indeed, to be marked with any label at all, even if he engaged in sexual acts with other men.

As a paragon of masculinity and symbol of the nation, the serviceman represented the ideals that men who presented themselves in terms of gender variance and sexual difference perceivably stood opposed to. Institutions and individuals were complicit in maintaining the national ideal of the soldier-hero, which gave the interwar serviceman some license to push the boundaries of sexual morality so long as he could ultimately fulfill his role as the "'symbolic centre' of Britishness . . . 'a cultural focus around which the national community could cohere.'"[65] Unlike in the Brigade of Guards scandal, there was no conspiracy at the institutional level that sought to protect the masculine integrity of Les Rouges as the ex-servicemen performers temporarily subverted their masculinity night after night. Instead, the company benefited from a more passive collective reverence for the soldier-hero.

The wartime service of the members of Les Rouges earned them admiration and attracted audiences who sought a connection to life on the front. However, the main focus of critics' praise was the impressive artistic quality of the troupe's performances. In particular, contemporary reviews unselfconsciously raved about the female impersonators'—especially Reg Stone's—ability to represent a beguiling idealized femininity. Despite the mostly comedic nature of the revues, Stone and his castmates' female impersonations never resembled broad caricature; they deliberately projected earnest beauty. "Compare any of the languid beauties of revue or musical comedy with the energetic charms of Mr. Reginald Stone as leading lady," the *Evening Standard* proclaimed of an engagement on the debut *Splinters* tour in 1919, "and it is obvious that the advantage belongs not to the former."[66] Another *Standard* review struck a similar tone: "There are many chorus beauties upon our London stage who might do worse than take a few hints from Reg. Stone. . . . Stone makes up into the most attractive girl with short dress, bewitching smile, and banded hair complete."[67] The *Daily Express* observed that the show "played to peals of laughter" and singled out Stone's "coquetry and demureness, without a trace of exaggeration, [which] nearly sent the ladies in the audience into hysterics. Mr. Stone could probably write a textbook on 'Hints to Actresses.'"[68] "Stone in particular . . . achieves a wonderful sexual transition, complete in all its details," gushed the *Brighton Standard*, "down to the white-powdered arms and polished manicured finger-nails, the dainty gestures and positively pretty little affectations of femininity."[69] The *London Opinion* also highlighted the ensemble's ability to mimic abstract "affectations of femininity," observing that "little captivating tricks that come unconsciously to the girl who has always been one are copied with excruciating fidelity by the temporary ladies of the company."[70]

Reviews like the ones written about Les Rouges' shows, with their lush and complimentary descriptions of the performers' bodies and feminine comportment, were similar to contemporary critical comment about erotically charged chorus line and "girlie" shows, a genre that took off in the United States and Britain between the 1890s and 1920s. Critics of the 1910s described the women who appeared in these shows as "lovely, shapely . . . superbly young and picturesque" and displaying a "fine carriage."[71] The reviews for Les Rouges also demonstrate how, by the interwar period, it had become increasingly acceptable for the male body to be seen as a site of eroticism and beauty.[72] Concepts like beauty and glamour, previously the preserve of women, were being frequently applied to men as well by the 1910s.[73] A consumption culture emerged around the objectification of the male physique, consisting of mass-produced photographs, magazines, and men's beauty competitions that women were sometimes invited to judge.[74] During the First World War many advertisers and photographers' studios went from showcasing beautiful women to displaying images of handsome young soldiers.[75] Organizations like the Men's Dress Reform Party complained that men had "abandoned their claim to be beautiful" by wearing utilitarian, muted clothing, while contemporary womenswear allowed for greater freedom and aesthetic individualism. The reformers encouraged men to be "as beautiful as women" by adopting a wardrobe of more loose-fitting, ornamental, colorful, and unique apparel.[76] These trends, combined with the carnivalesque fun of the theater milieu, made it increasingly acceptable for men to openly prize other men for aesthetic beauty, particularly if the subject was a virile young ex-serviceman.[77] What is more, in the case of Les Rouges, beauty was not just considered skin deep. In judging the attractiveness of these ex-servicemen performing femininity, critics not only considered the face, body, and clothing but also intangible facets of the ensembles' comportment, like "charms" and "affectations."[78] While these markers of superficial beauty could not be located on a specific part of the body, they were nonetheless deemed equally important as "bewitching smile[s]" and "white powdered arms" when the female impersonators' outward beauty was appraised.

Critics and audiences had no qualms about finding the female impersonators of Les Rouges attractive; indeed, they enjoyed it when they did. If a male audience member felt some form of desire, sexual or otherwise, for a cast member, it was not viewed as a crisis of sexuality but as part of the fun. The *London Opinion*, for instance, noted with amusement "the shock that [artist G. L.] Stampa had when he went round to the Stage Door afterwards" alongside a cartoon by Stampa depicting a lustful "Stage Door Johnnie's" amazement upon being greeted by masculine-presenting servicemen coming out of their dressing room. The caption read, "The Beauties in real life."[79]

The backstage area as a stark, reassuring dividing line where the veneer of theatrical feminine glamour was dropped to reveal the military man underneath was a reoccurring motif that Les Rouges played on. One scene in the first *Splinters* film depicts Reg Stone in his dressing room smoking a pipe after a performance, the picture of masculine leisure despite the fact that he is still cross-dressed. A Stage Door Johnnie, played by comedian Sydney Howard, and his lovelorn companion decide to pursue Stone to his dressing room after the artist blows Howard a flirtatious kiss onstage. In the offstage setting, however, Stone responds gruffly to the intruders' entreaties, yelling, "Now don't come back here again. . . . Now hop it!" at Howard's friend before physically assailing Howard.[80] *Splinters in the Navy* sees Howard trespassing backstage again. After he rips off a beauty chorus member's wig, the artist forcefully grabs it back and reprimands Howard, shouting, "What do you think you're playing at?!" in a gruff cockney baritone.[81] The backstage restoration of gendered normalcy was also highlighted in the film's promotion. Reg Stone "has so far managed to mislead three electricians and a carpenter as to his sex," stated one reporter while affirming that Stone's feminine guise was dropped once the cameras stopped rolling.[82] The momentary views of Les Rouges backstage tacitly acknowledged that some audience members may have inferred that the artists' theatrical effeminacy onstage was an indicator of disturbing behaviors offstage. Under the premise of providing a fly-on-the-wall backstage glimpse at the performers, audiences were assured that the company's femininity was purely an onstage affair; it was established that once the ensemble members de-wigged, they naturally reverted to a default masculinity, smoking pipes, fighting, and fulfilling their martial duties.[83]

The dressing room scenes, with their elements of voyeurism and depictions of partially undressed female impersonators, were sexually titillating to some audience members. One correspondent who wrote to *London Life* newspaper, for example, recalled with relish the backstage scenes in *Splinters* films. Writing in 1940, years after the films had been released, the correspondent remembered their favorite scenes in detail, albeit with some aspects embellished to make the proceedings sound more risqué. In describing what was probably the backstage scene from *Splinters in the Navy*, the writer recalled "[the scene] in the 'chorus girls'' dressing room, where the 'chorus' were to be seen in *every* stage of undress as they prepared for the stage."[84] Holding forth further on the topic of partially undressed drag artists in media, the letter writer also fondly remembered "one of those American 'shorts'" that depicted two young female impersonators revealing "their long silk-clad legs completely on view . . . not to mention frilly garters high up the leg, ribbon suspenders and chic 'unmentionables.'"[85] Les Rouges offered enjoyment to audiences who wanted to experience the fun of a temporary attraction to the performers, and those whose attraction was more profound, long lasting, and fetishistic.

Though Les Rouges received widespread critical acclaim, reviews were not always positive. Further, among the few negative assessments I have found, most cited discomfort with drag as a reason for their views. "The Splinters Concert Party," wrote one critic in 1932, "has once more been incorporated with the usual addition of female impersonation which always seems to me distasteful."[86] Other observers referenced negative connotations associated with drag but did so to reassure readers that Les Rouges provided only wholesome entertainment. "An important point is that there is nothing offensive about the 'beautiful young ladies' who are really stalwart young men," declared the *London Mail* in 1919, continuing, "How they have managed to eliminate all trace of that subtle unpleasantness so often associated with this type of thing I know not, but it has been done."[87] Another review of a stop on the troupe's 1919 tour, this time in the *Bournemouth Graphic*, chose to be more direct in its praise of Reg Stone for not evoking "the slightest suspicion of the 'Nancy' type."[88] In private correspondence Edith Thompson, whose 1922 murder trial would become a cause célèbre, reported on a Les Rouges performance she saw and compared the troupe favorably to other cross-dressed men she had seen. "Men usually dressed as women—especially in evening dress—look ridiculous," wrote Thompson, "but these were splendid—very clever and very funny—I did laugh such a lot—it was really dancing through the hours."[89] Negative views of female impersonation expressed in press coverage of Les Rouges remained stubbornly uncommon and muted from the late 1910s to the late 1930s, despite the press's increased focus on gender variance–related controversies from the mid-1920s.

One notable expression of unease came via the Lord Chamberlain's Office, which sometimes viewed the *Splinters* shows with skepticism but always inevitably licensed the revues with few edits. For instance, the Office reader's report on *Splinters* 1914–1933 determined that, despite show's inclusion of cross-dressing, "I do not see any unpleasant suggestiveness in this: it is simply a question of clever make-up. There is also mesmerism, 'illusionism,' sham thought reading, and a mannequin parade parodied by the men, in which it is definitely directed that there is to be no 'Nancy' business. . . . I find nothing to censor.'[90] The Lord Chamberlain cautiously agreed in a handwritten note at the bottom of the report. "I detest men making up as women," he wrote, "but if there is a caution about the avoidance of all suggestiveness and no 'Nancy' business, I suppose it is all right."[91] The chief constable of Manchester, who came to a staging of the show, saw it as "second-rate" and observed that some spectators were "disgusted," but nothing came of the complaints other than a meeting with the revue's producer at the Lord Chamberlain's Office during which it was agreed that just a couple of lines should be cut from the script.[92] A subsequent *Splinters* revue, though ultimately approved, was criticized by the Lord Chamberlain's Office for the inclusion of a "perversion joke." "No mercy with such trash," read a handwritten note on the reader's report in response to the alleged suggestiveness of the joke.[93]

With respect to the censor, the Lord Chamberlain's Office had an official ban on the representation of same-sex desire, and anything perceived to be indicative of it, on the stage until 1958.[94] These rules, however, were fairly nebulous and were applied inconsistently. Theater critic Nicholas De Jongh has argued that "effeminate and camp males generally appear to have been regarded as a virtual third gender that posed no threat to men."[95] De Jongh has cited the licensing of a Noël Coward script featuring quite obviously homosexual characters, *Bitter Sweet* (1929), as evidence that the censor was willing to turn a blind eye to displays of gender variance and even same-sex desire onstage as long as it was framed by middle- to upper-class mise-en-scène and represented a desexed, eccentric effeminacy. The perceived association between male cross-dressing and sexual immorality was observed by the Lord Chamberlain's Office, but it was not deemed explicit enough to warrant banning drag from the stage.[96] Les Rouges benefited from a censorship body that was tolerant of gender variance so long as it was mostly comic and was largely free of explicit references to sexuality.[97]

Extricating male cross-dressing from sexuality became increasingly difficult by the 1930s as the perception that gender variance was linked with sexual immorality became more culturally pervasive. As mentioned earlier in this chapter, in December 1932, shortly before *Splinters* 1914–1933 opened to fanfare, police arrested sixty people, many of them cross-dressed men, in a raid on an underground ball at Holland Park Avenue in London.[98] The ball's crossed-dressed male attendees were particularly fixated on by the police, the prosecution, and the media as symbols of immorality in London and the nation as a whole. The press reacted to the case with sensational headlines like "Men Dressed as Women," indicating that such a description could conjure up thoughts of lurid behaviors and types of people with no additional comment necessary.[99] During the trial the Recorder of London, Sir Ernest Wild, acknowledged the public's growing acknowledgment of sex between men—increasingly associated with gender variance—as a societal danger.[100] Contrasting the 1930s with Victorian times, he noted, "When gross indecency between males was made an offence nearly fifty years ago, many juries acquitted, because being decent-minded men they could not think such beastliness could exist."[101] Wild's comments specifically tied homosexual offenses to the accused men's feminine gender presentation and the women's clothing they wore while also comparing older understandings of gender and sexuality with newer ones. The British public of the 1930s, Wild argued, was now aware of the existence of men who engaged in acts of sexual immorality with one another and understood that gender variance signified the type of man who might commit these acts.

Even mainstream popular venues were not above suspicion regarding perceivably immoral presences. In 1933 a complaint was sent to Scotland Yard regarding "Degenerate Boys and men in female attire parading about" at that year's Lady Malcolm's Servants' Ball, an annual fancy dress ball for domestic servants in the Royal Albert Hall overseen by aristocrat Lady Malcolm.[102] A ban on male cross-dressing at the ball was imposed two years later, and former Criminal Investigation Department officers were hired to eject cross-dressed "sexual perverts" from the venue, thus clearly establishing the impetus behind the policy.[103]

Despite all these examples of gender variance being cast as a social ill, Les Rouges et Noirs remained hugely popular between the wars, and its legacy extended into the 1940s and 1950s. The widespread popularity of ex-servicemen's drag revues was sustained by Les Rouges from 1918 to the late 1930s and then surged again in the 1940s and 1950s with new touring productions such as *Soldiers in Skirts*, *Forces Showboat* (1947), and *Forces in Petticoats*.[104] In addition to being inspired by Les Rouges, the newer post–Second World War revues were also influenced by then-recent drag shows staged by American GIs. Female impersonation by Black and white American servicemen-performers figured prominently in the stage and film versions of the Irving Berlin "all-soldier musical show" *This Is the Army* (1942).[105] The British tour of *Skirts* (1943), a drag revue performed by American servicemen with music by songwriter Frank Loesser, also likely influenced British counterparts.[106] The newer British ex-servicemen's drag revues were widely popular, just as their post–First World War forerunners had been. *Soldiers in Skirts* and *This Was the Army* (1946) (figure 14), for example, both toured for nine uninterrupted years, while others, like *We Were in the Forces* (1944), employed multiple touring companies at once in order to keep up with demand.[107]

The ex-servicemen's drag revues of the 1940s and 1950s existed in a different cultural context than the Les Rouges shows, however. One pertinent development was the emergence of "the homosexual," "a relatively new category of selfhood" that emerged following the Second World War.[108] The homosexual cast himself as a respectable and discreet individual whose sexual and romantic desires, though abnormal, should not be subject to criminal penalty. For

FIGURE 14. Drag artists Sonny Dawkes and Tommy Rose featured in handbills for ex-servicemen's drag revue *This Was the Army* (1946) from 1950 (top) and 1953 (bottom). Note the earnest, glamorous femininity Dawkes and Rose exude in these images despite the show being mostly comedic. Credit: Images supplied by courtesy of Willson's Printers Newark Limited.

homosexual law reform campaigners like journalist Peter Wilde-blood, the homosexual identity was marked by opposition to gender variance.[109] Wildeblood criticized *Soldiers in Skirts* specifically as a "frankly homosexual" display while noting the show's popularity among mainstream audiences.[110] Further, the ex-servicemen of the 1940s and 1950s revues arguably had less immunity from accusations of sexual immorality than did their interwar counterparts. This is seen in the vilification of Royal Air Force servicemen Edward Mc-Nally and John Reynolds during the Montagu trial of 1953–54, where McNally was granted immunity in return for turning Queen's evidence against defendants Lord Montagu, Michael Pitt-Rivers, and Wildeblood for homosexual offenses.[111] Though the accused were the main focus of scorn, McNally and Reynolds were lumped together with them as "perverts, men of the lowest possible moral character," by the prosecution.[112] The prosecution also tried to link McNally's supposed effeteness to sodomitic behaviors, quipping that the serviceman "has a high voice naturally."[113] This treatment stood in contrast to the interwar guardsmen whose same-sex dalliances had been defended or explained away.

Despite this seemingly hostile cultural climate, the ultimate decline of ex-servicemen's drag revues in the mid-1950s was not due to concerns about cross-dressing, gender variance, or sexual morality. Instead, the craze had merely run its course, accelerated by the general decline of the variety theater. Drag entertainer Danny La Rue, who played in the revues prior to becoming a household name, recalled that the subgenre "petered out" after the shows ceased to be financially viable.[114] Newspaper coverage of the final show of *Soldiers in Skirts* in Preston reported that revue's demise "came as a shock to the whole company."[115] The growth of alternative forms of leisure, particularly privatized leisure, in the 1950s led to what contemporary observers saw as a "funeral atmosphere" in the theater as the public began to favor clubs, cinema, television, and other attractions over variety theaters.[116] Critic Richard Findlater bemoaned that by 1958 London theater audiences had declined to only 250,000 patrons nightly "compared to the two-and-a-half million at the cinema or the twelve million who are probably at home watching the telly."[117] Theater owners, sensing changing tastes, were increasingly booking acts that appealed to the youth market, like popular crooners, instead of plays and traditional variety entertainment.[118] Rather than being the victims of cultural anxieties, ex-servicemen's drag revues, which began with the remarkable success of *Splinters* in 1918, merely suffered the same fate as the industry to which its fortunes were tied.

3 Danny La Rue

Conservative Drag in the "Permissive Society"

Amid the apparent cultural, social, and political tumult of the 1960s, Britons who observed the ascendant "permissive" milieu with unease found an unlikely champion: a drag queen named Danny La Rue. La Rue, born Daniel Patrick Carroll in Cork, Ireland, was arguably the foremost drag entertainer in twentieth-century Britain in terms of cultural ubiquity. His act, which encompassed stage and screen, was known for its lavish costumes, song and dance numbers, blue-yet-benign humor, music hall references, and half-hearted impressions of celebrities. La Rue developed his penchant for female impersonation after playing the female lead in a concert party parody of the Hedy Lamarr film *White Cargo* (1942) during his stint with the Royal Navy.[1] After leaving the navy La Rue, still going by his birth name, joined the chorus of post–Second World War ex-servicemen's drag revues. Once the revues ceased touring, La Rue performed in a few more drag productions before becoming a mainstay in the floor show at Churchill's nightclub on Bond Street, London, in the mid-1950s, now performing under his stage name. Upon moving to rival club Winston's, La Rue was "emerging as the darling of the West End" by the late 1950s.[2] His club gigs led to appearances on television in the 1950s and early 1960s while the medium was in its infancy, and he starred in a number of Christmas pantomimes.[3]

La Rue eventually opened his own club, called Danny La Rue's, in 1964.[4]

From there La Rue established himself as one of the most ubiquitous figures in 1960s and 1970s popular culture. In addition to nightly appearances at his eponymous club, the entertainer starred in popular West End stage shows such as *Come Spy with Me* (1966) and the longest-running West End pantomime to that point, *Queen Passionella and the Sleeping Beauty* (1968), as well as being a featured act in the 1969, 1972, and 1978 Royal Variety Performances.[5] Outside of theater, he scored a top-forty single with his 1968 cover of "On Mother Kelly's Doorstep," was profiled in the September 1970 issue of American *Vogue*, and starred in his own film vehicle *Our Miss Fred* (1972). He was a fixture of televised light entertainment such as the ITV special *A Night Out with Danny La Rue* (1968), a 1969 television adaptation of *Charley's Aunt* in which he played Lord Fancourt Babberley, and *The Good Old Days* program (1953–83).[6] Further evidence of La Rue's ubiquity and popularity came in the form of various accolades: he received awards as the Variety Club of Great Britain's Show Business Personality of the Year (1969), Theatre Personality of the Year (1970), and Entertainer of the Decade (1979), in addition to being named honorary president of the London School of Economics Students' Union in 1971.[7] He was also given the title of King Rat in 1987 by the prestigious entertainment industry fraternity the Grand Order of Water Rats, received an OBE in 2002, and in 2013 was posthumously memorialized with a blue plaque in Twickenham.

Despite these achievements, La Rue has been openly derided in studies of drag performance. Scholars have justified overlooking La Rue's significance as a cultural figure because, they have argued, the artist's act was milquetoast and uninteresting. Theater historian Laurence Senelick has dismissed La Rue's "moss-grown music hall gags," comparing the entertainer unfavorably to edgier cross-dressed comics Dame Edna Everage and Lily Savage.[8] Journalist Roger Baker has offered a similarly negative appraisal in his expansive study of drag: "[La Rue] was a comedian who did not very good impressions highly dependent upon larger-than-life component parts, a passable singer who had appropriated the music hall song 'On Mother Kelly's Doorstep' as his theme tune and ultimately time moved on leaving him stranded with a diminishing audience and little claim on the West End or the *arrivistes* who took over smart society."[9] Though popular, La Rue was never considered hip. In the prime of his career the entertainer was mainly attracting "a well-dressed, respectable audience (few under thirty-five and many over fifty)."[10] His fan base only grew more geriatric from then on.[11] La Rue's conscious lack of trendiness was key to his success, but it has also discouraged serious interest in his career and legacy.

This chapter aspires to reorient historical interest in La Rue by taking a critical approach to his place within the cultural and sexual history of 1960s Britain. His massive popularity as a drag performer amid the backdrop of the so-called "permissive society" illuminates the wider history of the liberalization of social, cultural, and political attitudes in this period. The permissive society, which started roughly in the 1950s and gathered pace through the 1960s, was marked by a shift toward more relaxed cultural attitudes regarding sex and morality, an increasingly vibrant and conspicuous consumer culture, the waning influence of the church in public and private life, and the state taking a more liberal approach to the regulation of morality.[12] However, this process was not straightforward: permissive cultural and political attitudes did not emerge suddenly in the 1950s and 1960s but had earlier geneses, and changes associated with permissiveness were met with varying degrees of resistance and skepticism.[13] Permissiveness spread outside its nucleus in London, but the extent of its geographic reach has been contested. Also debatable is whether permissive attitudes were more prominent among certain classes, ages, and genders.[14] Though the question of how culturally transformative the 1960s was continues to be disputed by historians, contemporary media narratives promoted the idea that a profound cultural change was taking place, and the perception among everyday people was that a so-called "sexual revolution" and other such phenomena had occurred in the 1960s. In a 1970 poll, for example, at least 80 percent of respondents agreed that "people's attitudes towards sex in the last ten years have changed a lot."[15]

Instead of riding the wave of the ascendant liberal zeitgeist, La Rue achieved success by asserting himself as an unlikely cultural touchstone for those who were hesitant to fully embrace 1960s cultural liberalism. This La Rue–style conservatism was not as extreme or ideologically coherent as the hard-line traditionalism famously promoted by contemporary campaigner Mary Whitehouse and her National Viewers' and Listeners' Association or the largely evangelical Christian campaign group the Nationwide Festival of Light (NFOL).[16] Instead, the conservatism La Rue epitomized was felt and expressed as a more general discomfort with, rather than overt hostility toward, the perceived pace and nature of cultural change, while certain cultural shifts might be seen as tolerable or favorable.

The conservative ethos discussed here is akin to historian Alison Light's "conservative modernity."[17] Light, however, has defined conservative modernity as being an active, if genteel, agent of social and cultural transformation, whereas the 1960s cultural conservatism La Rue exemplified was more invested in critiquing certain real and perceived changes associated with permissiveness, while selectively acquiescing to others, rather than offering a clear, comprehensive alternative to contemporary liberalism. Further, Light has observed a "revolt against the past," especially against Victorianism, among interwar conservative modernists.[18] The conservatism of the 1960s epitomized by La Rue, on the other hand, was often marked by affection for the ethos and culture of the past, though 1960s cultural conservatives were still capable of favoring modern-day society and culture even as they expressed fascination with the past.

Some contemporary parallels with La Rue–style cultural conservatism could be seen in the realms of politics and economics in the "middle way" philosophy of Prime Minister Harold Macmillan, who was premier from 1957 through 1963. Though he was a Tory who saw his policy platform as a brake on the further nationalization of finance and industry, as well as a bulwark against other interventionist Labour agenda items that he described as "the totalitarian tendencies of modern socialism," Macmillan broadly supported or tolerated the postwar welfare state, some state intervention in the economy, and preexisting nationalization of industry and banking.[19] Prior to becoming prime minister, Macmillan regularly sought the counsel of Liberal economist John Maynard Keynes, whose views Macmillan accepted or entertained in part even though they often bucked Conservative orthodoxy and Macmillan's own belief in the importance of free enterprise and "personal responsibility."[20]

Doctrinaire conservative movements of the period struggled to engage those who espoused more casual, piecemeal conservative views. For example, the NFOL's evangelical Christian bent limited the group's appeal with "practical Christians" who had an affinity for Christian values but were not formally religious.[21] La Rue, despite being a churchgoing Catholic, regularly encouraged gentle mockery of doctrinaire social and political conservatives, often framing them as out of touch and rigid, even as he and his audience shared some of their views.

La Rue embodied the inconsistent nature of the permissive society-era conservative milieu he represented. He peddled an art form, drag, that held potentially subversive connotations, all while casting himself as a comforting, more traditional alternative to vogueish cultural trends such as "kitchen-sink drama" and the proliferation of live sexual entertainment as seen in venues like Soho's Raymond Revuebar, the eponymous nitery of strip club impresario Paul Raymond.[22] Perhaps no aspect of La Rue's career symbolically encapsulated the Janus-faced cultural conservatism of the era better than the March 1964 opening of La Rue's club, located at 17 Hanover Square near Soho, a neighborhood at the epicenter of the permissive society. The address had previously housed Raymond's risqué Bal Tabarin nightclub.[23] In establishing his club, La Rue took advantage of the favorable entrepreneurial environment offered by contemporary Soho while framing the venue as a bulwark against the permissive sexual culture of the surrounding area and Britain more widely. "We also gave dignity back to the sixties," the entertainer would later proclaim of his club, "at a time when society was in danger of running riot."[24]

In its analysis of a significant model of conservative drag, this chapter counters prominent present-day commentaries that frame drag as an inherently liberal or leftist art form.[25] Academic studies on drag, particularly since the 2000s, have tended to favor renderings of the medium that aim to advance progressive social and political change.[26] Even drag that has no overt sociopolitical message is praised for unsettling audiences' traditional conceptions of gender.[27] This is not to say that studying drag with progressive or disruptive aims is misguided, nor that it is wrong to frame the drag in this fashion when warranted. Drag, however—like all art forms—can also be rendered in unchallenging or blatantly conservative ways, including ways that reaffirm normative gendered boundaries, for example.[28]

The predominant media narrative surrounding La Rue was that he turned drag from an indecent practice into a widely palatable performance medium. This thesis had been firmly established by the height of the entertainer's career in the late 1960s. "[La Rue is] a star who has transformed the once-dubious minority art into something perfectly respectable," contemporary theater critic Michael Billington noted in a typical assessment.[29] "Getting geared up in drag and make up is, you will admit, a pretty freaky thing for a grown man to do," another critic argued. He continued, "But Mr. La Rue does not have the menace of a freak. He is safe and cosy and very pretty."[30] "Men who dress as women emerge grotesque, unless they are Danny La Rue," observed writer Nicholas de Jongh, reporting on a drag beauty contest he judged.[31] Obituaries following the entertainer's death on 31 May 2009 tended to echo the myth that La Rue popularized a newly respectable form of drag.[32] In addition to being propagated by critics, this myth was enthusiastically embraced by the entertainer himself. La Rue was constantly cultivating his respectable image by casting himself in opposition to a litany of perceived signifiers of moral decay. These included gay audiences ("I am not destructive enough for a gay audience. Because I love women. Gay audiences are over the moon when you take a woman and dissect her. I can't do that."); other drag acts ("The difference between me and the cheap end of the drag trade is that I'm wholesome, very wholesome."); transvestism and transgender people ("Transsexuals are sad, too, because they want to be girls. I'm not like that. I'm never seen out in my stage costumes. I leave the tits behind and am ordinary and quiet."); unkempt women ("If there's a bird in my show with a nick in her tights, they're off, not darned."); misbehaving celebrities ("If a person chooses to be in the public eye . . . they must behave themselves accordingly, or accept the consequences."); and even the abandonment of the Latin Mass after the Second Vatican Council.[33] The entertainer's tendency toward pontification led one commentator to astutely compare La Rue to "a slightly wayward but dynamic bishop."[34] La Rue's didacticism was not simply motivated by career preservation; his conservatism was genuine, no doubt influenced in large part by his staunch Catholicism. However, his need to moralize and defend himself in such fervent and persistent terms was likely driven by a neurotic urge to safeguard his career from being associated with immorality.

La Rue critiqued the permissive society obliquely and by name in his performances, such as his stage show *Danny La Rue at the Palace*, which ran from 1970 to 1972. The stand-up comedy segment of the

Palace show sees La Rue comment on the tumult of the previous decade and mock various popular culture icons and trends associated with the period, including Rolling Stones front man Mick Jagger ("He invited me to his wedding—I couldn't make it. I hear it was sensational. Long, flowing robes. Hair done up in pearls. And *she* looked beautiful as well."); spiritual guru Maharishi Mahesh Yogi ("He had a small spot on the Ganges. Was awfully painful."); former Beatle John Lennon and his wife, artist Yoko Ono ("[He] handed back his MBE, decided to hold onto Yoko. You know the last I saw of John and Yoko, they were dancing cheek to cheek backwards [pause] on the Isle of Wight ferry."); and women's fashion ("All the dolly little birds wore their skirts three inches above sea level.").[35] "Now what the sixties really gave us was permissive society," La Rue continues. "Permissive! I've got a friend who's [emigrating]. I said to him, 'Enoch,' I said. 'Enoch,' I said, 'why are you leaving this wonderful, wonderful country?' He said, 'I'll tell you: A hundred years ago they hung you for it, ten years ago they fined you for it, last year they made it legal, I'm going before they make it compulsory!'"[36] The "friend" in the joke is implied to be then–Tory MP Enoch Powell, popularly known for his xenophobic rhetoric, famously exemplified by his 1968 "Rivers of Blood" speech. The statement attributed to "Enoch" argues that the partial decriminalization of male homosexual acts in England and Wales as a result of the Sexual Offences Act 1967 will eventually lead to compulsory homosexuality.[37] Here La Rue gave voice to those who were uncomfortable with the pace and extent of cultural and political change during the 1960s, if not the changes themselves too, while ribbing, and thus gently distancing himself and his audience from, more doctrinaire conservative figures like Powell.[38] Both the first mention of the name Enoch and Enoch's diatribe elicited laughter from the crowd, suggesting that La Rue and his audience were in agreement that permissiveness had gone too far, too fast, even as they saw doctrinaire conservatives as being too reactionary.

The rest of *Danny La Rue at the Palace* is composed of dance numbers, songs, stand-up routines, and double entendre–laden comedy sketches, such as an American Old West–themed sketch with La Rue as "Fanny Oakley," which features exchanges like

> [COMEDIAN] JOE CHURCH: You must be the one they call the
>   fastest drawers in the West.
> LA RUE: I should be, they're always in me handbag!

and

> CHURCH: Sex is a pain in the neck!
> LA RUE: He must be doing it wrong! [Pause] And the next line's
>   been cut![39]

Additionally, the show takes another potshot at permissiveness in "Salute to the Stars," a sketch that sees La Rue performing impressions of Old Hollywood actresses such as Mae West, Ginger Rogers, and Marlene Dietrich (figure 15). *At the Palace*'s chorus caps the sketch with a song that unfavorably compares the "naked and slightly obscene" stars of the early 1970s whose films are "blue" (this can be interpreted to mean raunchy, depressing, or both) to the "magic" stars of yesteryear who provided glamour and escapism.[40]

To the extent that La Rue's often scattershot on- and offstage social commentary had a specific target of ire, it was the propagation of commercialized sexual entertainment in 1960s Britain, with Soho at the epicenter of this trend, that most raised his hackles. In his autobiography La Rue painted an almost bucolic picture of the pre-permissive Soho of his youth in the 1930s, writing, "Like a village, everyone in the community knew each other. It was a close-knit society based on friendship, like a large family."[41] This quaint snapshot of the area's past was given a slight edge by La Rue's appreciation for

There never was a woman like Danny

. . . but Danny La Rue, himself, skilfully conjures affectionate and hilarious portraits of many of the great ladies of the entertainment world. With astute recall of manner, gesture and costume, and a sly lyric or two, he has saluted such talents as Dorothy Squires, Barbra Streisand, Ginger Rogers, the legendary Marlene, Twiggy, Mae West and those supreme Shirleys, Bassey and Temple.

The Blue Angel . . .   *. . . angel in a tiger skin*   *. . . and the little angel !*

Cheek to cheek . . .   *. . . the cheeky chick*   *. . . and cheerfully cheekless !*

FIGURE 15. Danny La Rue impersonating various Old Hollywood and contemporary stars in *Danny La Rue at the Palace* (1970). Credit: Mander and Mitchenson / University of Bristol / ArenaPAL.

what he saw as a charmingly louche atmosphere. "On my walks back home in the small hours of the morning, I got to know many of the ladies of the night who patronized Soho—purely as friends, I hasten to add," La Rue recalled. "There was a kind of romance about the girls; they were part of the whole Soho scene, now sadly gone."[42] In contrast with these fond reminiscences about the area, La Rue despaired that in successive decades Soho "has all been allowed to disappear under a hail of sex shops, pornographic clubs, and rip-off joints. It saddens and amazes me that we could let it all go so easily . . . and [it] makes me very angry."[43] La Rue was not alone in this criticism. Members of the Soho Society, a community organization founded in 1970, indicated that Soho had crossed a vague threshold from endearingly "raffish" to unpleasantly sleazy.[44] As Soho Society vice-chair Dorothy Donaldson-Hudson remarked, "Soho has always been a slightly raffish area and we like it that way. We don't mind unobtrusive, well-run clubs that cater for the sex-trade. . . . But we do object to the way that most of these places have changed the environment for the community—the noise, the dirt, the kind of people they attract, the unpleasantness of being accosted."[45]

La Rue, the "slightly wayward but dynamic bishop," exemplified the mild ribaldry that was accepted by permissive society–era casual cultural conservatives. The entertainer constructed his entire performance style around exuding tasteful raffishness. "Devotees of Danny La Rue already know [his humour] is based to a considerable extent on good, clean English smut," reported one critic, summing up La Rue's blue, but never offensive, comedy stylings.[46] Predicting that La Rue's show *Come Spy with Me* would be a success, the Lord Chamberlain's senior examiner of plays C.D. Heriot declared that "the Great British Public does like a bit of dirt so long as it's clean."[47] Even when La Rue was seen to be getting too smutty, critics tended to chide him lovingly instead of expressing outrage. On the pantomime *Queen Passionella and the Sleeping Beauty*, the *Daily Mail* asked, "But what are the children to make of references to the *Kama Sutra*, whipping, Hugh Hefner and Playboy magazine? They are going to be bored stiff and annoyed that jokes are being made over their heads." Still, the *Mail* admitted that La Rue's "good humour is infectious. He has a likeable way with children."[48] Of the same show, the *Financial Times* observed, "This is not really a show for children," and yet, "I dare say they will enjoy it, since children seem to enjoy almost anything. But it's a great night out for their elders." "Although female impersonations are not to everyone's taste, it must be hard to resist Mr. La Rue's vivid and indeed oddly virile personality," the *Financial Times* added, "virile" arguably being a euphemism for "heterosexual-presenting" in this case.[49] "One can't help wishing, though . . . that there were a less heavy preponderance of jokes about Jewishness and homosexuality and that there were a storyline in which children could become gradually involved," noted the *Times* while remarking, "[La Rue has] made the art of glamorous transvestism acceptable to a mass audience. . . . Judged simply as a vehicle for Mr. La Rue this 'pantomime extraordinaire' offers splendid Yuletide entertainment."[50] For his part, La Rue "relentlessly insists that his humour is 'wholesome,'" as one typical profile of the entertainer observed. "He agrees the English like fruity material 'but not dirty jokes. English people are very clean-minded. Only dirty people think of dirty jokes. I don't think dirty at all, at any time.' He said the essence of any blue material was timing. 'If you sit on it it becomes vulgar. It must be sat on and then *right off*. Then it becomes a giggle.'"[51] This tendency to "[sit] on" a gag then get "right off" was a signature feature of La Rue's act, particularly as it related to his rendering of feminine glamour. One of the entertainer's catchphrases was "Wotcher mates!" intoned in the "booming voice of a brawny workman," which La Rue would often bellow a few seconds after appearing onstage in a new glamorous ensemble.[52] The artist described his delight at the "shattering of the vision" of femininity in this manner: "My favourite:

opening in Coventry, a gorgeous doll, platinum hair, hundreds of yards of chiffon, then, in my own voice, I say, 'Wotcher mates!' I could see the visual scream that went up from the audience; shattering of the vision. When I stop getting laughs [from this], I'll hang up all my gear."[53] Far from being a bad actor, as commentators like Roger Baker have argued, La Rue demonstrated an artistry in manipulating his audience through constructing and shattering his feminine illusion, frequently in the same joke. "[La Rue] can create the illusion, break it and then pick it up again, repeatedly; producing tension and release of tension that can be dramatic in the extreme and often very funny," biographer Peter Underwood observed.[54] La Rue's unwillingness to assume a stage persona or character distinct from his own personality had the effect of indicating an ambivalence toward the act of cross-dressing. Noting that La Rue portrayed "only slightly exaggerated feminine mannerisms," a *New York Times* reporter trying to explain the popularity of drag in Britain for curious American readers observed that "the purpose of [La Rue's] joke is, I suspect . . . [that] he is a man impersonating a man impersonating a woman."[55] The entertainer's noncommittal approach to his own performances served to reassure his audience that there was no deeper meaning to his cross-dressing than its entertainment value. "My costume is part of my act," he would often insist, "as a costume is to a clown. I don't get a kick out of wearing mine, as a transvestite might."[56]

Despite La Rue's ubiquitous association with the terms *drag* and *female impersonation* in the eyes of the public and critics, he insisted on distinguishing himself from that milieu, maintaining instead that he was a comic who just happened to wear frocks.[57] "I have always detested the term 'drag,'" the entertainer claimed with no evident self-awareness in his autobiography *From Drags to Riches* (1987), and he found "female impersonation" to be "a tiny bit suspect."[58] La Rue further emphasized the separation of his stage persona from his private self by regularly ending his club appearances out of women's clothes in men's formalwear. If audiences were still unclear about La Rue's feelings toward cross-dressing after this, La Rue went so far as to say that he disliked doing it. "Indeed he would like nothing better than never to wear women's clothing again; something he has recently threatened to do," his biographer reported.[59] Even La Rue's character Fred Wimbush in *Our Miss Fred*, a female impersonator in a military concert party, laments that he would rather be playing Titus Andronicus. Wimbush goes on to disguise himself as a woman offstage, but he does so reluctantly, and only after an appeal to his sense of patriotism ("Damn your trousers, this is for England!").[60] Yet La Rue's lavish feminine garb was a lynchpin of his appeal and the efforts he put into his wardrobe undercut his professed distaste for donning women's clothes. For instance, a news item about La Rue's film *Our Miss Fred* noted the entertainer's attention to sartorial detail: "[La Rue] chose all the clothes making sure the skirts were the right length for the [19]40's and the stockings seamed," while adding that the wardrobe budget for the "fashion show sequence" alone was £20,000.[61] *Danny La Rue at the Palace* boasted the entertainer's "million dollar wardrobe," including a dress, created by fashion designer Mark Canter, with a twenty-foot train made entirely of ostrich feathers that covered an entire staircase (figure 16).[62]

Another staple of La Rue's act was music hall and variety theater nostalgia, a feature that endeared him to audiences who sought reassurance by engaging with Britain's cultural heritage in the wake of 1960s permissiveness. La Rue's trademark top-forty hit "On Mother Kelly's Doorstep" was a cover of an early twentieth-century theater standard, and he usually interspersed his shows with other classics from the music hall and variety eras like "Ta-ra-ra Boom-de-ay," which often served as a politely raucous closing number.[63] La Rue also made frequent appearances on the BBC music hall nostalgia show *The Good Old Days* (1953–83), a perfect fit for the highly romanticized, polite interpretation of the music hall he peddled.[64] In the 1960s, nostalgia for

million dollar wardrobe

and the man responsible ....

The fabulous fantasies in silk and satin, sequins and furs which Danny La Rue brings to breath-takingly glamorous life in all his shows are the dream children of designer Mark Canter. Mark is a well-known personality in the publicity and advertising world of fashion. He collaborated some years ago with Disley Jones on a spectacular cabaret for Cecil Landeau, since when, concentrating on cabaret and intimate revue, his creations have supplied much of the essential sparkle of London nightlife.

This backstage photo of Danny 'rehearsing' one of his elaborate gowns gives some idea of the business involved, with six personnel and Danny himself to negotiate the manoeuvre.

FIGURE 16. Photograph of La Rue's costumer Mark Canter (top) and a demonstration of the logistics involved in maintaining La Rue's twenty-foot train for *Danny La Rue at the Palace* (bottom), 1970. Credit: Mander and Mitchenson/University of Bristol/ArenaPAL.

the music hall was part of a broader cultural trend of interest in the past, as exemplified by the popularity of BBC2's *The Forsyte Saga* (1967).

The twenty-six-episode television serial, based on the novels by John Galsworthy, was an immediate cultural sensation: six million out of a possible eight million viewers watched the BBC2 premiere in 1967, while seventeen million people, one-third of the British public, watched the repeat of the first episode when it was screened on BBC1 the following year.[65] Though the drama followed the travails of the Forsyte family from the late nineteenth century through the interwar period, it was the Victorian sections of the program that resonated most with viewers.[66] The popularity of *Forsyte* and other contemporary media that played on public fascination with the past, like the television program *Adam Adamant Lives!* (1966–67), was motivated in part by ambivalent attitudes toward 1960s permissiveness.[67] Such sentiments did not equate to uncritical wistfulness for a bygone age. *Forsyte* did not completely valorize the Victorian period, but it encouraged a more innocuous interest in the institutions and values of the era, such as its more rigid class structure.[68] Reflecting the contradictory nature of nondoctrinaire 1960s cultural conservatism, viewers of *Forsyte* were at once encouraged to find comfort in Victorian bourgeois society and to identify with the characters who sought to subvert its stuffy restrictions.[69] The series sentimentalized Britain's bygone status as an imperial superpower yet emphasized that "hearth and home rather than the sceptre and the sword" were the true "symbols of national existence."[70] *Adam Adamant Lives!*, an action-adventure serial in which a decorous Edwardian swashbuckler (Gerald Harper) awakens from suspended animation to fight crime in swinging London, reflected a similar conservative ambivalence about the ascendant cultural liberalism of the 1960s. The program oscillates between demonstrating appreciation for permissive culture and critiquing it.[71] Adamant's old-world values act as a check on the immaturity and bad judgment of his modish young female sidekick Georgie (Juliet Harmer). The show's rogues' gallery often represents trappings of permissive culture like consumerism, pop music, and cosmopolitanism.[72] Adamant's old-fashioned gentleman-liness and gallantry are portrayed as charming yet ridiculously anti-quated and naive, implying that these values are best left in the past even if present-day audiences find them pleasant.[73] *Adam Adamant Lives!* prompted viewers to see 1960s London from Adamant's be-mused perspective, thus encouraging critique of the permissive soci-ety, but these critiques mostly expressed ambivalence rather than outright hostility toward permissiveness.[74]

In addition to drawing upon popular unease with permissiveness, escapist entertainment like *Forsyte, Adam Adamant Lives!,* and La Rue's act revealed a backlash against the vogueish kitchen-sink drama of the 1960s, such as the kind shown on BBC's *The Wednesday Play* (1964–70).[75] "Above all," one *Forsyte* fan bemoaned, "we are sick to death of the sight and sound of scruffy teenagers and students and kitchen sink drama! No wonder we are happy to escape for 45 min-utes each week into a world of elegance and good manners."[76] "One knew instinctively," wrote another viewer to the *Radio Times,* "that the producer [of *Forsyte*] would not be a weird young man, wearing a black shirt, white tie, and sporting a frizzy hair style! This type, one presumes, is for *The Wednesday Play!*"[77]

In a period that saw the decay of the variety theater and the ascend-ancy of live sexual entertainment and realist countercultural drama, La Rue shrewdly identified a gap in the market for those yearning for inoffensive escapism—"elegance and good manners."[78] Contrasting himself with the black shirt–clad contemporary playwrights, La Rue insisted that "I bring colour to the stage when the world is drab. It's not memorable; it is a show for people who want a good laugh on their night out. I admire message theatre, but I haven't got any messages."[79]

For the medium of female impersonation, the permissive zeitgeist was a mixed bag. One 1970 poll on attitudes toward the permissive society found that 29 percent of respondents "approv[ed] of" "female impersonators," with 54 percent not approving.[80] These results are fairly positive considering that the poll invited interviewees to state whether they approved or disapproved of female impersonat*ors* as individuals instead of asking about the genre of female impersonat*ion* more generally. Further, in framing the question as a matter of approval or disapproval of female impersonators as people rather than, for instance, whether respondents enjoyed or did not enjoy shows featuring female impersonators, the pollsters coaxed respondents into making sweeping moral judgments on the imagined lifestyles of female impersonators instead of merely asking interviewees to comment on whether they thought drag was an entertaining or estimable art form. Also notable is that the poll results saw female impersonators being met with more approval than "unisex clothes" (27 percent), "cohabitation" (25 percent), "strip-clubs" (22 percent), "John and Yoko" (13 percent), "hippies" (8 percent), "young staying out all night" (8 percent), and several other supposed markers of permissiveness.[81] This suggests that female impersonators—whatever those polled associated with such a term—were not viewed as a particularly pressing social concern. Still, there is no suggestion that the cultural liberalism of the 1960s led to any increased acceptance of female impersonators either. Supporters of homosexual law reform of the 1950s and 1960s did not encourage any embrace of gender variance, as they clarified that it was the respectable, discreet "homosexual" who should benefit from the partial decriminalization of homosexual acts while effeminate men should be seen as a separate category of undesirables.[82] La Rue demonstrated, as did artists such as Les Rouges et Noirs and Arthur Lucan before him, that drag performers could be among the most prominent entertainers of their day, yet the artist's distinctness from the wider medium of female impersonation, as expressed by himself and the media, meant that his popularity did not translate directly into a swell of public goodwill toward the art form in general.

Upstart rivals to La Rue demonstrated that drag was seen as being commercially viable in the 1960s, but no other drag act resonated with the public to the extent La Rue did. Notable competitors included American female impersonator Ricky Renée (figure 17) whose eponymous club in Covent Garden opened in December 1966 and closed around half a year later, as well as several Paul Raymond–produced drag shows, such as the big-budget revue *Birds of a Feather* (1970), all of which were commercial disappointments.[83] The presence of female impersonators in the 1970 film *Goodbye Gemini*, a thriller that features a drag act at venerable London gay pub the Royal Vauxhall Tavern as well as Renée playing a transvestite sex worker, demonstrates that female impersonation that was more risqué than La Rue's act could get some national media recognition, though it was limited.[84]

La Rue–style glamour drag had contemporary international analogues as well. In 1970, when the *New York Times* remarked that Danny La Rue's glamour drag for straight audiences constituted "a few strange English tribal customs," the paper was neglecting similar contemporary trends in its own backyard.[85] Just two years before its article on La Rue, the *New York Times* published a review of the documentary *The Queen* (1968). The documentary covers a drag beauty pageant that took place at Broadway's The Town Hall—hardly an inconspicuous event or venue—for the benefit of the straight, mainstream cinemagoer.[86] In their review of *The Queen*, the *Times* reassured their readership that the documentary was an opportunity for them to take in a genuine, if novel, art form, and that there was nothing seedy about the film's content. "The drag queens are, of course, perfectly aware that they are not women," the paper clarified regarding the glamorous beauty pageant contestants, "and even their mannerisms—the flatted vowels, the relaxed wrist, the gait of the homosexual who wants it known—are not female imitations at all, but parodies. . . . [O]ne is watching actors, very conscious actors, at work."[87] Not far from The Town Hall, at Club 82 on the Lower East

TWO-WAY PORTRAIT

1966

Ricky Renee—following in Danny La Rue's high-heeled steps.

IT IS ASTONISHING, to say the least, how "drag" shows are the rage in London.

Danny La Rue, the cleverest of female impersonators, has his own night-club which is outrageously popular.

Now he is to have a rival in Ricky Renee, an American who has spent £50,000 buying and doing up Annie's Room in Covent Garden. Renee's transvestite act will be the main cabaret. With flashing nails and fluttering eye-lashes. Danny and Renee will fight it out for the drag trade.

FIGURE 17. Photograph of Ricky Renée with accompanying news article, 1966. Credit: Mander and Mitchenson/University of Bristol/ArenaPAL.

Side of Manhattan, crowds of mostly straight, respectable patrons, many of them tourists, had been entertained throughout the 1950s and 1960s by beautiful female impersonators as well as tuxedoed male impersonators.[88] Parisian drag club Le Carrousel attracted establishment fashion houses to outfit the drag artists and, like La Rue's club, boasted a guest list of contemporary celebrities, including comedian Bob Hope and playwright Tennessee Williams.[89] Even Japan, which has its own distinct traditional forms of male cross-dressing performance, had a 1960s glamour drag scene that would be legible to Western audiences, such as the kind seen in the film *Funeral Parade of Roses* (1969), starring gender-variant performer Pîtâ, and *Black Lizard* (1968), a showcase for drag artist Akihiro Miwa.[90]

Following on from the height of La Rue's career in the 1960s and early 1970s, the British drag scene for the rest of the twentieth century could be seen to be using La Rue as a reference point, either as a model of drag to aspire to or to reject. Those who hewed more closely to the La Rue mold included drag queens like Madame Jojo, hostess of the Paul Raymond–owned Madame Jojo's club in Soho, and Ruby Venezuela, the face of Soho club Ruby's. These artists embodied La Rue's extravagant glamour, his appeal to general audiences, and his entrepreneurial spirit into the 1980s and 1990s.[91] One of the most notable examples of anti–La Rue drag was Paul O'Grady's Lily Savage, whose persona approximated a woman who aimed for La Rue–like glamour on a working-class budget and reveled in her failure to conform to a staid, well-mannered disposition. Further along the anti–La Rue spectrum was the avant-garde drag that had grown in prominence by the 1990s, exemplified by artists such as Lindsay Kemp and Leigh Bowery.[92] Elements of La Rue's persona, though, were evident even in this milieu. For example, the host of the late-1980s and 1990s alternative London drag night Kinky Gerlinky, Black British Guyanese artist Winn Austin, appeared outwardly avant-garde but had a personal philosophy on drag that matched La Rue's almost word for word: "I am not one of those transvestites who get sexual kicks out of dressing up," Austin insisted in a magazine profile.[93] Evoking La Rue's comments on serious realist theater and other drag performers, Austin decried earnest transgender drag artists who "all sit around moaning about being men and talking about painful operations. It is supposed to be fun. They've made it terribly serious."[94]

Despite La Rue's pathological insistence on distancing himself from homosexuality and gay culture for most of his career, the entertainer was inspiring affectionate camp send-ups by the 1990s. Regina Fong, a character created by drag artist Reg Bundy, had a La Rue–themed act that saw her lip-synching to La Rue's rendition of "On Mother Kelly's Doorstep" interspersed with audio of a prickly interview La Rue once gave to talk radio station LBC. The DC Comics character Danny the Street (a play on La Rue's stage name), created by prodigious comic book writer Grant Morrison in 1990, is a "sentient transvestite thoroughfare" who speaks Polari and is surrounded by gender-variant fare such as hardware, military surplus, and gun stores festooned with lace curtains and fairy lights.[95] La Rue's reluctance to be seen as a gay icon, or transgressive in any way, renders these camp send-ups all the more absurd and amusing. Instead of overtly criticizing the entertainer, however, Bundy and Morrison's pastiches approach La Rue's conservatism with affectionate mockery and even sympathy, inviting us to imagine a loosened-up version of La Rue who is less burdened by oppressive societal expectations. Perhaps the key to reinvigorating the cultural legacy of La Rue, who confounds present-day cultural commentators by at once being an identifiable product of the swinging sixties while conspicuously resisting the permissive zeitgeist of the era, is to view his conservatism as these camp readings have done: with a mixture of bemusement, playful mockery, and understanding.

4 *Skirting the Censor*

Drag and the Censorship of the British
Theater, 1939–1968

In September 1968 the Lord Chamberlain approved the final play-script put before his Office, a one-act play entitled *As Long as I Live* (1968).[1] With this gesture, his famous blue pencil, which had annotated the works of numerous playwrights over the years, was retired.[2] The Stage Licensing Act of 1737 officially formalized the Lord Chamberlain's power to license plays. Over a century later, the Theatres Act 1843 repealed all previous laws relating to the regulation of the theater and codified and confirmed the Lord Chamberlain's role, charging his Office with the responsibility of approving every new script, or addition to an old one, which was intended to be produced or "acted for hire" at any theater in Great Britain.[3] Censorship amounted to less than twenty percent of the Lord Chamberlain's Office's overall duties, the rest being organizational tasks carried out on behalf of the sovereign in keeping with the Lord Chamberlain's position as part of the Royal Household. Yet between 1843 and 1968 theater censorship was what the Lord Chamberlain's Office was best known for.[4] As the twentieth century progressed, St James's Palace saw its influence diminish. This process was stimulated by the theater industry becoming ever bigger and more intricate from the time of the Second World War, with an unprecedented growth in the number of people involved in the theater industry, more people attending theater, and an increase in the economic power of the industry.[5] The Lord Chamberlain's Office found it difficult, and ultimately impossible, to assert dominance in this new environment to the point where Lord Cobbold, the last Lord Chamberlain to oversee theater censorship, felt his job was so untenable that he advocated for the removal of his own Office's censorship powers.[6] When the Lord Chamberlain's dominion over the theater ended with the passage of the Theatres Act 1968, the development met with little resistance from most observers—including from the Lord Chamberlain himself.[7] How was it that the regime of state censorship of the British theater appeared to crumble so suddenly in the late 1960s? In this chapter we will see that controversies about drag provide valuable insight into the opaque dynamics of theater censorship in twentieth-century Britain and help to explain why the system collapsed in 1968.

By investigating what the Lord Chamberlain's Office thought about drag, this chapter addresses a central concern of this book: was drag controversial, and to what extent? From the interwar period, male gender variance—and, with it, drag—was increasingly associated with sexual immorality, specifically same-sex desire. Among the observers who linked drag to sexual immorality, there was no consensus regarding the severity of the societal threat posed by drag and, if such a threat existed, what should be done about it. At the same time, the perception that drag was connected to sexual immorality was not culturally ubiquitous. Drag performance remained critically and commercially popular. A great number of consumers of popular culture, when it came to specific renderings of female impersonation or the art form in general, did not consider drag's sexual connotations, or they acknowledged drag's sexual connotations but were able to overlook them. There were also those who were attracted to female impersonation because of the art form's association with sexuality. A study of the censor's attitude toward drag illuminates the lack of cultural consensus on whether drag was controversial. St James's Palace was frequently at odds with other agents involved in the regime of state theater censorship over the extent to which drag was indecent. For the most part, female impersonation was allowed to continue entertaining theatergoers so long as the performances did not raise the ire of the Office by broaching issues that concerned the censor more than drag, such as nudity, explicit reference to same-sex desire, and vulgar dialogue.

Examining the state theater censor's views on the art form constitutes a logical, if imperfect, barometer for assessing wider cultural views of drag—"imperfect" because the views of the institution were not entirely reflective of broader society. The Lord Chamberlain and his employees tended to represent a certain elite point of view. Lords Chamberlain were frequently plucked from the aristocracy, and high-level Office employees were often older, retired military officers from the upper-middle classes. With that in mind, a study of the censor's views on drag over time is still instructive, and broader conclusions can be drawn from such a study. The perceptions of drag by the Office, as the chief regulator of the theater sector, held enormous political and cultural clout. St James's Palace had greater direct regulatory power over the day-to-day existence of drag performance than any other agent. Further, examining St James's Palace's attitudes toward drag does not solely provide us with the opinions of the Office, but it also enables us to understand the views of others who engaged in conversation with the institution. The Office's power was not absolute but part of a wider ecosystem of agents involved in the censorship of the British theater. This included the police and the judiciary, whom St James's Palace relied on to legally enforce its decisions, as well as those with more informal influence on theater censorship, such as arts critics in the press, pressure groups, and individual theatergoers who contacted the Office for one reason or another. The censor's policies often reflected an attempt, if not a mandate, to respond to the opinions of these other agents and to keep pace with public opinion in general.

Compared to average theatergoers and the press, the Office consistently expressed a more negative view of female impersonation, though the censor also disregarded extreme denunciations of drag performance by reactionary critics. Reflecting theatergoers' acceptance of female impersonation, St James's Palace tended to license drag shows, even if Office employees often expressed reservations about the artistic and moral merits of female impersonation. When the Office tried to stop certain drag shows from being staged, it tended to be in response to the production staging material that was not in the licensed script, or for reasons primarily pertaining to moral issues the censor found more pressing than male cross-dressing, like same-sex desire and nudity, although the inclusion of drag in a play could make the Office more suspicious of that production's overall moral propriety and artistic merit. Overall, drag was sometimes a source of controversy for the Office, but the censor's approach to the art form was mostly one of tolerance so long as drag shows were not perceived to have overtly crossed certain legal and moral boundaries, boundaries that were inconsistently defined.

St James's Palace was first given codified powers over stage censorship with the passage of the Stage Licensing Act of 1737. The legislation, passed in large part with the aim of protecting the monarchy and its government from ridicule and critique from the stage, ensured that only a select group of specially licensed patent theaters were allowed to present scripted plays.[8] The Lord Chamberlain's role, enshrined in the 1737 act and later clarified in the Theatres Act 1843 (which also broke up the strict patent theater system), was to approve or reject new scripts, or new additions to old scripts, that applicants wanted to stage.[9] Often the censor would accept scripts on the condition that certain objectionable lines or actions be cut from the final version. The Office's decisions could not be appealed. The Lord Chamberlain's Office was the final authority and its wishes had to be adhered to if a scripted production were to be staged for public consumption.[10]

There were no specific criteria for what merited objectionable material as detailed in either the 1737 or 1843 acts. The censor's decisions tended to be guided by a set of internally established guidelines, but, even so, what was considerable permissible in a script could be inconsistent. Three parliamentary select committees on stage censorship were organized between 1866 and 1909, but these did little to clarify a specific set of rules for the Lord Chamberlain to follow.[11] Successive Lords Chamberlain were reluctant to give interviews explaining their methodology and, since there was no appeals process available to applicants, Lords Chamberlain rarely had to explain their rationale to the playwrights, theater managers, producers, or others who contested official decisions.[12] Even after the Office's censorship powers were removed, Lord Cobbold, Lord Chamberlain from 1963 to 1971, refused to discuss stage censorship publicly outside of the House of Lords debate on the subject.[13] As this chapter will discuss, the opaqueness of the censor's decision-making processes caused consternation and confusion even among the Office's allies in the legal system who were tasked with enforcing the Lord Chamberlain's rulings.

There were a number of prominent criticisms leveled at the Office, both prior to and after 1968. Critics argued that successive Lords Chamberlain and their employees were unsuited to evaluate plays based on their lack of prior experience in the theater sector. Liberals and the left perceived the Office to be politically and culturally conservative. The rules relating to theater censorship were seen as vague and/or draconian. Further, critics argued that state theater censorship in general was illiberal and wrong.[14] St James's Palace also had its fair share of socially conservative critics, notably the purity campaign group the Public Morality Council (P.M.C.), which felt that the Office was being too permissive in its approach to theater censorship.

It is true that most high-level Office officials had no direct experience in the theater.[15] Employees of the Lord Chamberlain's Office were not necessarily hired based on prior knowledge of the theater sector. However, there were some distinguished members of the theater sector in the Lord Chamberlain's Office, such as Ifan Kyrle Fletcher, who founded the journal *Theatre Notebook* and the Society for Theatre Research; Lieutenant-Colonel Sir Thomas St Vincent Wallace Troubridge, who was president of the Stage Society; and Timothy Harward, who lectured in twentieth-century drama at Oxford University.[16] St James's Palace also consulted an official advisory board of critics, academics, and others from the theater sector to help guide their decisions, although the board's assistance was utilized to varying degrees depending on who the Lord Chamberlain was at the time, and Lords Chamberlain also selected board members themselves.

Accounts of the Lord Chamberlain's Office often portray the institution as one of stodgy, prudish political and cultural conservatism. To some extent this stereotype bears out. It is not uncommon, for example, to find overtly prejudiced views expressed in the Lord Chamberlain's documents, such as the anti-Semitic rhetoric directed against the producers of ex-servicemen's drag revue *Soldiers in Skirts* (1945).[17] In correspondence about the show *Strip Ahoy* (1940), which involved female impersonation, one Office employee primly remarked, "Too many jokes bearing on the eternal subject of sexual intercourse. There are moments when I wish God had not created Man and Woman, but had thought of something else!"[18] However, St James's Palace often came under fire from purity campaigners such as the P.M.C. for not being conservative enough. The Lord Chamberlain's Office, for its part, sometimes treated these traditionalists with the same amount of contempt it had for libertine playwrights and other countercultural figures. The case studies in this chapter demonstrate that St James's Palace was not beholden to traditionalist interest groups. Complaints made to the censor decrying the supposed immorality of certain drag shows were often dismissed or, more frequently, treated with skepticism by the Office.[19] Furthermore, the Lord Chamberlain's Office made overt attempts to reflect changing social mores. An example of this came when St James's Palace lifted its blanket ban on homosexual themes and characters on the stage after the publication of the Report of the Departmental Committee on Homosexual Offences and Prostitution (1957), known popularly as the Wolfenden Report.

Studies of the Lord Chamberlain's Office's censorship regime have tended to highlight plays that were banned or otherwise caused controversy.[20] The reasons for this are clear: unlicensed and controversial plays provide intriguing subject matter, and it is often easier to examine why a play was deemed objectionable than why a play was approved with little or no issue. It is important to emphasize that the overwhelming majority of scripts were licensed, albeit often on the condition that any objectionable material be cut. There were degrees to the Lord Chamberlain's Office's definitions of indecency and its reactions to perceived indecency; few scripts were refused a license outright. According to former Lord Chamberlain's Office comptroller John Johnston, from 1900 to 1968 55,394 scripts were given a license and 411 scripts were refused, with an annual average of 800 plays licensed and six refused per year.[21] There were a further 352 "waiting box" scripts that consisted of plays where cuts were stipulated by St James's Palace but the submitter of the script refused to comply, thus leaving the script in limbo. These waiting box scripts were sometimes performed in private theaters. Successive Lords Chamberlain supported the rights of private theaters to stage unlicensed plays and did not begrudge this system of circumventing their authority so long as the private theaters were run legitimately. For instance, they might be open only to members of a club rather than to the general public.[22]

The touring revue *Cosmopolitan Merry-Go-Round* (1939) was granted a license by the Lord Chamberlain shortly before its July

1939 premiere at the Chelsea Palace Theatre after some required cuts to the script, but nothing about the show elicited significant concern on the part of the censor. The production's thirteen scenes covered a range of light entertainment material, including a comedy routine that takes place in a maternity ward, a Cuban dance showcase, the nostalgic "Grandpa Takes You All into the Old-Time Music Hall" featuring "old-time acrobats" and "can-can girls," and a comedic scene about shipwrecked mariners stranded on a desert island.[23] None of the objectionable material initially flagged by the censor related to an act starring female impersonator Gerald De Vere performing the song "Lovely to Look At" accompanied by two female dancers, which was billed on the show's program as "Lovely to Look At" performed by "Three Beautiful ? ? ?"[24] Nevertheless, the subsequent controversy about the revue, which involved legal proceedings brought against the producers and De Vere, focused exclusively on this act. The *Cosmopolitan Merry-Go-Round* incident would demonstrate that the Lord Chamberlain's Office was one of several key agents involved in theater censorship, and its dominion over this regime was precarious in the run-up to the passage of the Theatres Act 1968.

Shortly after *Cosmopolitan Merry-Go-Round* opened at the Chelsea Palace Theatre in July 1939, the censor received a complaint from an "informant" claiming that either a man or woman (the informant could not tell) had stripped onstage. Comptroller George Titman was sent to investigate the allegations.[25] In his report on the performance he saw on 2 August 1939, Titman identified De Vere's act as obscene and recommended that it be removed from the show entirely. "The man slowly disrobed his feminine clothing. When the last top garment was removed he had let down hair from a wig which only partly covered dummy 'breasts.' He then put on a flimsy dressing jacket before removing the lower garment. . . . He then turned to face the audience displaying his body and with his legs close together. Although it was evident that his private parts were fastened with a jock strap, the exhibition was none the less disgusting."[26] Office employees sometimes included anecdotal information regarding audiences' reactions to certain material, and Titman did so in this case. "A very respectable-looking woman sitting beside me exclaimed 'Good God!'" he added.[27]

Based on Titman's report, St James's Palace decided to press charges against producer Joe Seymour, Chelsea Palace manager Adney Walter Gibbons, and De Vere himself for violations of the Theatres Act. The censor's reasons for objecting to De Vere's routine were twofold. First, St James's Palace accused De Vere and the revue's producers of staging unlicensed material. Since the script only described De Vere's act as a female impersonator singing the song "Lovely to Look At" accompanied by two female performers, with no description of actions or "business," St James's Palace argued that the license only extended to the performers singing the song and that anything extra was illegal.[28] Second, the Office felt that the act was obscene, not because it featured a perceivably nude man, but—intriguingly—because De Vere resembled a naked woman onstage. According to a Department of Public Prosecutions (D.P.P.) report, the Office complained that De Vere's appearance resembled that of a nude woman, with no issues being raised about De Vere's maleness specifically. "It was clear that [De Vere's] pubic hair had been shaved or covered, and his genital organs were held or attached behind him between his legs so that they were invisible and conveyed the impression that a naked woman was standing in front of the audience."[29] The account further stated that "Titman occupied [a seat] in the third row, it was difficult to tell the sex of the performer and the impersonation must have been more effective in those parts of the auditorium further removed from the stage. . . . [T]his exhibition disgusted members of the audience sitting in this vicinity."[30]

Given that, for the censor, the issue of male nudity onstage was mostly unprecedented while female nudity was not, it is understandable that the Lord Chamberlain's Office chose to interpret De Vere's performance within the familiar framework of female nude display. St James's Palace did not necessarily have fixed rules about the censorship of nudity, which made the regulation of nude performance difficult, as I will explain later. There were some instances of Lords Chamberlain at least attempting to articulate a policy on the matter over the years. According to evidence given to a 1966 parliamentary joint committee, proscriptions were as follows: "a) Actresses in movement must not wear less than briefs and an opaque controlling brassiere. b) Actresses may pose completely nude provided the pose is motionless and expressionless; the pose is artistic and something rather more than a mere display of nakedness; and the lighting must be subdued. c) Striptease as such is not allowed in a stage play. To date, requests for males to pose nude have not been received."[31]

In a similar vein, in response to a Cambridge professor who inquired about the Lord Chamberlain's policy on theatrical nudity in 1958, the Office replied, "His Lordship treats as nude any female whether otherwise clothed or not (i) who exposes the nipples, (ii) whose breasts are largely uncovered and not firmly supported, (iii) who exposes the region of the base of the trunk."[32] The only kind of nude female performance the censor allowed for public exhibition at the time of *Cosmopolitan Merry-Go-Round*'s debut in the late 1930s was static nudity in the form of *poses plastiques*, also known as *tableaux vivants*, or "living pictures."[33] This technique, popular since the 1840s, consisted of nude women striking poses, often imitating famous figures from antiquity. There were certain guidelines as to how the nude tableaux could be presented: stage lighting had to be subdued and a performer's movement had to be minimal. The only kineticism allowed was deliberate, inconspicuous movement into another static pose; the performer could not speak.[34] Nude dancing was not permitted in the public theater. Despite these restrictions, starting in the years of the First World War, erotic entertainment starring women became increasingly prolific in Britain, along with plays starring women more generally, as male actors were less readily available.[35]

Given what we know about the contemporary regulation of nude performance in the public theater, it is not entirely clear that De Vere's act broke the rules. Since he was a male, the policy for what parts of his body he was allowed to display was vague, and his jockstrap, false breasts, and wig meant that he was not technically nude. Still, the potential that audiences could interpret De Vere as a nude woman was enough for it to be considered obscenity in the view of the censor, who was not beholden to a rigid set of guidelines but could instead judge on a case-by-case basis.

Ultimately, however, the court altogether evaded the question of whether a partially clothed man could be considered, for the purposes of theater censorship, a nude woman. The magistrate dismissed the censor's case without even calling on the defense to testify. While acknowledging that he was of the opinion that De Vere's act was "extremely vulgar and obscene," the magistrate ruled that, since the producers of the show were on trial for putting on an unlicensed scene rather than for obscenity, the case was to be thrown out as the scene had been technically licensed.[36] The magistrate reasoned that De Vere was allowed to perform "any sort of female impersonation he wished," as the Office had approved a script with an act described as "a female impersonation by Gerald De Vere assisted by the two girls."[37] De Vere had been entitled to do anything within these parameters. According to the magistrate, accusing the producers and De Vere of performing unlicensed material was tantamount to "locking the stable door after the horse had gone."[38] The magistrate was clearly unwilling to lend a rubber stamp to whatever objections the censor had with regard to nudity in the theater, and the Office, rebuffed, was unable to do anything but accept the court's disregard for its authority. In response, St James's Palace expressed disappointment in the ruling but sheepishly resolved that "His Lord-ship will, however . . . ensure that more explicit details are furnished in the future when Plays of this nature are submitted for Licence."[39]

Through an examination of the *Cosmopolitan Merry-Go-Round* case, it is evident that fissures had already formed in the Office's au-thority over the regime of state theater censorship by the 1930s. The legal system, upon which the censor depended to enforce its judg-ments, could not be consistently depended upon as a partner in the Office's mission. There are other examples in the run-up to *Cosmo-politan Merry-Go-Round*'s premiere that place the September 1939 magistrate's court ruling within a wider trend of the courts and the police undercutting the censor's power.

In May 1937 the Metropolitan Police responded to reports of an indecent striptease performance on Regent Street in London. The show was defended by the performer on the grounds that it was no different from ones seen at the Windmill Theatre, a Soho venue fa-mous for its presentations of striptease and nude tableaux. This de-fense prompted the Metropolitan Police to send a letter to St James's Palace that carefully criticized the Office's standards on erotic dis-play. "Bottle parties are tending to introduce objectionable shows of this nature on the grounds that they are openly permitted at the Windmill theatre," stated the correspondence.[40] The Office's re-sponse, marked "Private & Confidential," rejected the insinuation that the Windmill was being given preferential treatment. "There is a considerable difference between what apparently is a sort of Strip Tease act given in the intimate surroundings of a Bottle Party—when probably most of the people were half tight," assistant comptroller N.W. Gwatkin insisted, "and what takes place on the stage [at the Windmill]." He then reiterated the Office's stance on kinetic nudity, noting that male cast members were not allowed to be onstage with a nude woman performer "except at the corner of the stage," but he admitted that the representation of nudity onstage was a "vexed and worried question, and I hope we can thrash out some *modus viviandi* now that the Coronation troubles are over."[41]

The following month, Lord Cromer, the Lord Chamberlain at the time, chaired a meeting with the London County Council (L.C.C.) on the topic of stage nudity. The invitees included representatives from the County Councils' Association, the Society of West End Theatre Managers, and the Hotels and Restaurants Association of Great Britain. It appears that this response to criticism from the police, though rapid, produced no gains as far as clarifying or codifying the censor's rules on erotic display. According to newspaper coverage of the meeting, "No definite steps about future action were decided upon" aside from a loose agreement that licensees "keep a sharper eye on the various types of entertainment presented."[42] This did not instill confidence in the Metropolitan Police, who displayed increasing reluctance to go after stage shows based on the Office's nebulous policies. The police reaction to a subsequent allegation of an illicit nude performance in Clapham in September 1938 was muted. "I am very strongly of the opinion," said a senior officer, "that on this general question we should stick to our policy of masterly inactivity."[43] Two years later St James's Palace again organized a meeting on the censorship of stage nudity attended by representatives from the Home Office, the police, county councils, and various theater industry bodies. This meeting was as ineffectual as the one in 1937. It ended with the Office's policies on nudity unclarified and no goals articulated other than a vague commitment to maintaining "a decent level of propriety" within the theater.[44]

As in the *Cosmopolitan Merry-Go-Round* case, the police and the courts would continue to be a significant roadblock, or at least a dissenting voice, when the Lord Chamberlain's Office wished to penalize future productions featuring female impersonation. The courts and the police often expressed open disagreement with the Office regarding the definition of indecency on the stage, and the censor resented the justice system for perceivably bungling cases or rejecting entreaties by the censor to pursue charges against indiscretions. These disagreements frequently left St James's Palace, which could not pursue proceedings against violators of the Theatres Act without the aid of legal bodies, toothless in the face of perceived violations of the Theatres Act.

For all that the *Cosmopolitan Merry-Go-Round* case tells the historian about cultural and legal debates over nude display and the decline of theater censorship, little indication is given regarding any of the involved parties' attitudes toward female impersonation. If the censor, the magistrate, or other spectators saw the art form as troubling, then that unease was not a primary concern when compared to the greater problem of female nudity. The magistrate's ultimate ruling and the censor's silence on the issue of female impersonation in this case indicate that the regulation of drag was not a moral imperative for those involved in the censorship of the British theater in the late 1930s, even if the practice raised suspicions.

If the reaction to *Cosmopolitan Merry-Go-Round* in 1939 failed to answer the question of whether the censor associated drag with sexual immorality, then the matter was clarified six years later when the producers of the ex-servicemen's drag revue *Soldiers in Skirts*—originally titled *Boys Will Be Girls*—applied for a license. "I think the title should be altered [from *Boys Will Be Girls*]," stated the script's reader.[45] A superior in the Office agreed, adding that "the title should be changed owing to its suggestion of perversion. . . . [W]e should not give way, as we try to eliminate everything referring to 'pansy' business."[46] Despite this skepticism, the Office generally concluded that the show's content presented "very little to object to," and *Soldiers in Skirts* was licensed with ease.[47] However, *Soldiers in Skirts* would ultimately prove to be a thorn in the side of the Lord Chamberlain's Office throughout the show's successful nine-year run. *Soldiers in Skirts* became a bête noire for the censor due to accusations that the show's performers were staging indecent and unlicensed material, but, as was the case with the *Cosmopolitan Merry-Go-Round* incident, St James's Palace had trouble convincing its partners in theater regulation that *Soldiers in Skirts* posed a threat. The censor, the courts, the police, theater critics, and theatergoers all had divergent opinions on the extent to which ex-servicemen's drag revues constituted an obscene display and whether drag was inherently transgressive. These disagreements illuminate the fatal fissures evident in the regime of theater censorship in the 1940s and 1950s.

Inspired by the success of interwar predecessors Les Rouges et Noirs, as well as shows performed by American GIs that involved drag, ex-servicemen's drag revues experienced a boom during and after the Second World War, with no less than a dozen theatrical drag shows touting casts entirely made up of ex-servicemen produced between the early 1940s and mid-1950s.[48] The shows tended to be lavish, well-produced affairs aimed at a general audience.[49] Some of the most successful of these, such as *Soldiers in Skirts* and *Forces Showboat* (1947), toured for several years continuously.[50]

Motivations for joining the revues varied among artists. For the many cast members who were entertainers prior to enlisting in the forces during the Second World War, touring in the all-male revues represented a resumption of their civilian careers. Some, like Danny La Rue, discovered their penchant for drag through entertaining in wartime concert parties. Others saw the shows as an exciting outlet for expressing gender variance.[51]

Many of the shows were produced by the same two agencies: Mannie Jay and Sydney Myers (later JMZ Productions) and the Ralph Marshall Agency. As a result, the theatricals often recycled the same content, sometimes at the same time as multiple ex-servicemen's drag revues ran concurrently. Recurring acts included variations on the "Mannequin Parade" (a fashion show of sorts featuring the cast in different dresses from various eras), the "Mermaid Sketch" (a patter with two female impersonators as mermaids featuring nautical-themed innuendo), "Eastern Scene" (a comedy sketch set in a harem or romanticized orientalist setting), "Dancing through the Ages" (a showcase of dance styles from different time periods, sometimes involving a comically inept cross-dressed male dancer), and impersonations of popular cultural figures such as Sophie Tucker and Carmen Miranda. Like the Les Rouges shows, the 1940s and 1950s revues were mostly comedic, but casts tended to project earnest feminine glamour. Performing in the revues was demanding work: casts typically staged two shows per evening (plus Saturday matinees), six days a week, with constant travel between venues. Salary was a fairly meagre £6 to £7 per week for most of the performers.[52]

The revues were critical as well as commercial successes. In particular, the press tended to hail the quality of the feminine illusion presented by the performers. For example, a *Hull Daily Mail* reviewer commented, "It is very hard to believe that that the company of 'Forces Showboat' at the Tivoli this week is an all-male one. Even in the finale when the 'girls' take off their wigs, the audience finds it difficult to accept the fact."[53] The *Western Morning News* also complimented *Forces Showboat* for "the ex-Service men who make up the cast [who] masquerade most convincingly as women and dance gracefully," while *This Was the Army* (1946), which toured for nine years, was praised by the *Aberdeen Press and Journal* for the cast's "amazingly good female impersonations."[54] *The Stage* praised the "all-male cast [of *Forces in Petticoats* (1952)], whose portrayals of various female roles are ingenious and skillful."[55]

Even the Lord Chamberlain's Office was at times capable of complimenting ex-servicemen's drag revues, or at least of viewing them as innocuous. "Surprisingly clean and reasonably funny," judged the reader's report for *Call Us Mister* (1953).[56] The Office's general attitude toward female impersonation and male effeminacy during this period, when the censor operated a blanket ban on homosexual themes in the theater, could be permissive as comedic, effete "maiden aunt" types were sometimes seen as an acceptable coded alternative to openly homosexual characters.[57]

An example of ambivalence expressed toward ex-servicemen's drag revues is seen in the censor's file on *We Were in the Forces* (1944). Police in Oldham and Blackpool visited the revue and found it to be "lewd" and "suggestive."[58] One scene in particular that was objected to was "Dancing through the Ages," which sees the cast undertake various dances from different historical periods, including "stone age," "waltz," "can-can," and "jitterbug." One police officer reported that during the "jitterbug" portion of the scene, female impersonator George Ellisia suggestively rubbed masculine-presenting comedian Hal Jones (of Les Rouges et Noirs fame) suggestively, "in front of [Jones's] middle" and "between [his] legs," with a large ostrich feather fan.[59] Another police officer agreed that the scene was indecent, reporting that *We Were in the Forces* was "in the main a more or less third-rate Show, and one which I am sure could be greatly improved upon by the elimination of the Can-Can Dance, which in my opinion is lewd when performed, as in this Show, by a male. The same could be said of the Specialty dances in the 'Jitterbug Club' dance scene."[60] After producer John D. Roberton and members of the cast were given a warning, the chief constable of the Oldham Borough Police nevertheless suggested that no legal proceedings should be taken against the show.[61] This disappointed the Lord Chamberlain's Office, which could now only resort to writing "a very strong letter" to Roberton to give him a "fright."[62] Despite the censor's desire to launch legal proceedings against *We Were in the Forces*, which was foiled by law enforcement's unwillingness to do so, St James's Palace appeared to forgive Roberton and the show rather quickly, if the incident was remembered at all. When Roberton put together a second touring company for the revue due to its popularity, and he asked the Office to license a revised version of the script, St James's Palace licensed it within two days of Roberton submitting it, with no indication that any prior issues concerning the show had occurred.[63] This incident highlights another example of the censor's desire to assert authority being hampered by law enforcement. It also demonstrates that even when female impersonation was deemed indecent, law enforcement and the Lord Chamberlain's Office were capable of shrugging it off rather than seeing lewd drag as a grave threat.

Ex-servicemen's drag revue *Forces Showboat* also fell afoul of the Theatres Act, but, despite this, the show was ultimately treated with leniency by the police and the D.P.P. The cast of *Forces Showboat* was found to be performing unlicensed material during an appearance at the Barnsley Theatre Royal on 4 April 1949.[64] Stars of the show Terry Bartlett and Colin Ross, along with other cast members, were visited backstage by police officer W. Tinker of the Barnsley County Borough Police and were warned against uttering unlicensed lines such as "I've got my points," in reference to a pair of false breasts.[65] On 5 April, Tinker viewed *Forces Showboat* again and found that unlicensed material was still being performed.[66] Finally, upon Tinker's third visit to the show on 7 April, he observed that the cast hewed to the licensed script and "there was nothing calling for adverse comment in the show."[67] *Forces Showboat*'s repeated infractions of the Theatres Act caused the Lord Chamberlain's Office to write to the D.P.P. to ask whether legal proceedings should be launched against the show.[68] The D.P.P. acknowledged that while "an offence has been committed . . . no useful purpose would be served by instituting proceedings in this case." "In my view the passages complained of are not unduly offensive and as they were not repeated after the police warning it is unlikely that any more than a nominal penalty would be inflicted," explained the D.P.P., even though the cast of *Forces Showboat* had, in fact, continued to perform unlicensed material after they had been issued with a warning.[69] Once again law enforcement were treating drag shows with a light touch even when such shows technically broke the law.

The Office's ongoing problems with the ex-servicemen's drag revue *Soldiers in Skirts* were focused mainly on unlicensed and indecent material in the show's "Cutting In" sketch and "Fan Fayre" routine, variations on two acts commonly seen in ex-servicemen's drag revues. The "Cutting In" sketch portrays a private and a sergeant, played by male comedians, competing for the attention of a woman played by a female impersonator. Throughout the scene the men take turns interrupting one another, punctuated by the line "You don't mind me cutting in," as each vies to court the woman. The men keep switching places at increasingly ludicrous junctures, such as the moment when the private and the woman are exchanging wedding vows. The sketch ends with the private cutting in just as the sergeant and the woman have disrobed and are getting into bed together. "Fan Fayre," a parody of the striptease fan dancing sequences popular at the Windmill Theatre, opens with a chorus of female impersonators "dressed in briefs and brassieres and carrying fans."[70] As they dance, the brassiere of one of the chorus girls comes undone, with socks falling out of the brassiere. The chorus girl frantically tries to continue the dance while adjusting the brassiere until the brassiere comes off completely, leaving the dancer flustered as she tries frantically to cover her bare chest.

The trouble for *Soldiers in Skirts* began when Inspector R. Strong of the L.C.C. Public Control Department paid a visit to a staging of the show at the Chelsea Palace Theatre on 6 December 1945. Along with "Cutting In" and "Fan Fayre," Strong reported seeing such sketches as female impersonator Archie Usher singing in falsetto, a Carmen Miranda impersonation, and a scene called "Little Nell" involving a young girl runaway who returns home with "a doll representing a baby which eventually turns out to be black."[71] The revelation leads to race-based gags such as "She must have been out with the Kentucky minstrels."[72] Despite the apparently risqué nature of this material, Strong stated explicitly that he did not think that *Sol-*

diers in Skirts was an indecent production. Of "Fan Fayre" in particular, Strong reported that he "saw nothing objectionable in this scene." "Judging the show in light of a music hall performance I saw nothing to cause offense," Strong concluded of the entire night's program.[73]

The Lord Chamberlain's Office expressed greater concern than did Inspector Strong. The word *pansy* was annotated in pencil on Inspector Strong's report by someone at the Office, and a St James's Palace employee who was sent to survey the show after Strong's visit complained that "the girl did disrobe and the comic 'cut in' half naked!"[74] However, the censor's subsequent warning to the producers of *Soldiers in Skirts* was ultimately moderate. "The Lord Chamberlain will not allow any undressing, stripping, or attempts to do so in the 'Cutting In' sketch," the Office said, adding that it would allow "the brassiere business" in "Fan Fayre" to continue "within reason," so long as the gag did not "run practically through the whole scene."[75] This warning to the producers appears especially light given that the censor was at the same time asking the L.C.C. Public Control Department whether the show could be taken to court for violations of the Theatres Act. The Public Control Department firmly shot down this inquiry.[76]

The Office got its wish the next month, in January 1946, however, when proceedings were launched against the *Soldiers in Skirts* producers in Chesterfield magistrates' court for violations of the Theatres Act in that locality. The case was dismissed unceremoniously within two hours, to the chagrin of St James's Palace, which blamed the loss on the ineptitude of the chief constable of Chesterfield and the prosecution.[77] Revealing an increasingly fraught relationship with legal institutions, St James's Palace was rebuffed several more times when it tried to initiate further legal proceedings against *Soldiers in Skirts*. In July 1946 the Chesterfield town clerk advised the censor against pursuing an appeal of the earlier case against the revue's producers.[78] The D.P.P. also declined to pursue a separate case on behalf of the censor after the theater manager of the Accrington Hippodrome in Lancashire complained to the Office about unlicensed material in performances of *Soldiers in Skirts* at his theater.[79] A police officer sent to view a performance of the show in Blackpool that month agreed with the D.P.P. that *Soldiers in Skirts* posed no threat to public decency, though the officer noted that "this show is definitely of a second class type."[80]

St James's Palace again found fault with the "Fan Fayre" sketch six years after the short-lived Chesterfield case, in March 1952, when it was reported by Sergeant F. Slack of the Sheffield police that female impersonator Eric Lloyd "handl[ed] his fan as though he was stroking his private parts" and "show[ed] his own nipples." Still, despite judging that "the programme generally is of a poor standard of entertainment," Slack surmised that "there is little in it which can be said to be obscene or seriously suggestive."[81] Of "Fan Fayre" specifically, "the action of the fan near the private parts" was deemed by Slack to be "not necessarily evident enough to attract the attention of a member of the public attending merely for entertainment and without any motive for concentrated attention. The actions of the man concerned were more in the way of slapstick comedy and were only slightly suggestive."[82] This assessment mirrored R. Strong's earlier opinions of the act and the revue in general. The censor once again found the business described to be a matter of graver concern than the police felt it was, and St James's Palace reached out to the D.P.P. about launching another round of legal proceedings. "I do not consider that this is a suitable case for criminal proceedings," responded the director firmly, citing the failure of the previous case as well as his view that the excesses in the "Fan Fayre" sketch would probably be seen as only "a technical offence" as the reasons for his decision.[83]

As opposed to the Lord Chamberlain's Office, the press and public generally viewed *Soldiers in Skirts* positively. Mirroring the media response to Les Rouges et Noirs, critics regularly praised the convincing female impersonations by the revue's cast. "So adequately do the artists impersonate the glamorous women of the stage, that one feels their skirts become them nearly as well as their battle dresses did," raved one typical review.[84] Another critic declared, "There is no doubt that in the nine years of its existence this company has brought the art [of female impersonation] to a very high pitch. So completely has the cast absorbed even the mannerisms of women that when the compere introduced the chorus as 'the boys' it was still difficult to believe that they were, in fact, only men in disguise."[85] *Soldiers in Skirts* proved popular with average theatergoers as well. One newspaper review, while mostly negative, noted that *Soldiers in Skirts* attracted a respectable audience of "wives and sweethearts" to the theater.[86] P. C. William Marsden, who observed a staging of the show in Blackpool at the censor's behest, noted that "the audience are very appreciative and the show is generally well received. On leaving the Theatre we mingled with the people and no adverse criticism of any description was heard."[87] Toward the end of the show's run in 1953 and 1954, newspaper columns were noting that *Soldiers in Skirts* was still drawing packed houses around the country.[88] "It has . . . built up an enormous fund of goodwill among music hall audiences, and there is no mistaking the genuine warmth of the welcome with which this novel presentation is received on all sides," observed the *Stage*.[89] Even detractors who explicitly associated female impersonation with homosexuality, such as homosexual law reform campaigner Peter Wildeblood, agreed that the revue was well received by the public. "The popularity in Britain since the war of frankly homosexual entertainments such as the 'Soldiers in Skirts' revues," Wildeblood grumbled, "suggests that such men (i.e. homosexuals) are now regarded by middle- and working-class audiences with tolerant amusement instead of with scorn."[90] Testifying to its popularity amongst the public, the revue ran uninterrupted from May 1945 through April 1954.

Soldiers in Skirts elicited some harshly negative direct audience responses, but the severe tenor of these critiques was extraordinary compared to mainstream opinion. For instance, a letter sent to St James's Palace in January 1947 from a complainant identifying themselves as S. Oakes of Sheffield decried the perceived perversity of *Soldiers in Skirts*, citing the "matrimony" and "fan" scenes (likely to be "Cutting In" and "Fan Fayre," respectively) as being particularly "disgusting" and "disgraceful." "What an insult to our soldiers who died for this country," Oakes bemoaned. "We expect to see genuine discharged men, not a Bunch of Filthy Puffs . . . Can't you stop these menaces?"[91] Additionally, a military officer, Captain Gray, publicly echoed Oakes' skepticism as to whether the *Soldiers in Skirts* cast was genuinely composed of ex-servicemen as they were "moral perverts . . . [who] would be a menace to any self respecting body of men."[92] In the same year that Oakes wrote his letter, a similarly dramatic complaint was mailed to St James's Palace regarding *Forces Showboat*. The correspondent in question, George Richardson of 232 Upper Brook Street, Manchester, lamented that "it is not in the best interests of *clean variety* that the principal comedian (*with black hair*) dressed as a female should be allowed to: 1) pull up clothes and exhibit Red FLANNEL DRAWERS. 2) pull up clothes, exhibit painted on White DRAWERS. (THE ATOM BOMB) 3) pull up drawers EXHIBIT ON PINK DRAWERS (LOCK + CHAINS) followed by old gent round the stage—we are not prudes but these FEMALE SHOWS by men are not in the best taste anyhow and especially since the CORNOCK disclosures Educating to the young."[93] The Lord Chamberlain's Office pursued some of these complaints but its reaction was mild, especially compared with the tone of the letters. A few of Oakes's allegations were raised in a letter sent by St James's Palace to the producers of *Soldiers in Skirts*. The producers responded indignantly, retorting, "May I point out to you that the previous proceedings were proved by the court to be pure fabrications, and one cannot go against the court's decision," while brushing off Oakes's grievances as "somebody . . . trying to manufacture trouble."[94] After this the matter of Oakes's complaints was dropped. Richardson's letter regarding *Forces Showboat* was deemed important enough to warrant a visit to the show by senior examiner of plays H. C. Game from the Lord Chamberlain's Office, but the allegations were mostly dismissed thereafter. "Disappointment attended my official visit to the Wood Green Empire last evening," reported Game wryly, who concluded "there was no sign of the questionable business alleged by Mr Robinson [sic]."[95] Game went on to suggest that Richardson could have fabricated the complaints due to "professional jealousy," as the letter was written on the back of a small advertisement for "Richardson's World Famous Stringed Marionettes." Game even paid *Forces Showboat* some compliments: "I found a very clean show, with some excellent variety turns, certainly above the usual standard of touring Revue."[96]

Despite the potential of these complaints to appeal to the censor's distrust of drag, the Office was restrained in its reaction to them; the producers of *Soldiers in Skirts* received a perfunctory letter of warning as a result of Oakes's accusations, while Richardson's grievances were quickly dismissed. The response from St James's Palace in these cases was in keeping with its lukewarm relationship with contemporary moral purity campaigners who were always agitating for the censor to take a more aggressive approach toward regulating the theater. The Lord Chamberlain's Office often viewed such campaigners as a nuisance. Of these moral crusaders, the P.M.C. was the most vocal and organized.[97] Founded in 1899, the P.M.C. was made up of church officials, ordinary citizens, and even paid officers who actively surveilled public places—including theaters—to report any indecent activities to the censor and other authorities.[98] St James's Palace often saw the P.M.C. as tiresomely overzealous. "You cannot confine the drama to plays about children for children," stated one

Lord Chamberlain employee in a typical dismissal of the P.M.C.[99] But the Lord Chamberlain's Office was still guardedly receptive to some of the organization's entreaties, sometimes following up complaints with a visit from a representative of St James's Palace, as was the case after George Richardson's letter was received.[100]

The Lord Chamberlain's Office, with its tolerant but often wary approach to drag, as well as the harsher, more vocal opponents of ex-servicemen's drag revues, appear out of step with the broadly positive views of theatergoers, with whom the shows resonated. The press too generally praised ex-servicemen's drag revues, or at least found the shows innocuous, if lowbrow, entertainment.[101] The censor's partners in the enforcement of theater censorship—the judiciary, the police, the L.C.C., and the D.P.P.—mostly did not view ex-servicemen's drag revues as a serious threat to public decency, and these institutions hindered the Lord Chamberlain's Office's attempts to regulate drag performance.

John Osborne's play *A Patriot for Me* (1965) was denied a license multiple times, starting with its first submission in 1964. The Lord Chamberlain's Office specifically highlighted act 2, scene 1 as the reason for withholding a license.[102] The scene in question takes place at a "drag ball."[103] The play would not be presented in a public theater in Britain until the Lord Chamberlain's Office lost its censorship powers in 1968. Unlike the shows previously discussed in this chapter, *A Patriot for Me* is a narrative drama. The play is set between 1890 and 1913 and centers upon the real-life personality of Colonel Alfred Redl, an Austro-Hungarian intelligence officer whose homosexuality made him subject to a Russian blackmail scheme.[104] In the scene in question, Redl attends a drag ball, which is overseen by host Baron von Epp dressed as Queen Alexandra of Denmark (figure 18), and which gives the audience a glimpse of the Viennese male homosexual underworld of 1902, which is made up of a mix of characters from various walks of life, including "rich, discreet queens," military

FIGURE 18. Leonard Rosoman, *Portrait with Candelabra: George Devine as Baron von Epp, Act 2, Scene 1* (1968). Credit: Photograph © Pallant House Gallery, Chichester UK.

officials, and "paid bum boys."[105] The scene is meant to be performed earnestly, with Osborne's script taking care to describe the specific social groups attending the ball in detail and specifically calling for high-quality outfits to be worn by the actors.[106] The submission of *A Patriot for Me* for licensing was one of the first tests of the Office's new, more permissive policy regarding the portrayal of homosexuality in the theater, though the policy was ultimately not liberal enough for *A Patriot for Me* to obtain a license.

Six years before *A Patriot for Me*'s application for a license, in 1958, the Lord Chamberlain had officially decided to lift his Office's blanket ban on homosexual themes and characters on the stage, allowing the subject of homosexuality to be referenced openly under certain circumstances. The Lord Chamberlain's Office was in a reflective mood regarding the matter on the heels of events that helped to spur public discussions on homosexual law reform, such as the Montagu trial of 1953–54, the subsequent publication of trial defendant Peter Wildeblood's memoir *Against the Law* (1955), and the formation of the Wolfenden Committee in 1954. The Office's official position until 1958 was that any play about homosexuality, or one that included homosexual characters, would be denied a license, though in practice this policy was inconsistently applied.[107] It appears that the 1957 publication of the Wolfenden Report was a catalyst for the end of the censor's blanket ban on homosexual themes in the theater. In this sense, St James's Palace was revealing a desire to keep pace with public opinion. "Up to now I had maintained a rigid attitude, as had my predecessors, on this subject, and allowed no mention of it on the stage," explained Lord Scarbrough, the Lord Chamberlain between 1952 and 1963. However, Scarbrough went on to acknowledge that homosexuality was now "much talked about" and it would thus appear "ostrich-like" to continue the total ban. Furthermore, "an increasing number of plays, some of them good, and dealing seriously with this subject, were being written."[108]

In a memorandum issued on 31 October 1958, Scarbrough laid out a set of rules dictating the parameters for the portrayal of homosexuality in the theater. These were:

(a) Every play will continue to be judged on its merits and only those dealing seriously with the subject will be passed;
(b) Plays violently homosexual will not be passed;
(c) Homosexual characters will not be allowed if their inclusion in the piece is unnecessary to the action or theme of the play;
(d) Embraces between homosexuals will not be allowed.[109]

Further rules included "No funny innuendos," "'Pansy' to be allowed but not 'bugger,'" "Criticism of the present laws on the subject *to be allowed*" unless the play constituted straightforward propaganda, and "Embarrassing displays by male homosexuals *not* to be allowed," particularly if such "displays" applied to male prostitutes.[110]

The censor's pre-1958 approach to homosexual themes on the stage frustrated cultural liberals while doing little to appease cultural conservatives who felt the Office was being lax in its defense of public decency. The Office's new policy on homosexual themes in the theater from 1958 similarly appeased few across the political spectrum. It raised the hackles of conservatives, while liberals remained unsatisfied. Labour MP Frederick John Bellenger criticized the Lord Chamberlain's decision in a parliamentary debate. "I am of the opinion that there are too many presentations on the stage . . . portraying homosexuality as their central theme," Bellenger observed. "I notice that the Lord Chamberlain has recently permitted the public performances of certain plays. I regret that."[111] The Archbishop of Canterbury warned the Lord Chamberlain that, as "homosexual vice is still a criminal offence," the censor could be taken to court "for allowing incitements to homosexuality."[112] Conversely, the Office's liberal critics took the new development as another opportunity to question the entire enterprise of theater censorship. The *Stage* newspaper, for example, greeted the policy change with some appreciation, but the paper and theater professionals it interviewed for comment ultimately took the news as an opportunity to agitate for the full abolition of theater censorship. "Other restrictions may well be lifted as time goes on," the paper mused hopefully, "to give the theatre even greater freedom and to treat the serious playgoer as an adult capable of deciding for himself."[113] "I hope, it will prove to be a big move towards abolition of the censorship," added actress Dame Peggy Ashcroft.[114] The reactions to the censor's policy change of 1958 presaged the subsequent debate over the staging of *A Patriot for Me*, which would bring into relief the Office's tendency to aggravate opponents of theater censorship while pleasing few supporters.

In addition to St James's Palace's objections to *A Patriot for Me*'s generally sympathetic, earnest portrayal of homosexuality and "scenes in which men embrace each other and are seen in bed together," the Office was primarily concerned by the play's drag ball scene. "He [the Lord Chamberlain] cannot allow such scenes as a homosexual Ball at which some of the men are dressed as women (including one who portrays Lady Godiva dressed in a gold lamé jockstrap)," the Office warned the managers of the Royal Court Theatre, where the play was due to be staged.[115] St James's Palace's main concerns about the drag ball scene centered upon the notion of female impersonation as a propagandistic tool for seducing the vulnerable audience member into homosexuality. Secretary Ronald John Hill observed, "The transvestite ball is not essential to the action, but only to the atmosphere of the piece and by presenting homo-sexuals in their most attractive guise—dressed as pretty women, will to some degree cause the congregation of homo-sexuals and provide the means whereby the vice may be acquired. . . . The homosexual has no lack of advocate today, and assistance from the stage is unnecessary."[116] Another Office memo echoed this sentiment, stating, "The homosexual ball will give a homosexual thrill to homosexuals or near homosexuals."[117] Senior examiner of plays C. D. Heriot agreed, arguing that "the very fact that the homosexual scenes, especially the 'drag' ball, are presented in their best terms would certainly attract all the perverts in London and might even persuade the young and ignorant that such a life would not be so bad, after all. It is thus a corrupting play."[118] Despite these criticisms, some high-ranking employees in the Office admired *A Patriot for Me*, deeming it "dramatically an excellent play," though its high quality only made it more likely to corrupt viewers, it was argued.[119]

Within St James's Palace, homosexuality was predominantly framed as a pernicious and communicable vice. The theater, Office employees argued, had the potential to induce impressionable individuals to adopt a homosexual lifestyle. Cultural elites, among whom homosexuality was allegedly propagating, were conspiring to use the theater for this sinister purpose, and the Lord Chamberlain's Office saw itself as a bulwark against this plot.[120] Internal memos from May 1966 relating to *A Patriot for Me* illuminate these views. Secretary Hill, citing a "British Medical Association report on homo-sexuals," alleged that a homosexual lifestyle was often adopted by certain individuals as a result of "seduction," "imitation," and "cultural aspirations." "Some people adopt homo-sexual practices because they think such activity denotes superiority of mind and the possession of cultured and artistic instincts." He warned that those most susceptible to corruption included individuals with "jaded appetites" seeking "new sensations."[121] Reflecting the view that homosexuality was increasingly a bourgeois affectation, Hill noted that "homosexuals in positions of authority give preferential treatment to homo-sexuals or require homo-sexual subjection as expedient for promotion. The existence of practicing homosexuals in. . . . . . press, Radio, stage. . . . constitutes a special problem."[122] When reviewing plays that depicted homosexuality, St James's Palace tasked itself with considering the needs of impressionable audience members, such as children or those with misguided "cultural aspirations," who might "acquire" the "vice."

The notion that the state should protect vulnerable individuals from corrupting influences was not merely an issue when it came to homosexuality but it had long been at the heart of legal definitions of obscenity. Between 1857 and 1959 the Obscene Publications Act (1857) was the primary legislative means of regulating indecent materials in Britain. The legal framework relating to the enforcement of the act was strongly informed by the 1868 court case *Regina v. Hicklin*. In that case Chief Justice Alexander Cockburn ruled that obscenity law should be enforced with the aim of protecting "those whose minds are open to such immoral influences, and into whose hands a publication of this sort may fall," a standard known commonly as the "Hicklin test" or the "Cockburn test."[123] Therefore, the circumstances of publication—how and where the material was circulated and displayed—played a critical role in whether it was legally considered obscene. If, for example, a medical text covering sexual matters or a picture book containing artful nudity was only made available to specialist consumers or otherwise high-minded individuals, then those publications would be less likely to be considered legally obscene. If those materials made their way to general bookshops, newsagents, or other venues accessible to consumers perceived as vulnerable (for example, youth or women), however, then they were more likely to be obscene in the eyes of the law.[124] In 1959 a revised Obscene Publications Act was passed in Britain. This law still employed the Hicklin Test as a standard by which obscenity should be measured, but, importantly, material alleged to be obscene could now be defended on the basis that it held wider artistic, literary, or other merits that served the "public good." This standard was soon put to the test in 1960 when the publishers of an unbowdlerized new edition of the novel *Lady Chatterley's Lover* (1928) were taken to court under obscenity charges but won the case based on the artistic and literary merit provision of the 1959 act.

In July 1965 the Royal Court changed from a public theater to a club in order to stage *A Patriot for Me* with the drag ball scene intact.[125] St James's Palace doubted that the Royal Court was being run as a legitimate private theater club, and Assistant Comptroller John Johnston was sent to investigate. Johnston reported that he and a companion were able to enter the venue without showing membership cards.[126] The Lord Chamberlain's Office concluded that the "'club' arrangement in this case was a subterfuge," but that to prosecute the Royal Court would appear to be spiteful and an attack on all private theater clubs in general, which, "like my predecessors, I consider a valuable contribution to the Theatre if properly managed."[127] It appeared that St James's Palace changed its mind later that month when the attorney general was consulted about the prospect of prosecuting the theater and the play's producers. "The way in which this play is being presented at the Royal Court Theatre constitutes a 'public performance,'" agreed the attorney general. "They [the law officers in the attorney general's office] are, however, strongly of the opinion that it would be inexpedient to institute such a prosecution in connection with the performance of this play which has attracted a great deal of public interest and a good deal of support and which has been running for some time."[128] The Office was wounded by this rejection. "This seems to me to be a quite outspoken statement of lack of faith in the Censor's decisions and is I think the most complete official disavowal of this Office that I have seen," remarked Hill.[129] The Lord Chamberlain's Office pleaded with the D.P.P. and the attorney general's office to take up a case against *A Patriot for Me* in autumn 1965, going so far as to say that the entire administration of theater censorship was at risk over the issue. Again, the censor was rebuffed, with the D.P.P. replying that "it is undesirable to do this."[130]

St James's Palace, stifled by the D.P.P. and the attorney general's office once again, also found few friends in the press. "If I did not know it to be untrue, I should think that the Lord Chamberlain was mad," remarked the *Sunday Times* in a harsh assessment of the censor's decision. "It is ludicrous and pathetic that the Lord Chamberlain should have refused to allow John Osborne's *A Patriot for Me* to be performed publicly at the Royal Court." Perhaps alluding to the drag shows and performances featuring maiden aunt types that St James's Palace had previously tolerated, the article went on to articulate a criticism of the case that was typical in the press: "One cannot protest too strongly against that double moral standard which prevails in the government of the English theatre, by which it is permissible to treat a difficult and delicate subject frivolously, but of which any thoughtful consideration is almost automatically penalised."[131] The *Western Mail* (Cardiff) surmised, "[The Lord Chamberlain] need not have worried; only an extraordinarily loutish and prurient mind could possibly find smut in this production."[132] The *Tribune* criticized the Lord Chamberlain, Lord Cobbold, as inept due to his prior experience, not in theater, but as governor of the Bank of England. "It would much surprise me if, after a lifetime as a writer, I were to be invited in my late fifties to become supreme arbiter of financial policy and veto the actions of people who have gained experience and distinction in that sphere," the journalist mused spitefully.[133] More than merely critiquing the censor's decision regarding *A Patriot for Me* specifically, the press used the affair to question the entire enterprise of theater censorship.

Even commentators who opposed homosexuality were bemused by the censor's actions. Contrary to the fear that the play might corrupt vulnerable theatergoers, these observers felt that the play—particularly the drag ball scene—portrayed homosexuality in a negative light. Public intellectual Lord Annan argued, "I cannot conceive of any play less sentimental towards homosexuality. . . . The transvestite scene, to which particular exception was taken, was both pathetic and comical, but it was entirely integral to the play."[134] Some journalists agreed. "The homosexual ball scene which opens the second act . . . says more, in purely dramatic terms about the tragedy, pathos, absurdity, and comicality of male homosexuality," declared the *Times Educational Supplement* in its critique of St James's Palace, "than 500 owlish journalists, television performers, and psychologists would together be capable of."[135] This barrage of pointed criticism from multiple quarters appeared to take the censor by surprise, but the Office did not concede defeat. *A Patriot for Me* was not staged in the public theater in Britain until the Theatres Act 1968 had passed.

The abolition of the Lord Chamberlain's Office's powers over theater censorship in 1968 was the result of a prolonged process of deterioration. The increasing size and complexity of the theater sector and the difficulty in maintaining control over the levers of theater censorship, composed of a varied array of agents, institutions, interest groups, and opinions, inexorably diminished the authority of St James's Palace. The Office's confusing system of rules and lack of appeasement of observers across the political spectrum abetted censorship's decline. By the mid-twentieth century, Lords Chamberlain Scarbrough and Cobbold, as well as those under their employ, were pessimistic about the future of the Office's control over censorship and were petitioning the Home Office to end the regime in as dignified a fashion as possible.[136] When the Office's dominion over theater censorship was finally taken away, few observers, including the Lord Chamberlain himself, were disappointed.[137]

The Theatres Act 1968 is often invoked as one of several examples of late-1950s and 1960s "permissive" legislation that signified the state's increasingly libertarian approach to matters of cultural and sexual morality in the period. Other, more frequently discussed, laws of this kind include the abolition of the death penalty, the partial decriminalization of homosexual acts between men, and the legalization of abortion.[138] The fact that countercultural works such as *Hair: The American Tribal Love-Rock Musical* (1967) and *Oh! Calcutta!* (1969) were among the first stage productions to debut publicly in Britain after the passage of the 1968 act has added to a Whiggish narrative that the Lord Chamberlain's loss of power constituted a victory for permissive sexual revolutionaries over the reactionary values of the past.[139] Yet the evidence points to a less teleological narrative: theater censorship was being undermined not by some irrepressible current of permissive sentiment, but rather by established institutions over the course of several decades prior to the late 1960s. These institutions, namely the courts, the police, the press, and parts of the theater industry—with the legislature ultimately stripping the Office of its censorship powers—questioned and contravened the censor's decisions, preventing, in some cases, the Office from exerting its authority.

The Office's messy and inconsistent relationship with drag performance reflected the administrative issues involved in the British regime of state-run theater censorship. Drag was held in higher esteem by average theatergoers and theater critics than by St James's Palace, yet the censor's relationship with drag still reflected some of the wider culture's complex views regarding the connection between drag and sexual immorality. St James's Palace consistently associated female impersonation with sexual immorality and was thus skeptical of the art form. The inclusion of drag could render a show more susceptible than it would have otherwise been to legal proceedings or other manner of heightened scrutiny by the Lord Chamberlain's Office. However, when St James's Palace pursued shows involving drag for purported violations of the Theatres Act, female impersonation tended to be at best a secondary motivation for such actions. Usually concerns about homosexual content, nudity, lewd humor, unlicensed additions to a script, or other issues were foremost. The Office was also capable, with notable exceptions as in the case of *A Patriot for Me*, of looking past its personal prejudices and licensing shows involving female impersonation, often viewing such plays as innocuous, if lowbrow, entertainment, with some receiving earnest praise. The perceptions of and reactions to drag by the Lord Chamberlain's Office and other observers illuminate the lack of consensus over what drag meant from the start of the Second World War through the 1960s. The sense that female impersonation connoted sexual immorality, particularly same-sex desire, was pervasive, though not ubiquitously acknowledged. Further, there was no consensus on how and whether to respond to the threat of drag, if the art form indeed constituted one. This ambivalent attitude toward drag extended to state institutions as well as the general public.

Epilogue

How Queer Is Drag?

We were finding a new way of doing drag that wasn't offensive to women, that wasn't about false tits and distasteful jokes. We saw ourselves as a new type of man. We could wear frocks and make-up and be silly and funny, but we had a serious message, too. That tradition continues today in performers from David Hoyle down, who are doing what you could loosely call drag, but it's not that aggressive form of "female impersonation." That still goes on, and I still don't like it.

BETTE BOURNE

By 1970 a new kind of drag was coming into its own. Inspired in part by the drag queens and gender nonconforming people who took part in the 1969 Stonewall riots in New York City, practitioners of "radical drag" were a key part of the gay liberation movement of the early to mid-1970s in Britain. Notably, radical drag practitioners were involved in the British Gay Liberation Front (GLF) from the activist group's inception in 1970. Arguably the most prominent example of radical drag as a method of protest came during the GLF disruption of the inaugural meeting of the Nationwide Festival of Light (NFOL) on 9 September 1971 in Westminster Central Hall. There, GLF activists and their allies infiltrated the hall where NFOL supporters had gathered. The activists proceeded to carry out a series of disruptive actions, including dancing the cancan dressed as nuns and initiating a melodramatic mock religious epiphany performed by a cross-dressed man.[1] For its practitioners, radical drag was both a lifestyle and a tool for protest. Radical drag practitioners populated a GLF commune in a former film studio in Notting Hill Gate, named "Colvillia" after nearby Colville Terrace, where they cross-dressed as part of their everyday routine, such as while "stagger[ing] down to the newsagents in our high heels and distressed make-up to get the Sunday papers" after coming down from an LSD trip.[2] Radical drag practitioners later helped to precipitate the GLF's dissolution in 1973 after they, along with women in the GLF, left the group due to what they perceived as disrespect and outright hostility toward them from masculine-presenting male GLF members.[3]

As the above quote by drag artist and activist Bette Bourne indicates, exponents of radical drag saw the practice as a distinct break from the tradition of female impersonation that had defined drag from the nineteenth century up to the 1970s. Radical drag was rooted in feminist philosophy. The practice was meant to provoke reflection on socially informed gender roles for wearers and observers, in addition to marking the wearer as a "visible homosexual."[4] This was in contrast to female impersonation, which, according to radical drag practitioners, was colored by misogyny and tackiness.[5]

Though the rise of radical drag did not signify the death knell for more traditional female impersonation, and drag continued to hold meanings for practitioners and observers that had little or nothing to do with queer sexualities, radical drag represented a significant cultural shift for the art form. Drag was being overtly claimed as the preserve of gay culture and politics. Drag performances in venues for leisure like pubs were also becoming more explicit about the art form's ties to gay culture, even if the acts were not straightforwardly political.[6]

Following suit, academia and popular scholarship were, by the 1970s, viewing drag through the lens of what we would today call queer studies. Anthropologist Esther Newton's influential *Mother Camp: Female Impersonators in America* (1972) studied "the gay male world" through an investigation of drag and drag artists.[7] "Professional drag queens are, therefore, professional homosexuals," Newton has argued, thus essentializing drag as a gay art form.[8] Author Peter Ackroyd has indirectly expressed agreement with Newton in his 1979 text *Dressing Up: Transvestism and Drag: The History of an Obsession*, stating, "Drag is primarily a homosexual performance."[9] There have been some notable examples of scholarship on cross-dressing performance that has not followed this trend; Marjorie Garber's *Vested Interests: Cross-Dressing and Cultural Anxiety* (1992) and Laurence Senelick's *The Changing Room: Sex, Drag and Theatre* (2000), for instance, belong more to cultural and theater studies than queer studies. However, academic considerations of drag since *Mother Camp* have tended to fall under the domain of queer studies or related fields.[10]

But to what extent was drag *always* "queer"? While this book has shown that the history of drag cannot be reduced to the art form's real or perceived association with same-sex desire, it was the case that, in the past, drag held particular fascination for same-sex desiring and gender-variant audience members and performers.[11]

For Victorian female impersonators Ernest Boulton and Frederick William Park, to name two examples, performing drag on the stage was an outlet for the pair's feminine gender presentations that they exuded offstage as well. Boulton and Park were also regularly involved in same-sex relationships.[12] The post–Second World War ex-servicemen's drag revues were seen by same-sex desiring and gender-variant men, as well as people who identified as trans women later in life, as a forum for the safe and open expression of feminine gender presentation.[13] Participants in the shows recalled that the choruses in particular were made up of effete homosexuals who routinely engaged in sexual liaisons with Stage Door Johnnies and could be heard speaking Polari backstage.[14] This culture that surrounded the post–Second World War ex-servicemen's drag revues is confirmed by the novel *Chorus of Witches* (1959), which was published not long after the decline of all-male revues and was written by an author who appears to have had insider knowledge about the shows.[15] Late in his career, Danny La Rue divulged that he had been in a long-term relationship with his manager, Jack Hanson, until Hanson's death in 1984. Despite the secrecy around their relationship, La Rue was deeply loyal to Hanson. The entertainer threatened to leave his beloved Catholic Church after Hanson was initially not allowed to be buried in a plot at St Patrick's, London, where La Rue too had planned to be buried. A cardinal personally granted La Rue's request for Hanson to be buried in the plot after a "battle."[16] La Rue and Hanson were eventually interred together underneath the same tombstone at St Mary's Catholic Cemetery in London.

Drag is a queer art form. Drag is also many other things. In reading present-day commentaries on drag and discussing the medium with others, I am often struck by the extent to which drag is essentialized, more so than other art forms, as having a precise meaning or intent. Watercolor painting, for example, is not widely perceived as having one or a few reasons for being, yet drag has been affixed with descriptions like "always a protest" or "primarily a homosexual performance."[17] If an actor plays a medical doctor, for instance, that is not usually seen as a statement on the actor's offstage emotional life, yet present-day audiences (and many in the past) are liable to make assumptions about an artist's personal and inner life if that artist performs drag. This book has not aimed to be contrarian, to tell readers that the concepts they associate with drag are wrong. The book has instead aspired to historically contextualize preconceived notions readers might have about drag and to illuminate other meanings drag has held. Historically, the meanings of drag have been capacious. Drag flourished as a mass cultural form in large part because it could mean different things to different observers, including pro-gressivism, conservatism, exciting sexual and gender possibilities, glamour, pertinent social and political commentary, frivolity, pro-fundity, pathos, comfort, and discomfort. Drag has long entertained us—all of us, of every background—and the enduring pertinence, adaptability, and dynamism of the art form ensure that it will con-tinue to flourish.

Notes

Introduction

1. The Lord Chamberlain's Office has often been described as an institution that censored plays. This is true enough in spirit but technically incorrect. The Lord

Chamberlain's Office would review newly written scripts or additions to old ones and then, if any material was found to be objectionable, license the scripts for performance on the public stage on the condition that indecent content was removed or altered in the final script—that is, unless the Office thought a script was irredeemable, which was a rare occurrence. Playwrights, producers, or other agents involved in producing the play censored themselves at the behest of the Lord Chamberlain. For more information on the Lord Chamberlain's Office, see chapter 4.

2. Reflecting the cultural language of their time, most of the entertainers discussed in this book saw themselves as "men dressed as women," or something approximating this, when they performed drag. Audiences also tended to perceive the performers in this way, except in some circumstances. One exception to this was, for example, when audience members were convinced that a female impersonator was a "genuine" woman. I will use traditional gendered and sexed terms to refer to the figures discussed in this book (e.g., "male," "men," "female," "women"). If there is any indication that a certain figure identified as anything other than what we would today call a cisgender man or woman, then their identity will be respected.

3. British Library Manuscript Collections (BL MC), Lord Chamberlain's Plays Correspondence files (LCP Corr) 1958/667, *We're No Ladies* by Phil Starr, Report by Ronald John Hill of the Lord Chamberlain's Office, 7 February 1958.

4. BL MC, Lord Chamberlain's Plays (LCP) 1958/3: *We're No Ladies* by Phil Starr, Script, Licensed 22 January 1958.

5. For more on the definitions and etymology of female impersonation and female impersonators, see Michelle Liu Carriger, "'The Unnatural History and the Petticoat Mystery of Boulton and Park': A Victorian Sex Scandal and the Theatre Defense," *TDR: The Drama Review* 57:4 (2013): 141–42; H.G. Cocks, *Nameless Offences: Homosexual Desire in the Nineteenth Century* (London: I. B. Tauris, 2003), 99; Laurence Senelick, "Boys and Girls Together: Subcultural Origins of Glamour Drag and Male Impersonation on the Nineteenth-Century Stage," in *Crossing the Stage: Controversies on Cross-Dressing*, ed. Lesley Ferris (London: Routledge, 1993), 82.

6. BL MC, LCP Corr 1958/667, *We're No Ladies*, Report by Ronald John Hill, 7 February 1958. This transcription has been slightly altered from the original for the sake of readability.

7. BL MC, LCP Corr 1958/667, *We're No Ladies*, Report by Ronald John Hill, 7 February 1958.

8. BL MC, LCP Corr 1958/667, *We're No Ladies*, Report by Ronald John Hill, 7 February 1958 (punctuation in the original). For more on cruising and cottaging, see Matt Houlbrook, "The Private World of Public Urinals: London 1918–57,"

London Journal 25:1 (2000): 52–70; Frank Mort, "Mapping Sexual London: The Wolfenden Committee on Homosexual Offences and Prostitution: 1954-7," *New Formations: Sexual Geographies* 37 (1999): 92–113.

9. BL MC, LCP Corr 1958/667, *We're No Ladies*, Report by Ronald John Hill, 7 February 1958.

10. BL MC, LCP Corr 1958/667, *We're No Ladies*, Memorandum by Ronald John Hill, 7 February 1958; BL MC, LCP Corr 1958/667, *We're No Ladies*, Report by Ronald John Hill, 7 February 1958.

11. BL MC, LCP Corr 1958/667, *We're No Ladies*, Report by Ronald John Hill, 7 February 1958.

12. BL MC, LCP Corr 1958/667, *We're No Ladies*, Memorandum by Ronald John Hill, 7 February 1958.

13. BL MC, LCP Corr 1958/667, *We're No Ladies*, Report by Ronald John Hill, 7 February 1958.

14. BL MC, LCP Corr 1958/667, *We're No Ladies*, Report by Ronald John Hill, 7 February 1958.

15. BL MC, LCP Corr 1958/667, *We're No Ladies*, Letter from H.C.R.A. Bennett of 22 Warwick Chambers, Peter St., Kensington to the Lord Chamberlain's Office, 6 February 1958.

16. BL MC, LCP Corr 1958/667, *We're No Ladies*, Letter from H.C.R.A. Bennett, 6 February 1958.

17. BL MC, LCP Corr 1958/667, *We're No Ladies*, Letter from Brian Boss of 88 St James's Street, London to the London County Council (L.C.C.) and forwarded to the Lord Chamberlain's Office, 6 February 1958.

18. BL MC, LCP Corr 1958/667, *We're No Ladies*, Letter from A.P.J. Rydekker to the L.C.C. and forwarded to the Lord Chamberlain's Office, 5 February 1958.

19. A second edition of the show was staged three years later and does not appear to have aroused controversy. "A touring revue featuring two male 'dames.' Nothing here is newer than 1939," wrote the reader upon examining the second-edition script. See BL MC, LCP Corr 1961/1660, *We're No Ladies* (second edition) by Terry Dennis, Reader's Report, 23 March 1961. A discussion of *We're No Ladies* has also appeared in Steve Nicholson, *The Censorship of British Drama 1900–1968, Volume Three: The Fifties* (Exeter: University of Exeter Press, 2011), 125–27; Dan Rebellato, *1956 and All That: The Making of Modern British Drama* (London: Routledge, 1999), 185–89. For a later interview with Starr in which he expresses a preference for "a normal audience" over "a camp audience," see Twitter, BBC Archive, https://twitter.com/BBCArchive/status/1222459370837069827, 29 January 2020 (accessed 17 October 2021).

20. Peter Ackroyd, *Dressing Up: Transvestism and Drag: The History of an Obsession* (London: Thames and Hudson, 1979), 14. See also the epilogue of this book.

21. Marjorie Garber, *Vested Interests: Cross-Dressing and Cultural Anxiety* (New York: Routledge, 1992), 4–5. Laurence Senelick's *The Changing Room: Sex, Drag and Theatre* (London: Routledge, 2000) is another notable example of scholarship on drag that goes well beyond the realm of queer studies.

22. See, for example, Elaine Aston, "Male Impersonation in the Music Hall: The Case of Vesta Tilley," *New Theatre Quarterly* 4:15 (1988): 247–57; Susan A. Glenn, *Female Spectacle: The Theatrical Roots of Modern Feminism* (Cambridge, MA: Harvard University Press, 2000), 9–39; Senelick, *The Changing Room*, esp. 326–49.

23. Jim Davis, "'Slap On! Slap Ever!': Victorian Pantomime, Gender Variance, and Cross-Dressing," *New Theatre Quarterly* 30:3 (2014): 220–23, 227–28; Garber, *Vested Interests*, 165–85.

24. Historian Gillian Rodger's recent work on the history of male impersonation in the United States has gone some way toward alleviating this. See Gillian M. Rodger, *Just One of the Boys: Female-to-Male Cross-Dressing on the American Variety Stage* (Urbana: University of Illinois Press, 2018).

25. A recent example of scholarship that moves on from viewing drag through the lens of cultural repression is Kayte Stokoe, *Reframing Drag: Beyond Subversion and the Status Quo* (Abingdon, Oxon: Routledge, 2020).

26. Cross-dressing was not inherently an antiestablishment practice, but there are conspicuous examples of cross-dressers resisting oppression. See, for example, Alan Bray, *Homosexuality in Renaissance England* (London: Gay Men's Press, 1982), 97.

27. Britain's lack of legal prohibition of cross-dressing stands in contrast to the legal traditions of some other countries, such as the United States. See, for example, William N. Eskridge Jr., "Privacy Jurisprudence and the Apartheid of the Closet, 1946–1961," *Florida State University Law Review* 24:4 (1997): 723; History .com, Hugh Ryan, "How Dressing in Drag Was Labelled a Crime in the 20th Century," 25 June 2019; Clare Sears, *Arresting Dress: Cross-Dressing, Law, and Fascination in Nineteenth-Century San Francisco* (London: Duke University Press, 2015).

28. Thomas A. King, "Performing 'Akimbo': Queer Pride and Epistemological Prejudice," in *The Politics and Poetics of Camp*, ed. Moe Meyer (London: Routledge, 1994), 23; Rictor Norton, *Mother Clap's Molly House: The Gay Subculture in England* 1700–1830 (London: GMP Publishers, 1992), 10–11.

29. Norton, *Mother Clap's Molly House*, esp. 92–105.

30. Literary scholar Thomas A. King has disputed the concept of a coherent molly culture, arguing instead that molly houses constituted venues where several distinct segments of the contemporary demimonde congregated. See Thomas A. King, *The Gendering of Men, 1600–1750: Volume 2, Queer Articulations* (London: University of Wisconsin Press, 2008), 146.

31. Edward Ward quoted in Norton, *Mother Clap's Molly House*, 97. Ward is also discussed in Bray, *Homosexuality in Renaissance England*, 100; Thomas A. King, *The Gendering of Men, 1600–1750: Volume 1, The English Phallus* (London: University of Wisconsin Press, 2004); King, *The Gendering of Men, 1600–1750: Volume 2*, 148–49; Randolph Trumbach, "Modern Sodomy: The Origins of Homosexuality, 1700–1800," in *A Gay History of Britain: Love and Sex between Men Since the Middle Ages*, ed. Matt Cook, H.G. Cocks, Robert Mills, and Randolph Trumbach (Oxford: Greenwood World Publishing, 2007), 79–81.

32. *The Yokel's Preceptor: Or, More Sprees in London! Being a . . . Show-up of All the Rigs and Doings of the Flash Cribs in this Great Metropolis*, quoted in Charles Upchurch, *Before Wilde: Sex between Men in Britain's Age of Reform* (London: University of California Press, 2009), 164. See also "A Few Words about Margeries, c.1855," in *Homosexuality in Nineteenth-Century England: A Sourcebook*, ed. Rictor Norton (29 October 2017), http://rictornorton.co.uk/eighteen/yokel.htm (accessed 12 October 2021); H.G. Cocks, "Secrets, Crimes and Diseases, 1800–1914," in *A Gay History of Britain*, ed. Matt Cook, H.G. Cocks, Robert Mills, and Randolph Trumbach, 116. The guidebook's author also told readers where the "monsters" were located and some of their names. Thus, this passage could be seen as both a warning and as an invitation for the curious.

33. See Dominic Janes, *Oscar Wilde Prefigured: Queer Fashioning and British Caricature, 1750–1900* (Chicago: University of Chicago Press, 2016). Extravagant male fashions were also parodied in the contemporary theater. For example, see Jeffrey Richards, *The Golden Age of Pantomime: Slapstick, Spectacle and Subversion in Victorian England* (London: I.B. Tauris, 2014), 36.

34. Janes, *Oscar Wilde Prefigured*, 13–18.

35. Upchurch, *Before Wilde*, 76.

36. Norton, *Mother Clap's Molly House*, 66–68. Margaret Clap, who ran the molly house, was charged with and found guilty of keeping a disorderly house. Various attendees were charged with and found guilty of homosexual offenses. See Rictor Norton, "Mother Clap's Molly House," *The Gay Subculture in Georgian England* (5 February 2005), http://rictornorton.co.uk/eighteen/mother.htm (accessed 4 October 2022). Norton has noted that enthusiastic support for harsh

sentences was widespread in the early eighteenth century, so the hostile press response to Mother Clap's molly house case can be seen as indicative of this gestalt rather than as proof of a unique revulsion toward male gender variance. On the "light and diversionary" press treatment of male cross-dressing, see Upchurch, *Before Wilde*, 166–67.

37. For example, see Cocks, *Nameless Offences*, 102, 109; "'Queen of Camp,' 1874," in *Homosexuality in Nineteenth-Century England: A Sourcebook*, ed. Rictor Norton (4 December 2018; expanded 30 October 2019), http://rictornorton.co .uk/eighteen/1874camp.htm (accessed 12 October 2021).

38. Historian Randolph Trumbach has asserted that the 1725/26 raids of seventeen houses led to fifty-six men being charged with or arrested for homosexual offenses, with over a dozen individuals charged with keeping molly houses. See Trumbach, "Modern Sodomy," 84.

39. Upchurch, *Before Wilde*, 75–76, 162–63. See also Bray, *Homosexuality in Renaissance England*, 102.

40. Upchurch, *Before Wilde*, 76. Concurrent with nineteenth-century drag balls that occasionally came to the attention of the British press, similar events were coming to public attention in American cities. Some of the most prominent nineteenth-century American drag balls were run by African Americans, including former slave William Dorsey Swann. Swann's regular Washington, D.C., drag balls were interrupted when police raided one of the events in 1888. See Garber, *Vested Interests*, 300; Channing Gerard Joseph, "Swann, William Dorsey," *Oxford African American Studies Center* (20 May 2021), https://oxfordaasc.com/view /10.1093/acref/9780195301731.001.0001/acref-9780195301731-e-79001 (accessed 11 November 2021); Kevin J. Mumford, *Interzones: Black/White Sex Districts in Chicago and New York in the Early Twentieth Century* (New York: Columbia University Press, 1997), 75.

41. Upchurch, *Before Wilde*, 75–76.

42. Upchurch, *Before Wilde*, 159.

43. Cocks, *Nameless Offences*, 102, 107; Upchurch, *Before Wilde*, 165.

44. Upchurch, *Before Wilde*, 183.

45. Upchurch, *Before Wilde*, 74, 162–63, 166–67, 183.

46. See Carriger, "The Unnatural History and the Petticoat Mystery of Boulton and Park," 135–56; Cocks, *Nameless Offences*, 107; Senelick, "Boys and Girls Together," 86.

47. Sean Brady, *Masculinity and Male Homosexuality in Britain, 1861-1913* (Basingstoke: Palgrave Macmillan, 2005), 72; Cocks, *Nameless Offences*, 109; Senelick, "Boys and Girls Together," 87.

48. Brady, *Masculinity and Male Homosexuality in Britain*, 71; Cocks, *Nameless Offences*, 108–9; Senelick, "Boys and Girls Together," 87. Boulton and Park were acquitted of conspiracy to commit sodomy at their 1871 trial. They pled guilty to a misdemeanor charge of "an offence against public morals and common decency," for which they received a fine of five hundred guineas each and a two-year probation that obliged them to cease cross-dressing during that period, as well as to generally avoid further legal trouble. See Judith Rowbotham, "A Deception on the Public: The Real Scandal of Boulton and Park," *Liverpool Law Review* 36 (2015): 123–45; Charles Upchurch, "Forgetting the Unthinkable: Cross-Dressers and British Society in the Case of the Queen vs. Boulton and Others," *Gender & History* 12:1 (2000): 143.

49. Nina Auerbach, "Before the Curtain," in *The Cambridge Companion to Victorian and Edwardian Theatre*, ed. Kerry Powell (Cambridge: Cambridge University Press, 2004), 6; Dennis Denisoff, "Popular Culture," in *The Cambridge Companion to Victorian Culture*, ed. Francis O'Gorman (Cambridge: Cambridge University Press, 2010), 135–55; Barry J. Faulk, *Music Hall and Modernity: The Late-Victorian Discovery of Popular Culture* (Athens: Ohio University Press, 2014), 1; Dave Russell, "Popular Entertainment, 1776–1895," in *The Cambridge History of British Theatre. Volume 2: 1660 to 1895*, ed. Joseph Donahue (Cambridge: Cambridge University Press, 2015), 372. Gillian M. Rodger has similarly cited the 1870s as the start of a boom period for male impersonation in both Britain and the United States. See Rodger, *Just One of the Boys*, 27, 99–100.

50. See Caroline Radcliffe, "Dan Leno: Dame of Drury Lane," in *Victorian Pantomime: A Collection of Critical Essays*, ed. Jim Davis (Basingstoke: Palgrave Macmillan, 2010), 118–34.

51. See Senelick, *The Changing Room*, 241–42; John Russell Stephens, "Thomas, (Walter) Brandon," *Oxford Dictionary of National Biography* (3 January 2008), https://doi.org/10.1093/ref:odnb/51459 (accessed 15 October 2021). On dame Malcolm Scott, see Derek Sculthorpe, *Malcolm Scott: The Woman Who Knows* (Orlando, FL: BearManor Media, 2022).

52. Laypeople who expressed these views tended not to cite sexual theorists, or they cited theorists' ideas in a piecemeal, diluted manner. However, some especially curious nonspecialists, such as writer Ralph Werther, became well versed in nineteenth- and twentieth-century sexology. See Ralph Werther, *Autobiography of an Androgyne*, ed. Scott Herring (New Brunswick, NJ: Rutgers University Press, 2008). For more on wider public knowledge of sexology, see Heike Bauer, *English Literary Sexology: Translations of Inversion, 1860–1930* (Basingstoke: Palgrave Macmillan, 2009); H.G. Cocks, "Saucy Stories: Pornography,

Sexology and the Marketing of Sexual Knowledge in Britain, c. 1918–70," *Social History* 29:4 (2004): 465–84; Ivan Crozier, "Nineteenth-Century British Psychiatric Writing about Homosexuality before Havelock Ellis: The Missing Story," *Journal of the History of Medicine and Allied Sciences* 63:1 (2008): 65–102; Anna Katharina Schaffner, *Modernism and Perversion: Sexual Deviance in Sexology and Literature, 1850–1930* (Basingstoke: Palgrave Macmillan, 2012); Lisa Z. Sigel, *Making Modern Love: Sexual Narratives and Identities in Interwar Britain* (Philadelphia: Temple University Press, 2012), esp. 43–45.

53. Michel Foucault, *The History of Sexuality, Volume 1: An Introduction* (London: Allen Lane, 1979), 43. See also Eve Kosofsky Sedgwick, *Epistemology of the Closet* (Berkeley: University of California Press, 1990), 133; Jay Prosser, "Transsexuals and the Transsexologists: Inversion and the Emergence of Transsexual Subjectivity," in *Sexology in Culture: Labelling Bodies and Desires*, ed. Lucy Bland and Laura Doan (Chicago: University of Chicago Press, 1998), 119; Robert Deam Tobin, *Peripheral Desires: The German Discovery of Sex* (Philadelphia: University of Pennsylvania Press, 2015), 1–26.

54. Quoted in Ralph M. Leck, *Vita Sexualis: Karl Ulrichs and the Origins of Sexual Science* (Urbana: University of Illinois Press, 2016), 40. Ulrichs later updated his sexual classification system to acknowledge other sexual types and ways of experiencing same-sex desire, including "Mannlings [masculine types who are attracted to feminine men]" and "Uriasters, heterosexual men who participate in homosexual acts." See Leck, *Vita Sexualis*, 43.

55. Tobin, *Peripheral Desires*, 19–22. There is some confusion in the historiography regarding Foucault's pronouncement. Foucault cited 1870 as the year Westphal's landmark article was published and thus the year constituting the "date of birth" of homosexuality. However, as historian Robert Deam Tobin has observed, "Foucault not only gets the year wrong, but he also cites the journal [which published Westphal's article] incorrectly." Since the 1976 publication of Foucault's *The History of Sexuality, Volume 1*, subsequent works that discuss early sexology have repeated his error. See Tobin, *Peripheral Desires*, 18.

56. Prosser, "Transsexuals and the Transsexologists," 119–20.

57. Magnus Hirschfeld, *Transvestites: The Erotic Drive to Cross-Dress*, trans. Michael A. Lombardi-Nash (Buffalo, NY: Prometheus Books, 1991), 148.

58. Hirschfeld, *Transvestites*, 148. See also pp. 219–23.

59. Hirschfeld, *Transvestites*, 235.

60. Hirschfeld, *Transvestites*, 359–60.

61. Sigel, *Making Modern Love*, 135. The term *eonism* was a reference to eighteenth- and nineteenth-century gender nonconforming French diplomat

the Chevalier d'Éon. For more on d'Éon, see Jonathan Conlin, "The Strange Case of the Chevalier d'Éon," *History Today* 60:4 (2010): 45–51.

62. Sigmund Freud quoted in Vern L. Bullough and Bonnie Bullough, *Cross Dressing, Sex, and Gender* (Philadelphia: University of Pennsylvania Press, 1993), 214. See also Prosser, "Transsexuals and the Transsexologists," 120.

63. Quoted in Bullough and Bullough, *Cross Dressing, Sex, and Gender*, 214–15.

64. Prosser, "Transsexuals and the Transsexologists," 121. See, for example, ONE National Gay & Lesbian Archives, University of Southern California Libraries (ONE), Magazine cover story collection, Coll2013-027, *Dare*, "A Composite: Christine Jorgensen in a Bathing Suit," July 1953, 8; ONE, Magazine cover story collection, Coll2013-027, *People Today*, "People in Medicine: New Sex Switches," 5 May 1954, 17; ONE, Magazine cover story collection, Coll2013-027, *Uncensored*, Carroll Hotchkiss, "His or Hers: Christines in Reverse: The Hush-Hush Choice 150,000 'Girls' Must Make," October 1955, 32.

65. See, for example, ONE, Magazine cover story collection, Coll2013-027, *Whisper*, Louie Bolinger, "Why Some Men Dress Like Women," July 1960, 37.

66. Bullough and Bullough, *Cross Dressing, Sex, and Gender*, 215.

67. Bullough and Bullough, *Cross Dressing, Sex, and Gender*, 216–19.

68. Quoted in Chris Waters, "Disorders of the Mind, Disorders of the Body Social: Peter Wildeblood and the Making of the Modern Homosexual," in *Moments of Modernity: Reconstructing Britain, 1945–1964*, ed. Becky Conekin, Frank Mort, and Chris Waters (London: Rivers Oram Press, 1999), 145. This view was also articulated in contemporary gay novels. See, for example, Paul Buckland, *Chorus of Witches* (Richmond, VA: Valancourt Books, 2021), 66, 187, 198, 216; *The Gay & Lesbian Review Worldwide*, Michael Schwartz, "Drag Shows and Illicit Love in a 1959 Novel," 2 May 2022.

69. David M. Halperin, *How to Do the History of Homosexuality* (Chicago: University of Chicago Press, 2002), 18.

70. "Dublin" quoted in Peter Farrer, ed., *Men in Petticoats: A Selection of Letters from Victorian Newspapers* (Liverpool: Karn Publications Garston, 1987), 32.

71. Quoted in Farrer, ed., *Men in Petticoats*, 32.

72. "W. M. G." quoted in Peter Farrer, ed., *Cross-Dressing between the Wars: Selections from* London Life *Part II, 1934–1941* (Liverpool: Karn Publications Garston, 2006), 142–43.

73. Quoted in Farrer, ed., *Cross-Dressing between the Wars: Selections from* London Life *Part II*, 77.

74. "One More Victim," quoted in Farrer, ed., *Men in Petticoats*, 34–35.

75. "H. E." quoted in Farrer, ed., *Cross-Dressing between the Wars: Selections from* London Life *Part II*, 358. For more examples of male cross-dressing and its relation to sexual humiliation and sadomasochism, see Farrer, ed., *Men in Petticoats*, 32–33, 39; Farrer, ed., *Cross-Dressing between the Wars: Selections from* London Life, 1923–1933 (Liverpool: Karn Publications Garston, 2000), 71, 78; Farrer, ed., *Cross-Dressing between the Wars: Selections from* London Life *Part II*, 276–77, 313–15.

76. For example, see Farrer, ed., *Men in Petticoats*, 41; Farrer, ed., *Cross-Dressing between the Wars: Selections from* London Life, 1923–1933, 43–46, 52, 100–101.

77. See, for example, Farrer, ed., *Men in Petticoats*, 11–12, 35–36, 39; Peter Farrer, ed., *Borrowed Plumes: Letters from Edwardian Newspapers on Male Cross Dressing* (Liverpool: Karn Publications Garston, 1994), 75; Farrer, ed., *Cross-Dressing between the Wars: Selections from* London Life, 1923–1933, 89, 113, 152; Farrer, ed., *Cross-Dressing between the Wars: Selections from* London Life *Part II*, 79, 219–20, 309, 318–19.

78. "Hal" quoted in Farrer, ed., *Cross-Dressing between the Wars: Selections from* London Life *Part II*, 316.

79. "Gay Deceiver" quoted in Farrer, ed., *Cross-Dressing between the Wars: Selections from* London Life *Part II*, 347–48.

80. George Chauncey, *Gay New York: Gender, Urban Culture, and the Makings of the Gay Male World*, 1890–1940 (New York: Basic Books, 2019), 328.

81. ONE, Magazine cover story collection, Coll2013-027, *People Today*, "Exclusive: U.S. Homosexuals on the Increase," March 1957, 31.

82. BL MC, LCP Corr 1958/667, *We're No Ladies*, Report by Ronald John Hill, 7 February 1958. See also Frank Mort, *Capital Affairs: London and the Making of the Permissive Society* (London: Yale University Press, 2010), 181.

83. "Drag, n," *OED Online* (Oxford: Oxford University Press, September 2021), www.oed.com/view/Entry/57406 (accessed 12 October 2021). See also Michael Quinion, *Port Out, Starboard Home: The Fascinating Stories We Tell about the Words We Use* (London: Penguin, 2005), 103. The first published use of the term "camp" was also used in relation to an 1870s court case involving male cross-dressing. See Norton, "Queen of Camp."

84. The *Times* quoted in Upchurch, "Forgetting the Unthinkable," 155. See also Carriger, "The Unnatural History and the Petticoat Mystery of Boulton and Park," 137.

85. Senelick, *The Changing Room*, 302, 321n35; Upchurch, "Forgetting the Unthinkable," 136.

86. Senelick, *The Changing Room*, 302.

87. J. Redding Ware quoted in Senelick, *The Changing Room*, 302. Another relevant contemporary etymological turn was the development of the term *female*

impersonator, and variations thereof, from around the 1850s. Earlier definitions of impersonation tended to refer to the assumption of certain traits or characteristics, whereas from the mid-nineteenth century impersonation tended to connote taking on or mimicking a fully realized character. The term *female personator* was still in popular usage in the 1870s, with *personator* being a now-outdated term for one who assumes a theatrical role. See Carriger, "The Unnatural History and the Petticoat Mystery of Boulton and Park," 141–42; Cocks, *Nameless Offences*, 99; Senelick, "Boys and Girls Together," 82.

88. David Kathman, "How Old Were Shakespeare's Boy Actors?," in *Shakespeare Survey Volume 58. Writing about Shakespeare*, ed. Peter Holland (Cambridge: Cambridge University Press, 2005), 220–21.

89. Senelick, *The Changing Room*, 210.

90. Senelick, "Boys and Girls Together," 81–82.

91. Pantomime's genealogy is complex and somewhat messy. Theater historian Jeffrey Richards has observed that pantomime as it would be familiar to present-day audiences developed in the 1840s as a blend of three earlier theatrical genres: the harlequinade, the extravaganza, and the burlesque. By the 1890s pantomimes had become a fixture of British popular entertainment. See Richards, *The Golden Age of Pantomime* (London: I. B. Tauris, 2015).

92. See Patrick Newly, *Bawdy But British! The Life of Douglas Byng* (London: Third Age Press, 2009); Robert V. Kenny, *The Man Who Was Old Mother Riley: The Lives and Films of Arthur Lucan and Kitty McShane* (Albany, GA: BearManor Media, 2014).

93. Victoria and Albert Theatre and Performance Archives (V&A), Blythe House, Theatre and Performance Biographical Files: BIOG LUCAN, *Daily News*, "Old Mother Riley Dies," 18 May 1954; Stefan Szczelkun, *The Conspiracy of Good Taste: William Morris, Cecil Sharp, Clough Williams-Ellis and the Repression of Working Class Culture in the 20th Century* (London: Working Press, 1993), 10–11.

94. See Robert James, *Popular Culture and Working-Class Taste in Britain, 1930–39: A Round of Cheap Diversions?* (Manchester: Manchester University Press, 2010), 166, 204.

95. Senelick, "Boys and Girls Together," 82; Senelick, *The Changing Room*, 295–96.

96. Stephen Gundle, *Glamour: A History* (Oxford: Oxford University Press, 2008), esp. 158–59.

97. Neil McKenna, *Fanny & Stella: The Young Men Who Shocked Victorian England* (London: Faber and Faber, 2013), 341–43; Senelick, *The Changing Room*, 305.

98. British Pathé, Film ID 868.20, "Ringing in the Changes," 20 April 1922; Anthony Slide, *Great Pretenders: A History of Female and Male Impersonation in the Performing Arts* (Lombard, IL: Wallace-Homestead, 1986), 38; Frances Gray, "Errol, Bert [*real name* Isaac Whitehouse] (1883–1949)," *Oxford Dictionary of National Biography* (8 January 2015), https://doi.org/10.1093/ref:odnb/64569 (accessed 15 August 2022).

99. *Eastern Daily Press*, "The Hippodrome," 17 April 1906. For more on non-white female impersonators who made an impression in early twentieth-century Britain, see Donyale Bartíra's "Claudius Modjesko: The Creole Patti" on her blog Black Jazz Artists (19–20th Century), http://blackjazzartists.blogspot.com/2019/09/claudius-modjesko-creole-patti.html, 13 October 2020 (accessed 3 January 2023).

100. *Leeds Mercury*, "Music Halls," 10 January 1905 (emphasis added); *Dundee Evening Telegraph*, "The Palace Theatre," 20 March 1906. Gauze sometimes shared a bill with other racialized entertainments, such as "Madame Maro's Piccanninies [*sic*]" and the "Akimoto Japanese troupe." See *Belfast News-Letter*, "Extraordinary Holiday Attractions First Visit to Belfast," 27 December 1904; *Eastern Daily Press*, "The Hippodrome," 17 April 1906. It is unclear to me at this time whether Gauze was an Indigenous Canadian or a nonwhite person of another race who was promoted as being an Indigenous Canadian. "Canadian Indian" and "Indian" would have been common ways of describing Indigenous Canadians in the early twentieth-century British press. I am grateful to Professor David Stirrup for his insights on this matter.

101. Mander & Mitchenson Theatre Collection, University of Bristol (M&M), Drag: MM/REF/TH/SU/SP/2, *Photo Bits*, "Men Who Wear Petticoats: Amusing and Curious Gossip Regarding the Questionable Lind," 7 January 1905.

102. *New York Times*, "A Theater's Muses, Rescued; Mural Figures Recall Celebrity of a (Well-Painted) Face," John Holusha, 24 March 2000. For more on Eltinge and other female impersonators of the turn of the century, see Sculthorpe, *Malcolm Scott*, 66–69.

103. Bill Ellis, *Entertainment in Rhyl and North Wales* (Chalford: Chalford Publishing Company, 1997), 23–33. Catlin's Royal Pierrots also performed in other seaside towns such as Scarborough and Great Yarmouth. Local historian Bill Ellis has stated that Manders got his first big break performing with the Catlin's Royal Pierrots troupe as early as 1908, though Ellis has also recounted that Manders "was spotted by [troupe founder] Will Catlin" while the female impersonator was "on demobilisation" during the First World War. The earliest record I have found of Manders performing with Catlin's is a reference to a performance in 1912, for which he used his earlier stage name, Willie Manders. See Ellis, *Entertainment in Rhyl and*

North Wales, 23, 28; University of East Anglia Archives and Special Collections (UEA), Norwich, UK, Tinkler and Williams' Theatre Collection (T&W), Tinkler box 17, Great Yarmouth (Histories), History of Gt. Yarmouth Britannia Pier 1858–1969, compiled by H.T.G. Tinkler, 1969. Though Manders was closely associated with Rhyl, he and his troupe were well received in other areas. The Quaintesques were voted "the most popular holiday entertainment party in the British Isles" by *Sunday Dispatch* newspaper readers in 1934. See Bruce Anderson, Rusholme & Victoria Park Archive, "Harry Leslie's Rusholme Pavilion," https://rusholmearchive.org /harry-leslie-and-the-rusholme-pavilion, n.d. (accessed 15 June 2022).

104. BBC.co.uk, Programme Index, https://genome.ch.bbc.co.uk/search/0 /20?order=first&q=billie+manders#top (accessed 15 June 2022). For more about female impersonation on early radio, see Sculthorpe, *Malcolm Scott*, 151–53.

105. For example, see British Library Newsroom (BL NR), *Sketch*, "The Famous Spanish 'Female Impersonator': Derkas—In One of His Amazing Costumes," 18 January 1928; BL NR, *Sketch*, "A Charming 'Deceiver': Babette [*sic*], The Mystery of the Olympia Circus," 22 December 1926. Barbette was also said to affect an "astounding" Marlene Dietrich impression. See M&M, Drag, uncredited newspaper clipping, "Lots of Good Things in 'The Jack Pot,'" May 1932.

106. Gilbert Oakley, *Sex Change and Dress Deviation* (London: Morntide, 1970), 9.

107. Alkarim Jivani, *It's Not Unusual: A History of Lesbian and Gay Britain in the Twentieth Century* (London: Michael O'Mara Books, 1997), 175–76. See also Sasha Geffen, *Glitter Up the Dark: How Pop Music Broke the Binary* (Austin: University of Texas Press, 2020); Senelick, *The Changing Room*, 409–58. Mick Jagger has been compared to a "drag mother." See Judith A. Peraino, "Mick Jagger as Mother," *Social Text* 33:3 (2015): 82. Whether Jagger was indeed wearing a dress during the 1969 Hyde Park concert has been disputed. See Michael A. Langkjær, "A Case of Misconstrued Rock Military Style: Mick Jagger and his Evzone 'Little Girl's Party Frock' *Fustanella*, Hyde Park, July 5, 1969," Endymatologika: Endyesthai (To Dress): Historical, Sociological and Methodological Approaches, Conference Proceedings, Athens, Greece, 9–11 April 2010, Nafplion: Peloponnesiako Laographiko Hidryma / Peloponnesian Folklore Foundation, vol. 4 (2012): 111–19.

108. Lavinia Co-op, Crystal, and Stuart Feather, "Drag: Power & Politics," panel discussion, Newington Green Meeting House, London, 25 October 2021; *Time Out London*, Rupert Smith, "Bette Bourne: Interview," 27 May 2008.

109. For example, one of the most significant contributions to the study of drag performance has been the *Journal of Homosexuality*'s special double issue on drag. See *Journal of Homosexuality* 46:3–4 (2004).

110. For more on current drag scenes, see Mark Edward and Stephen Farrier, eds., *Contemporary Drag Practices and Performers: Drag in a Changing Scene, Volume* 1 (London: Bloomsbury, 2020).

111. See, for example, Axios, Selene San Felice, "Florida and Texas Republicans Want to Ban Kids from Drag Shows," 13 June 2022.

112. See, for example, *Guardian*, Tim Jonze, "'I'm Just Trying to Make the World a Little Brighter': How the Culture Wars Hijacked Drag Queen Story Hour," 11 August 2022.

113. See, for example, Joe Parslow, "Dragging the Mainstream: *RuPaul's Drag Race* and Moving Drag Practices between the USA and the UK," in *Contemporary Drag Practices and Performers: Drag in a Changing Scene, Volume* 1, ed. Mark Edward and Stephen Farrier, 19–31.

114. For some of the numerous examples of this argument, see *Globe and Mail*, Elio Iannacci, "Long Live the Queens: How Drag Culture Went Mainstream," 24 June 2018; *Guardian*, Amelia Abraham, "'Finally! A Sport for Us Gay People!' How Drag Went Mainstream," 10 August 2019; Mark McCormack and Liam Wignall, "Drag Performers' Perspectives on the Mainstreaming of British Drag: Towards a Sociology of Contemporary Drag," *Sociology* 56:1 (2022): 3–20; *Quartz*, Carolina Are, "No Tea, No Shade: How 'RuPaul's Drag Race' Changed the Way We Speak," 2 October 2019. For more on the present-day visibility of drag, see Niall Brennan and David Gudelunas, eds., *RuPaul's Drag Race and the Shifting Visibility of Drag Culture: The Boundaries of Reality TV* (Basingstoke: Palgrave Macmillan, 2018).

115. For more on the importance of the unstated as it relates to studying the history of sexuality, see Laura Doan, *Disturbing Practices: History, Sexuality and Women's Experience of Modern War* (Chicago: University of Chicago Press, 2013), 160–61.

116. Nick Cherryman, "The Tranimal: Throwing Gender Out of Drag?," in *Contemporary Drag Practices and Performers: Drag in a Changing Scene, Volume* 1, ed. Mark Edward and Stephen Farrier, 150.

Chapter 1

Epigraph: Victoria & Albert Theatre and Performance Archives (V&A), Blythe House, Theatre and Performance Biographical Files: BIOG LUCAN, *Daily Express*, 18 May 1954. After Lucan collapsed, his understudy, Frank Seton, took his place, and that night's performance continued after a brief delay of an alleged eight minutes. See V&A, BIOG LUCAN, *Daily Express*, 18 May 1954; V&A, BIOG

LUCAN, *Daily Mail*, "'Old Mother Riley' Dies Just Before Show," 18 May 1954; Robert V. Kenny, *The Man Who Was Old Mother Riley: The Lives and Films of Arthur Lucan and Kitty McShane* (Albany, GA: BearManor Media, 2014), 270-71. I am grateful to Lucan biographer Robert V. Kenny not only for sharing his insights through his book, but also for our correspondence, which has benefited this chapter significantly.

1. Lucan's adopted surname was inspired by the Dublin-based Lucan Dairy. See Anthony Slide, *Great Pretenders: A History of Female and Male Impersonation in the Performing Arts* (Lombard, IL: Wallace-Homestead, 1986), 80.

2. As this chapter is concerned with the pantomime dame and Arthur Lucan's characterization of the dame, Kitty McShane will not be analyzed in depth, except when necessary. As a performer she was generally considered to have been capable at best, if she was mentioned by critics at all. More recent critical opinion has not been kind to Kitty either. Film scholar Anthony Slide has crudely described her as "a lifeless lump." As an additional insult, Donald Towle, Lucan and McShane's son, refused to pay for his mother's gravestone or attend her funeral after Kitty died on 24 March 1964. Lucan and McShane's tempestuous marriage was the subject of the play and television movie *On Your Way, Riley* (1985). Their relationship has also been covered extensively in biographer Robert V. Kenny's book on the pair. See British Film Institute Reuben Library (BFI RL), *Kinematograph Weekly*, "Old Mother Riley in Paris," 25 August 1938; BFI RL, *Kinematograph Weekly*, "Old Mother Riley's Circus," 30 October 1941; Slide, *Great Pretenders*, 80; *On Your Way, Riley* (dir. John Glenister, Yorkshire Television, 1985); Kenny, *The Man Who Was Old Mother Riley*, 294. McShane did not appear in the final *Old Mother Riley* film, *Mother Riley Meets the Vampire* (1952). The Old Mother Riley comic strip appeared regularly in the comic book series *Film Fun* in the 1940s and 1950s. Riley also graced the cover of several *Film Fun* annual issues.

3. BFI RL, *Daily Herald*, "Mother Riley 'in a Spot,'" 19 August 1953; Richard Farmer, *Cinemas and Cinemagoing in Wartime Britain, 1939-45: The Utility Dream Palace* (Manchester: Manchester University Press, 2016), 203-4; V&A, BIOG LUCAN, *Daily News*, "Old Mother Riley Dies," 18 May 1954.

4. *Leamington Spa Courier*, "New Hippodrome Coventry," 28 October 1938.

5. BFI RL, Archibald Haddon, *Old Mother Riley, MP* (1939) press release, 31 January 1939; BFI RL, *Call Boy*, Ellis Ashton, "In Me Bonnet and Shawl," March 1966; *Grantham Journal*, "Rutland Cinema, Uppingham," 1 October 1938; *Motherwell Times*, "La Scala," 21 January 1938. An earlier example of a male actor playing a leading female role in film is Wallace Beery as Sweedie the Swedish Maid in the 1910s. However, all of Sweedie's appearances were in silent short films.

6. See *Dundee Courier*, "Curtain Up—But Old Mother Riley Was Dead," 18 May 1954; *Yorkshire Evening Post*, "Old Mother Riley Owes £15,000 Tax," 28 August 1953; BFI RL, *Sunday Mirror*, Trevor Reynolds, "Life of Riley! Dead Comic 'Haunts' Tax Office," 1 April 1979.

7. Quoted in BFI RL, *Hull Times*, Anthony Slide, "Children Still Place Posies on His Grave," 10 May 1968.

8. V&A, BIOG LUCAN, *Daily News*, "Old Mother Riley Dies," 18 May 1954. See also Laurence Senelick, *The Changing Room: Sex, Drag and Theatre* (London: Routledge, 2000), 245.

9. For views on the dame that differ from the argument asserted here, see Millie Taylor, "Continuity and Transformation in Twentieth-Century Pantomime," in *Victorian Pantomime: A Collection of Critical Essays*, ed. Jim Davis (Basingstoke: Palgrave Macmillan, 2010), 186; Senelick, *The Changing Room*, 245.

10. Peter Holland, "The Play of Eros: Paradoxes of Gender in English Pantomime," *New Theatre Quarterly* 13:51 (1997): 201.

11. Jeffrey Richards, *The Golden Age of Pantomime: Slapstick, Spectacle and Subversion in Victorian England* (London: I. B. Tauris, 2014), 2.

12. Prior to the passage of the Theatres Act 1843, under the regime of the Licensing Act of 1737, only a select group of licensed playhouses were allowed to present plays with dialogue. The Drury Lane, the Covent Garden, and the Haymarket in the summer season are the most oft-cited examples of this privileged coterie of patent theaters, but many other theaters still managed to stage scripted plays under the 1737 act by simply breaking the law, finding loopholes, taking advantage of subsequent legislation that loosened restrictions, securing special legal allowances, or other means. See David Thomas, David Carlton, and Anne Etienne, *Theatre Censorship: From Walpole to Wilson* (Oxford: Oxford University Press, 2007), 42–59.

13. Richards, *The Golden Age of Pantomime*, 4, 69, 77, 80.

14. Senelick, *The Changing Room*, 229.

15. Senelick, *The Changing Room*, 232–33.

16. BFI RL, *Monthly Film Bulletin*, "Old Mother Riley in Paris," August 1938.

17. *Stagedoor* quoted in Kenny, *The Man Who Was Old Mother Riley*, 315.

18. Mander & Mitchenson Theatre Collection, University of Bristol (M&M), Dan Leno: MM/REF/PE/VA/146, *Observer Magazine*, Richard Findlater, "The Star of Christmas," 21 December 1975.

19. Claude J. Summers, ed., *The Queer Encyclopedia of Music, Dance & Musical Theatre* (San Francisco: Cleis Press, 2004), 264. Minstrelsy was also home to purposefully alluring glamour drag. Cultural scholar Claude J. Summers has argued

that "in the United States minstrelsy can properly be regarded as the origin of glamour drag" (*The Queer Encyclopedia of Music, Dance & Musical Theatre*, 264). See also Eric Lott, *Love & Theft: Blackface Minstrelsy and the American Working Class* (New York: Oxford University Press, 2013), 55, 170–71.

20. Olive Logan quoted in Lott, *Love & Theft*, 166 (first ellipsis added).

21. Leno played male roles as well, but his dame characterizations in Drury Lane pantomimes have been widely considered by both his contemporaries and more recent critics to be the crowning achievements of his entire career. See Barry Anthony, *The King's Jester: The Life of Dan Leno, Victorian Comic Genius* (London: I. B. Taurus, 2010), 190; Caroline Radcliffe, "Dan Leno: Dame of Drury Lane," in *Victorian Pantomime*, ed. Jim Davis, 120.

22. Anthony, *The King's Jester*, 163–65.

23. Anthony, *The King's Jester*, 175–77.

24. *Northern Echo*, Chris Lloyd, "Nothing Like a Dame—'til Dan Dared," 21 March 2009. For more on the Electrophone, see *New Scientist*, Denys Parsons, "Cable Radio—Victorian Style," 23/30 December 1982.

25. Roger Baker, *Drag: A History of Female Impersonation in the Performing Arts* (London: Cassell, 1994), 162; Holland, "The Play of Eros," 201; Radcliffe, "Dan Leno: Dame of Drury Lane," 120.

26. Clement Scott quoted in Radcliffe, "Dan Leno: Dame of Drury Lane," 127.

27. Quoted in Holland, "The Play of Eros," 201.

28. Anthony, *The King's Jester*, 73. For a description of Stanislavski's system, see Rose Whyman, *Stanislavski: The Basics* (London: Routledge, 2013), 113.

29. Louise Peacock, *Slapstick and Comic Performance: Comedy and Pain* (Basingstoke: Palgrave Macmillan, 2014), 27. Slapstick comedy as it is currently understood has distant origins in commedia dell'arte. See, for example, Peacock, *Slapstick and Comic Performance*, esp. 62–63, 129–31.

30. Peacock, *Slapstick and Performance*, 158.

31. M&M, Dan Leno, *Observer Magazine*, Findlater, "The Star of Christmas," 21 December 1975. *Charley's Aunt* also got comedic mileage out of portraying a shockingly athletic dame, but, in the case of that play, the audience knows that the older woman is a man in disguise. See Benjamin Poore, "Reclaiming the Dame: Cross-Dressing as Queen Victoria in British Theatre and Television Comedy," *Comedy Studies* 3:2 (2012): 180.

32. M&M, Dan Leno, *Observer Magazine*, Findlater, "The Star of Christmas," 21 December 1975. Leno's experience in clog dancing—a "Northern athletic pastime" in the late nineteenth century—informed the physicality of his dame

performances. He won the title of "Greatest Clog Dancer in the World" several times over the course of his career. M&M, Dan Leno, *Observer Magazine*, Findlater, "The Star of Christmas," 21 December 1975; M&M, Dan Leno, uncredited newspaper clipping, "Death of Mr Dan Leno," ca. 31 October 1904. For more on nineteenth-century clog dancing, see Caroline Radcliffe, "The Ladies' Clog Dancing Contest of 1898," in *Step Change: New Views on Traditional Dance*, ed. Georgina Boyes (London: Francis Boutle, 2001), 87–116.

33. Quoted in M&M, Dan Leno, *Observer Magazine*, Findlater, "The Star of Christmas," 21 December 1975.

34. Anthony, *The King's Jester*, 69; M&M, Dan Leno, *Observer Magazine*, Findlater, "The Star of Christmas," 21 December 1975. "General paralysis of the insane" was a euphemism for neurosyphilis. See Anthony, *The King's Jester*, 193.

35. *Kinematograph Weekly* quoted in Kenny, *The Man Who Was Old Mother Riley*, 176.

36. See *Bath Chronicle and Weekly Gazette*, "Some Show," 9 January 1926; *Western Daily Press*, "Stage & Screen," 16 October 1928.

37. British Library Manuscript Collections (BL MC), Lord Chamberlain's Plays (LCP) 1941/16, *Old Mother Riley and Her Daughter Kitty* by Arthur Lucan and Kitty McShane, Script, Licensed 13 October 1941. Lucan performed various iterations of this scene throughout his career. The basic premise and many of the lines remained mostly unchanged from the 1920s through the 1950s. However, some versions contained a more tragic ending in which the bride does not reunite with her fiancé, while others feature a wedding portion. For examples of these variations, see BL MC, LCP 1952/9, *Going Gay* by J. Gaston, Script, Licensed 19 February 1952; BL MC, LCP 1933/8, *Old Match Seller* by Arthur Lucan, Script, Licensed 25 February 1933.

38. BL MC, LCP 1941/16, *Old Mother Riley and Her Daughter Kitty*, Script, Licensed 13 October 1941.

39. Lucan and McShane were singled out for praise in media coverage of the event. "The scena greatly amused the King and Queen," reported one critic on "Bridget's Night Out," then billed as "A Domestic Comedy Episode." Another praised the sketch as "Exceedingly diverting, and gets the audience in roars of laughter from the whirlwind comedy it provides. With it there is a splendid piece of characterisation by Mr Arthur Lucan." Biographer Kenneth Rose has observed that King George V possessed "a salty humour" to which Riley's antics may well have appealed. See M&M, Arthur Lucan and Kitty McShane: MM/REF/PE/VA/157, Royal Variety Performance program, 8 May 1934; M&M, Arthur Lucan

and Kitty McShane, uncredited newspaper clipping, "The King's Music Request," May 1934; M&M, Arthur Lucan and Kitty McShane, uncredited newspaper clipping, "The Night's Royal Variety Show: Special Picture," May 1934; *Western Morning News*, "Appeal of Variety—Popular Programme at Palace Theatre," 13 November 1934; *Telegraph*, William Shawcross, "Kenneth Rose: We'll Miss His Wit, Warmth, and Wry Sense of Humour," 1 February 2014.

40. My description of this scene and transcription of lines from it is based on its appearance in *Stars on Parade* (dir. Oswald Mitchell, Butcher's Film Service, 1936). The dialogue presented here was written by Arthur Lucan. However, Lucan did not write all of his own material. Many of the films in the *Old Mother Riley* film series, for instance, were written by experienced screenwriter Con West. Lucan, for his part, was known to regularly improvise, and he provided a great deal of creative input for each project regardless of whether he received an official writing credit. See Frank J. Dello Stritto and Andi Brooks, *Vampire Over London: Bela Lugosi in Britain* (Houston: Cult Movies Press, 2015), 303; Kenny, *The Man Who Was Old Mother Riley*, 233. "Bridget's Night Out" was later revived several times by Danny La Rue, who played Bridget, with entertainer Roy Rolland as Riley. For an example, see *Danny La Rue: The Ladies I Love* (dir. David Bell, London Weekend Television, 1974).

41. Riley's manic physicality translated surprisingly well to radio and gramophone, where frenetic wordplay effectively stood in for the physical slapstick of Riley's stage and screen appearances. Such memorable lines of dialogue included "The [gas] inspector said that if he found any more tiddlywinks in the gas metre, he'd 'tiddlywink' me! Oh daughter, I wonder what it feels like to be tiddlywinked. I've been hoodwinked by the coal man, I've been winked at by the tally man, but I've never been tiddlywinked by a gas man!" and "[Recounting how she met her husband] I met him by the pale moon, I was engaged by the new moon, I got married on the full moon, and I lost him on the honeymoon." British Library Sound Archive (BL SA), 1CS0034745/1CS0034746, *Old Mother Riley's Budget*, Recorded August 1941 (dialogue transcribed by me); BL SA, 1CS0034706/1CS0034707, *Old Mother Riley's Past*, Recorded July 1941 (dialogue transcribed by me). See also Kenny, *The Man Who Was Old Mother Riley*, 299–308.

42. Peacock, *Slapstick and Comic Performance*, 22–24; Millie Taylor, *British Pantomime Performance* (Bristol: Intellect, 2007), 41.

43. Lucan usually acquired unglazed china for "Bridget's Night Out" so it would smash more easily, though he was forced to use tin plates in the years immediately following the Second World War due to postwar rationing. The crockery was usually cleaned up by stagehands after the scene was over. During the

1934 Royal Variety Performance, the noise made by the sweeping of the crockery was allegedly so loud that the act following Lucan and McShane was rendered inaudible. It was advertised in advance of the Royal Variety Performance that Lucan and McShane would break 250 pieces of crockery during their scene. See Kenny, *The Man Who Was Old Mother Riley*, 153–54, 157, 222; M&M, Arthur Lucan and Kitty McShane, uncredited magazine clipping, "A Very Odd Couple," 18 April 1982.

44. Senelick, *The Changing Room*, 245; Taylor, "Continuity and Transformation in Twentieth-Century Pantomime," 186.

45. For the incongruity, anticipation, and relief theories of humor, see Simon Critchley, *On Humour (Thinking in Action)* (London: Routledge, 2001), 3; Peacock, *Slapstick and Comic Performance*, 6, 42–43.

46. Douglas Byng quoted in Slide, *Great Pretenders*, 50. Unlike Lucan, Byng was a keen media hound and granted interviews freely. On his reading habits, he stated unapologetically, "[I] usually have three or more books on the go, mostly about theatre, my favourites being those that mention me." See V&A, Theatre and Performance Biographical Files: BIOG BYNG, *Sunday Times Magazine*, "A Day in the Life of Douglas Byng," 20 March 1983. For more on Byng, see Patrick Newly, *Bawdy But British! The Life of Douglas Byng* (London: Third Age Press, 2009).

47. For a thorough analysis of Evans's dame, see Paul Matthew St. Pierre, *Music Hall Mimesis in British Film, 1895–1960: On the Halls on the Screen* (Madison, NJ: Farleigh Dickinson University Press, 2009), 130–33, 151–58. It was common for male comedians in the early to mid-twentieth century to have dame studies among their range of comic personae.

48. Though Lucan's dame would not technically be called Old Mother Riley until the release of the film *Old Mother Riley* (1937)—she was called Mrs. O'Flynn before screenwriter Con West came up with the name Old Mother Riley—Lucan had been developing the character since at least the late 1910s, and by the 1930s he was almost exclusively playing his dame role. A rare exception to this was Lucan's brief cameo in a male role in *Old Mother Riley's Ghosts* (1941). Kenny, *The Man Who Was Old Mother Riley*, 86–91; *Old Mother Riley's Ghosts* (dir. John Baxter, British National Films, 1941).

49. In a notable example of this phenomenon, the Kinks vocalist Ray Davies, who name-dropped Riley in the band's hit song "The Village Green Preservation Society," expressed surprise upon learning that she was played by a man. "I thought it was a real old lady until I saw a documentary about her and discovered it was a man," Davies recalled, "not a drag queen but a female impersonator. Definitely not camp or queenie. Just a bloke in a frock. There is a difference to the art

form of the drag queen. Old Mother Riley was an extremely ugly man who looked even uglier as a woman." See *Magnet*, "Ray Davies revisits The Kinks' 'Village Green Preservation Society': Old Mother Riley," December 2009.

50. *Portsmouth Evening News*, "Old Mother Riley Joins the Home Guard," 18 March 1952.

51. *Grantham Journal*, "Rutland Cinema, Uppingham," 1 October 1938.

52. *Motherwell Times*, "La Scala," 21 January 1938.

53. Marcia Landy, *British Genres: Cinema and Society, 1930–1960* (Princeton, NJ: Princeton University Press, 1991), 356.

54. Many, if not most, newspaper articles that reported on Lucan's death in May 1954 mentioned only Riley, rather than Lucan, in the headline.

55. Kenny, *The Man Who Was Old Mother Riley*, 180. It was claimed that Kitty McShane "never lets Old Mother Riley appear without wig and shawl on the set. Even his stand-in for three films doesn't recognise [Lucan] in ordinary clothes." This account seems somewhat exaggerated but, even so, it indicates the extent to which Lucan's offstage identity was obscured by his character. See *Daily Express*, Guy Morgan, "Britain Finds a New Big-Money Screen Team," 16 August 1939. During the filming of *Mother Riley Meets the Vampire*, Lucan unnerved his costar Bela Lugosi and others by arriving on set in the full costume of Riley and staying in character the whole time. Dello Stritto and Brooks, *Vampire Over London*, 295–96, 306.

56. Kenny, *The Man Who Was Old Mother Riley*, 159–60. For other historical examples of seriously injurious slapstick comedy, see Peacock, *Slapstick and Performance*, 157–58.

57. Uncredited source quoted in Kenny, *The Man Who Was Old Mother Riley*, 41.

58. Arthur Ladds quoted in Kenny, *The Man Who Was Old Mother Riley*, 41.

59. M&M, Arthur Lucan and Kitty McShane, uncredited magazine clipping, "A Very Odd Couple," 18 April 1982.

60. Uncredited source quoted in Kenny, *The Man Who Was Old Mother Riley*, 198.

61. Slide, *Great Pretenders*, 80.

62. Although most dames in the interwar and postwar periods dressed drably, there were some exceptions. Douglas Byng, for instance, eschewed the traditional working-class washerwoman occupation. Byng admitted to being "a bit of a snob about my dame characters." "I won't play the maid," he claimed, "I always make her the governess. I won't play the cook, I always make her the housekeeper." See BL SA, F2218–F2220, Vicinus Music Hall Interviews, Douglas Byng interviewed by

Martha Vicinus, Recorded 4 July 1975. For more on the decline of real-life washer-women and the rise of mechanized washing techniques, see Joy Parr, "What Makes a Washday Less Blue? Gender, Nation, and Technology Choice in Postwar Canada," *Technology and Culture* 38:1 (1997): 153–86; Norma Tilden, "Maytag Washer, 1939," in *From Curlers to Chainsaws: Women and Their Machines*, ed. Joyce Dyer, Jennifer Cognard-Black, and Elizabeth MacLeod Walls (East Lansing: Michigan State University Press, 2016), 2–7; C.G. Woodson, "The Negro Washer-woman, a Vanishing Figure," *Journal of Negro History* 15:3 (1930): 269–77.

63. M&M, Arthur Lucan and Kitty McShane, uncredited magazine clipping, "A Very Odd Couple," 18 April 1982. The dame "striptease" routine dates back to the nineteenth century. See, for example, Anne Varty, "Pantomime Transformations: Genre, Gender and *Charley's Aunt*," *Nineteenth Century Theatre and Film* 39:2 (2012): 45.

64. BL MC, LCP 1944/10, *Old Mother Riley and Her Daughter Kitty* by Arthur Lucan and Kitty McShane, Script, Licensed 6 April 1944. Riley's wardrobe was slightly updated in the film *Old Mother Riley in Business* (1940). As Kenny has observed, the film sees Riley wearing Edwardian clothing, which was, at the time, "[only] forty years out of date." Lucan was said to have worn outfits donated to him by real elderly women. See Kenny, *The Man Who Was Old Mother Riley*, 176, 182.

65. Roy Rolland, who sometimes acted as Lucan's understudy and assumed the role of Riley after Lucan's death, was said to have played the dame in a camp manner, unlike his predecessor. Rolland played Riley opposite Kitty McShane in some stage appearances and performed with Danny La Rue. See BFI RL, *Sunday People*, Tony Purcell, "Ghost Behind the New Mother Riley," 9 September 1974; V&A, BIOG LUCAN, *Times*, "Roy Rolland," 26 August 1997. The fascinating 1961 film *The Impersonator*, in which a pantomime dame is unmasked as a sexually motivated stalker and killer of women, suggests that dames had the potential to be seen in a sinister light, though this perception was not widespread. See Steve Chibnall and Brian McFarlane, *The British "B" Film* (Basingstoke: Palgrave Macmillan, 2009), viii–x, 278–80.

66. Charlotte Greenhalgh, *Aging in Twentieth-Century Britain* (Oakland: University of California Press, 2018), 106–8.

67. Ruth M. Ayers quoted in Greenhalgh, *Aging in Twentieth-Century Britain*, 107.

68. Quoted in Greenhalgh, *Aging in Twentieth-Century Britain*, 111.

69. Greenhalgh, *Aging in Twentieth-Century Britain*, 111–19.

70. Antonia Lant, *Blackout: Reinventing Women for Wartime British Cinema* (Princeton, NJ: Princeton University Press, 1991), 75–85.

71. At their career peak in the early 1940s, Lucan and McShane were reportedly earning £30,000 per annum. To put that in perspective, barristers and GPs (the "well-to-do") earned an average of approximately £1,090 per annum during the mid to late 1930s. See BFI RL, *Sunday People*, Purcell, "Ghost Behind the New Mother Riley," 29 September 1974; John Burnett, *A History of the Cost of Living* (Harmondsworth: Penguin Books, 1969), 295–98.

72. *Derby Daily Telegraph*, "'Old Mother Riley' Is in the Money," 4 February 1950. Each of the first ten *Old Mother Riley* films reportedly cost between £8,000 and £30,000 to make, totaling £270,000. See BFI RL, *Daily Mail*, "The Lucans Stepping Out," 5 December 1949. The first three films in the *Old Mother Riley* series were produced by Butcher's Film Service, eight were produced by British National Films, and the subsequent four by Renown Pictures Corporation. A planned sixteenth film in the series, *Mother Riley's Trip to Mars*, was never made due to Lucan's death. See Kenny, *The Man Who Was Old Mother Riley*, 242.

73. Kenny, *The Man Who Was Old Mother Riley*, 178–84. Radio and gramophone usage in Britain was surging during this period. By 1939, about nine million radio licenses had been issued and around 75 percent of households had a license (compared with just thirty-five thousand licenses in 1926). At the start of the 1930s, around eight hundred thousand gramophones and sixty million records were being sold in a year—more than one record per person in Britain. See James Nott, *Going to the Palais: A Social and Cultural History of Dancing and Dance Halls in Britain, 1918–1960* (Oxford: Oxford University Press, 2015), 105–7.

74. BFI RL, *Kinematograph Weekly*, "Old Mother Riley in Paris," 25 August 1938.

75. BFI RL, *Kinematograph Weekly*, "Old Mother Riley's Circus," 30 October 1941.

76. BFI RL, *Daily Film Renter*, "Old Mother Riley Meets the Vampire," 26 June 1952. For reasons unknown the film was marketed widely as *Mother Riley Meets the Vampire*, with "Old" left out of Riley's name. It was also released under the title *Vampire Over London* and, bizarrely, rereleased in the United States in the early 1960s as *My Son, the Vampire* in order to capitalize on the popularity of song parodist Allan Sherman's album *My Son, the Folk Singer* (1962). Sherman even recorded an introduction, trailer, and original song for the American rerelease. The film has received some renewed interest recently. It inspired an essay that won The Observer/Anthony Burgess Prize for Arts Journalism in 2014 and a play, *The Vampire and Mrs. Riley* (2013), depicting a fictionalized account of Lugosi and Lucan's relationship. See *Observer*, Roger Lewis, "Observer/Anthony Burgess

Prize-Winning Essay: Freaks by Roger Lewis," 11 May 2014; Dello Stritto and Brooks, *Vampire Over London*, esp. 303–15.

77. Kenny, *The Man Who Was Old Mother Riley*, 172–73. Comedian Cyril Fletcher has described one of Lucan's failed attempts to break into the West End. According to Fletcher's account of a revue at the London Palladium in which he appeared on the bill with Lucan and McShane, "Our part of the audience did not like Lucan and McShane," while the provincial audiences Lucan and McShane drew to the West End "hated our half of the show." "Oil did not mix with water," Fletcher despaired, referring to his "rather quietly artistic" comedy that contrasted with the "strong visual comedy" of Old Mother Riley. See Cyril Fletcher, *Nice One Cyril: Being the Odd Odyssey and Anecdotage of a Comedian* (London: Barrie & Jenkins, 1978), 56–57. Lucan has sometimes been misleadingly labeled a "northern [English] comic" even though he was popular across Great Britain, as well as in Ireland. See Kenny, *The Man Who Was Old Mother Riley*, 12, 199.

78. V&A, BIOG LUCAN, *Daily Telegraph*, "'Old Mother Riley' Dies in Theatre," 18 May 1954.

79. BFI RL, *Daily Mail*, "The Lucans Stepping Out," 5 December 1949. *Old Mother Riley's New Venture* received a New York premiere in 1952, three years after it was first released in Britain. See Slide, *Great Pretenders*, 82.

80. *New Society*, vol. 32, 1975, cited in Kenny, *The Man Who Was Old Mother Riley*, 347; William Bell quoted in *Marylebone Mercury*, "But It's Shudders for Old Mother Riley," 20 June 1975.

81. *New Society* quoted in Kenny, *The Man Who Was Old Mother Riley*, 347.

82. *New Society* quoted in Kenny, *The Man Who Was Old Mother Riley*, 347.

83. Irene Chaplin quoted in *Marylebone Mercury*, "But It's Shudders for Old Mother Riley," 20 June 1975.

84. For criticism of working-class entertainment, see Stefan Szczelkun, *The Conspiracy of Good Taste: William Morris, Cecil Sharp, Clough Williams-Ellis and the Repression of Working Class Culture in the 20th Century* (London: Working Press, 1993), 10–11; Robert James, *Popular Culture and Working-Class Taste in Britain, 1930–39: A Round of Cheap Diversions?* (Manchester: Manchester University Press, 2010), 2–3, 24–25.

85. See, for example, *Mother Riley Meets the Vampire* (dir. John Gilling, Renown Pictures Corporation, 1952). Riley directing her chaotic energies toward taking on authority figures contrasts with Regency-era clowns like Joseph Grimaldi, who targeted both the vulnerable and the powerful in their acts. See Jane Moody, "Grimaldi, Joseph [Joe] (1778–1837), actor and pantomimist," *Oxford Dictionary of*

National Biography (29 May 2014), https://doi.org/10.1093/ref:odnb/11630 (accessed 13 October 2021); Richards, *The Golden Age of Pantomime*, 36.

86. According to the script of the 1954 version of *Old Mother Riley in Paris*, for instance, the landlord's entrance is meant to elicit "boos from the crowd." See BL MC, LCP 1954/19, *Old Mother Riley in Paris* by Con West, Script, Licensed 12 February 1954.

87. David Sutton, *A Chorus of Raspberries: British Film Comedy, 1929–1939* (Exeter: University of Exeter Press, 2000), 120, 123.

88. Sutton, *A Chorus of Raspberries*, 187–88, 191.

89. *Old Mother Riley, MP* (dir. Oswald Mitchell, Butcher's Film Service, 1939). See also Steven Fielding, *A State of Play: British Politics on Screen, Stage and Page, from Anthony Trollope to* The Thick of It (London: Bloomsbury, 2014), 89–90.

90. *Old Mother Riley in Business* (dir. John Baxter, British National Films, 1940).

91. Quoted in Geoff Brown and Tony Aldgate, *The Common Touch: The Films of John Baxter* (London: BFI Publishing, 1989), 73.

92. James, *Popular Culture and Working-Class Taste in Britain*, 45–46.

93. James, *Popular Culture and Working-Class Taste in Britain*, 46.

94. *Old Mother Riley* road shows, made to capitalize on the success of the dame's film series, consisted mostly of what were known as "revues-with-a-plot." They contained a central story based around Old Mother Riley, some of which was lifted liberally from the plots of the films, interspersed with assorted variety acts. Scripts for various *Old Mother Riley* productions name an eclectic mix of variety turns, including: "Dancing Scene—Girls," "Music Hall Acrobatic Act," and "Anna and her Performing Dogs." These routines could be inserted into the plot of the show or could be arbitrary. See BL MC, LCP 1950/38, *Old Mother Riley and Her Daughter Kitty* by Kitty McShane, Script, Licensed 28 August 1950; BL MC, LCP 1944/10, *Old Mother Riley and Her Daughter Kitty*, Script, Licensed 6 April 1944; BL MC, Lord Chamberlain's Plays Correspondence files (LCP Corr) 1950/1865, *Old Mother Riley and Her Daughter Kitty*, Licensed 28 August 1950; BL MC, LCP Corr 1944/5467, *Old Mother Riley and Her Daughter Kitty*, Licensed 6 April 1944.

95. *Nottingham Evening Post*, "The Empire," 19 March 1940.

96. BL MC, LCP 1944/10, *Old Mother Riley and Her Daughter Kitty*, Script, Licensed 6 April 1944. The punctuation is reproduced from the original source. How Lucan chose which pawnbroker and street to mention beforehand is unknown.

97. BL MC, LCP 1950/38, *Old Mother Riley and Her Daughter Kitty*, Script, Licensed 28 August 1950.

98. Lucan died during a staging of this play on 17 May 1954. After his death the title of the show was changed to *Paradise Row to Paris*. See BL MC, LCP Corr 1954/6512, *Old Mother Riley in Paris*, Letter from Gaston and Andree Productions to the Lord Chamberlain's Office, 28 May 1954.

99. BL MC, LCP 1954/19, *Old Mother Riley in Paris*, Script, Licensed 12 February 1954.

100. By 1954, Lucan and his wife Kitty were separated after much domestic strife. They made their last film together, *Old Mother Riley's Jungle Treasure* (1951), while operating on different shooting schedules and performed onstage together for the last time in January 1952. During a performance of *Going Gay* (1952), in which Lucan was appearing without Kitty, Kitty ran onstage from the stalls and swung her handbag at Lucan, hitting him and drawing blood. Kitty was also alleged to have set fire to more than one theater where Lucan was performing without her. See Kenny, *The Man Who Was Old Mother Riley*, 215, 243, 252.

101. BL MC, LCP 1954/19, *Old Mother Riley in Paris*, Script, Licensed 12 February 1954.

102. Ruth Shade, "Take My Mother-In-Law: 'Old Bags,' Comedy and the Sociocultural Construction of the Older Woman," *Comedy Studies* 1:1 (2010): 72–73.

103. Kathleen K. Rowe, "Roseanne: Unruly Woman as Domestic Goddess," *Screen* 31:4 (1990): 410; Sutton, *A Chorus of Raspberries*, 151. On similar considerations regarding filmmaker and playwright Tyler Perry's dame-like Madea character, see Timothy Lyle, "'Check with Yo' Man First; Check with Yo' Man': Tyler Perry Appropriates Drag as a Tool to Re-Circulate Patriarchal Ideology," *Callaloo* 34:3 (2011): 943–58. Cultural scholar Timothy Lyle has ultimately been more skeptical of Madea's status as an agent for positive societal change than Rowe has been regarding Barr.

104. On Riley's debated Irish heritage, see BFI RL, uncredited newspaper clipping, 19 May 1954; V&A, BIOG LUCAN, *Daily News*, "Old Mother Riley Dies," 18 May 1954; Kenny, *The Man Who Was Old Mother Riley*, 310; St. Pierre, *Music Hall Mimesis in British Film*, 118–19. For examples of Irish themes in Lucan's act, see *Kathleen Mavourneen* (dir. Norman Lee, Argyle British Productions, 1937); BL MC, LCP 1944/10, *Old Mother Riley and Her Daughter Kitty*, Script, Licensed 6 April 1944; BL MC, LCP 1950/38, *Old Mother Riley and Her Daughter Kitty*, Script, Licensed 28 August 1950. The dialogue in the Old Mother Riley *Film Fun* comic strip emphasized Kitty's Irish dialect. See Dello Stritto and Brooks, *Vampire Over London*, 301.

105. David Hayton, "From Barbarian to Burlesque: English Images of the Irish c. 1660–1750," *Irish Economic and Social History* 15 (1988): 5–31. For stage

Irish*women*, see M. Alison Kibler, "The Stage Irishwoman," *Journal of American Ethnic History* 24:3 (2005): 5–30.

106. Geraldine Maschio, "Ethnic Humour and the Demise of the Russell Brothers," *Journal of Popular Culture* 26:1 (1992): 81–92. For more on cross-dressed stage Irishwomen and the dame in American theater, see Gillian M. Rodger, *Just One of the Boys: Female-to-Male Cross-Dressing on the American Variety Stage* (Urbana: University of Illinois Press, 2018), 124–26.

107. Kenny, *The Man Who Was Old Mother Riley*, 164–65, 360–61.

108. See Michael Rogin, "Blackface, White Noise: The Jewish Jazz Singer Finds His Voice," *Critical Inquiry* 18:3 (1992): 417–53.

109. BFI RL, *Hull Times*, Slide, "Children Still Place Posies on His Grave," 10 May 1968. Slide has recalled that attending children's matinees was one of the few ways he was able to watch *Old Mother Riley* films in his adulthood. See Anthony Slide, "Foreword," in Kenny, *The Man Who Was Old Mother Riley*, x.

110. The punctuation was added by me. This inscription was chosen by Kitty McShane, to whom Lucan was still technically married at the time of his death, although the two had been estranged for years by that point. Lucan and McShane's only son, Donald, an adult and also estranged from Kitty in May 1954, reportedly referred to the epitaph as "vulgar little lines" shortly after it was commissioned. See Kenny, *The Man Who Was Old Mother Riley*, 281.

111. Oliver Double, *Britain Had Talent: A History of Variety Theatre* (London: Bloomsbury, 2012), 41, 82–87.

112. James, *Popular Culture and Working-Class Taste in Britain*, 205.

113. *Sunderland Daily Echo and Shipping Gazette*, "Grand Entertainment for Children at the Empire," 18 January 1938.

114. See BFI RL, *Call Boy*, Ashton, "In Me Bonnet and Shawl," March 1966. There has been an enduring notion of pantomime constituting children's entertainment, but this perception is not entirely true. For example, principal boy roles, traditionally played by young women, were often made to be sexually alluring for the benefit of male audience members. See Jim Davis, "'Slap On! Slap Ever!': Victorian Pantomime, Gender Variance, and Cross-Dressing," *New Theatre Quarterly* 30:3 (2014): 220–23, 227–28; Holland, "The Play of Eros," 203; Senelick, *The Changing Room*, 258–91.

115. Roger Baker quoted in Simon Sladen, "Wicked Queens of Pantoland," in *Drag Histories, Herstories and Hairstories: Drag in a Changing Scene, Volume 2*, ed. Mark Edward and Stephen Farrier (London: Bloomsbury, 2021), 198.

116. See Richard Anthony Baker, *Old-Time Variety: An Illustrated History* (Barnsley: Pen & Sword Books, 2011), 159–60; BL SA, 1LP0173066 and

2LP0011983, *A Drop of the Hard Shuff... For Adults Only: Mrs. Shufflewick Live! At the New Black Cap*, 1973; Patrick Newly, *The Amazing Mrs Shufflewick: The Life of Rex Jameson* (London: Third Age Press, 2007).

117. See *Irish Times*, Bernice Harrison, "It's Not That Mrs Brown's Boys Is Too Mainstream. It's Just Not Funny," 12 February 2011; *Guardian*, Ryan Gilbey and Bruce Dessau, "*Mrs Brown's Boys* v *Mulholland Drive*: A Culture Showdown," 23 August 2016; *Guardian*, Brian Logan, "Mrs Brown's Boys Live? They'll Need More Than Malaprops and Mincing to Thrill an Entire Arena," 6 July 2017. A similar public discussion has emerged around Perry's Madea. See NPR.org, Jimi Izrael, "Tyler Perry vs. Spike Lee: A Debate Over Class and 'Coonery,'" 22 April 2011.

Chapter 2

1. According to theater historian Rebecca D'Monté, the genre's popularity lay partly in its perceived timeliness. "The revue's episodic and fragmentary structure," D'Monté has noted, "reflected the insecurity of the times, and the informal and intimate style enacted a break with past hierarchies." See her chapter "First World War Theatre" in Rebecca D'Monté, ed., *British Theatre and Performance: 1900–1950* (London: Bloomsbury, 2015), 64.

2. For more on cross-dressing performance among servicemen during wartime, see Lisa Z. Sigel, "'Best Love': Female Impersonation in the Great War," *Sexualities* 19:1–2 (2016): 98–118; David A. Boxwell, "The Follies of War: Cross-Dressing and Popular Theatre on the British Front Lines, 1914–1918," *Modernism/Modernity* 9:1 (2002): 1–20; Laurel Halladay, "A Lovely War: Male to Female Cross-Dressing and Canadian Military Entertainment in World War II," *Journal of Homosexuality* 46:3–4 (2004): 19–34; Clare Makepeace, "'Pinky Smith Looks Gorgeous!' Female Impersonators and Male Bonding in Prisoner of War Camps for British Servicemen in Europe," in *Men, Masculinities and Male Culture in the Second World War*, ed. Linsey Robb and Juliette Pattinson (London: Palgrave Macmillan, 2017), 71–95; Alon Rachamimov, "The Disruptive Comforts of Drag: (Trans)Gender Performances among Prisoners of War in Russia, 1914–1920," *American Historical Review* 111:2 (2006): 362–82; Emma Vickers and Emma Jackson, "Sanctuary or Sissy? Female Impersonation as Entertainment in the British Armed Forces, 1939–1945," in *Gender and the Second World War: The Lessons of War*, ed. Corinna Peniston-Bird and Emma Vickers (London: Palgrave, 2017), 40–52.

3. For more on the drag scene during the interwar period, such as drag performed at universities, see Dominic Janes, "The 'Curious Effects' of Acting: Homosexuality, Theatre and Female Impersonation at the University of Cambridge,

1900–39," *Twentieth Century British History* 33:2 (2022): 169–202; Dominic Janes, "The Varsity Drag: Gender, Sexuality, and Cross-Dressing at the University of Cambridge, 1850–1950," *Journal of Social History* 55:3 (2022): 695–723; Chris O'Rourke, "Exploiting Ambiguity: *Murder!* and the Meanings of Cross-Dressing in Interwar British Cinema," *Journal of British Cinema and Television* 17:3 (2020): 289–312.

4. Major Les Rouges productions included the stage shows *Splinters* (1918), *Splinters* (1920), *Super Splinters* (1927), *Splinters* 1914–1933 a.k.a. *Splinters* 1914–1934 a.k.a. *Which Is Which* (1933), and *Splinters* (1937).

5. Victoria and Albert Theatre and Performance Archives (V&A), Blythe House, Theatre and Performance Company Files: CORP LES ROUGES ET NOIRS, Engagement book, January 1919 to November 1924.

6. V&A, LES ROUGES, *Pall Mall Gazette*, "'Splinters' at the Savoy: Capital Performance by 'Les Rouge Et Noir [*sic*],'" 5 August 1919.

7. V&A, LES ROUGES, "Les Rouges et Noirs" Savoy Theatre program, August 1919.

8. Matt Houlbrook, "'The Man with the Powder Puff' in Interwar London," *Historical Journal* 50:1 (2007): 160.

9. Matt Houlbrook, *Queer London: Perils and Pleasures in the Sexual Metropolis: 1918–1957* (London: University of Chicago Press, 2005), esp. 33–34, 139–66; quoted in Houlbrook, "The Man with the Powder Puff," 160.

10. Matt Houlbrook, "'Lady Austin's Camp Boys': Constituting the Queer Subject in 1930s London," *Gender and History* 14:1 (2002): 31–61.

11. Matt Cook, "Queer Conflicts: Love, Sex and War, 1914–1967," in *A Gay History of Britain: Love and Sex between Men Since the Middle Ages*, ed. Matt Cook, H.G. Cocks, Robert Mills, and Randolph Trumbach (Oxford: Greenwood World Publishing, 2007), 152; Houlbrook, "Lady Austin's Camp Boys," 36.

12. See British Library Manuscript Collections (BL MC), Lord Chamberlain's Plays Correspondence files (LCP Corr) 1933/12058, *Splinters* 1914–1933 by L. Arthur Rose, Reader's Report, 19 April 1933.

13. British Film Institute Reuben Library (BFI RL), South Bank, *Picturegoer*, 13 February 1932; V&A, LES ROUGES, *London Mail*, 23 August 1919.

14. Susan Kingsley Kent, *Aftershocks: Politics and Trauma in Britain, 1918–1931* (Basingstoke: Palgrave Macmillan, 2009), 153. For other examples of this kind of narrative, see Lucy Bland, *Modern Women on Trial: Sexual Transgression in the Age of the Flapper* (Manchester: Manchester University Press, 2013); Lesley Hall, *Sex, Gender and Social Change in Britain Since* 1880 (Basingstoke: Palgrave Macmillan, 2000), 123–24; Houlbrook, "Lady Austin's Camp Boys," 31–61; Houlbrook, "The

Man with the Powder Puff," 145-71; John Johnston, *The Lord Chamberlain's Blue Pencil* (London: Hodder & Stoughton, 1990), 131-32, 205-9; Susan Kingsley Kent, *Making Peace: The Reconstruction of Gender in Interwar Britain* (Princeton, NJ: Princeton University Press, 1993), esp. 41-43; Marek Kohn, *Dope Girls: The Birth of the British Drug Underground* (London: Granta Books, 2003); Angus McLaren, *The Trials of Masculinity: Policing Sexual Boundaries, 1870-1930* (Chicago: University of Chicago Press, 1997), esp. 208-31; Martin Pugh, *We Danced All Night: A Social History of Britain between the Wars* (London: Vintage, 2009), esp. 152-60.

15. Some notable studies have discussed predominantly positive responses toward certain renderings of gender variance in interwar Britain. For example, historian Alison Oram has asserted that "until the late 1930s, women passing as men in Britain continue to be represented in the popular press as entertaining, fascinating and even admirable." However, in contrasting this phenomenon with the contemporary reaction to drag, Oram has largely repeated the narrative that male gender variance and female impersonation were seen as social problems. "Alongside this anxiety about male effeminacy [in the 1920s]," she has argued, "came a retreat by the press from its previous approval of female impersonation on the stage." See Alison Oram, *Her Husband Was a Woman! Women's Gender-Crossing in Modern British Popular Culture* (London: Routledge, 2007), 82, 87.

16. For an exploration of "a literature of convalescence," see Alison Light, *Forever England: Femininity, Literature and Conservatism between the Wars* (London: Routledge, 1991), 65-75.

17. The name "Les Rouges et Noirs" referred to the regimental colors of the First Army, as the troupe was affiliated with the First Army Concert Party. The individual performers, however, were initially recruited "from many regiments and army corps." See V&A, LES ROUGES, Savoy Theatre program.

18. J.G. Fuller, *Troop Morale and Popular Culture in the British and Dominion Armies 1914-1918* (Oxford: Clarendon Press, 1991), 96, 188. Entertainment for the forces became increasingly professionalized after the war with the establishment of the Navy, Army, and Air Force Institutes (NAAFI) in 1921 and the Entertainments National Service Association (ENSA) in 1939. See the chapter "Second World War Theatre and After," in Rebecca D'Monté, ed., *British Theatre*, 153-55.

19. Fuller, *Troop Morale*, 95.

20. Fuller, *Troop Morale*, 96-98.

21. Sigel, "Best Love," 103, 109.

22. Les Rouges had a Canadian counterpart, The Dumbells, who embarked upon a London tour in 1918. See Jason Wilson, *Soldiers of Song: The Dumbells and*

Other Canadian Concert Parties of the First World War (Waterloo, Ontario: Wilfrid Laurier University Press, 2012), 65-67.

23. Les Rouges' Savoy Theatre program insisted that the members of the company "were all artistes, NOT AMATEURS, before the war." See V&A, LES ROUGES, Savoy Theatre program; for some information on Jones's and Stone's theatrical backgrounds, see V&A, LES ROUGES, *Empire News*, 10 August 1919.

24. Les Rouges appears to have garnered a good degree of institutional support by the end of the war. The *Times* reported that "when the end came the party was demobilized as a complete unit" so they could tour together in Britain. Furthermore, General Sir Henry Horne, commander of the First Army during the end of the war, personally gave the troupe £1,000 in funds once they were discharged, and he addressed the audience at Les Rouges' first night at the Savoy Theatre in August 1919. The ensemble's friends in high places probably aided them significantly when it came to securing their initial British theatrical engagements at the Beaver Hut Theatre and Windsor Castle. See V&A, LES ROUGES, *Times*, "'Les Rouges Et Noirs' Army Entertainers at the Savoy," 5 August 1919; V&A, LES ROUGES, *Era*, 24 September 1919; V&A, LES ROUGES, *Era*, "Les Rouges et Noirs. General's Appreciation," n.d.

25. V&A, Les Rouges, Engagement book, January 1919 to November 1924.

26. The first *Splinters* film functions largely as a fictionalized account of the company's founding and features several scenes from their stage shows. *Splinters in the Navy* depicts Les Rouges backstage and showcases a few concert party performances aboard a navy vessel, but troupe members are relegated to minor parts supporting star comedian Sydney Howard. *Splinters in the Air*, the final *Splinters* film, also stars Howard and barely involves Les Rouges at all aside from a scene set in a concert party. See *Splinters* (dir. Jack Raymond, British and Dominions Films Corporation, 1930); *Splinters in the Navy* (dir. Walter Forde, Twickenham Film Studios Productions, 1932); *Splinters in the Air* (dir. Alfred Goulding, Herbert Wilcox Productions, 1937).

27. V&A, LES ROUGES, Savoy Theatre program; Les Rouges were not alone in their eagerness to emphasize the fact that their cast was made up of genuine ex-servicemen. According to D'Monté, during the Great War actors were "fearful of being handed the 'white feather,' a sign of cowardice, by a member of the audience," and it was not uncommon for theater programs to clarify that all male cast members had served or had legitimate reasons for not serving. D'Monté, ed., *British Theatre*, 71.

28. V&A, LES ROUGES, Savoy Theatre program.

29. V&A, LES ROUGES, Savoy Theatre program.

30. V&A, LES ROUGES, Savoy Theatre program.

31. V&A, LES ROUGES, *Brighton Standard*, "Brighton Palace Pier," 15 May 1919.

32. V&A, LES ROUGES, *Sussex Daily News*, 9 September 1919.

33. V&A, LES ROUGES, *Sussex Daily News*, 9 September 1919; BL MC, Lord Chamberlain's Plays (LCP) 1920/17, *Splinters* by Eric Barber, Script, Licensed 26 June 1920.

34. V&A, LES ROUGES, *Sporting Times*, 1919.

35. V&A, LES ROUGES, *Brighton Standard*, "Brighton Palace Pier," 11 September 1919. Allan, a Canadian dancer, gained fame in North America and Europe for her "Dance of the Seven Veils" routine. She is also remembered for her failed 1918 libel case against British MP Noel Pemberton Billing, who accused her of leading a Sapphic cult. The *Standard* critic's wistfulness was likely a response to the ending of Allan's stage career, which had been precipitated by the recent trial. It is therefore significant that Hives, as a female impersonator, was deemed to be a worthy successor to Allan given this context. See Judith R. Walkowitz, "The 'Vision of Salome': Cosmopolitanism and Erotic Dancing in Central London, 1908–1918," *American Historical Review* 108:2 (2003): 337–76.

36. V&A, THM/LON/CHP: Chelsea Palace Theatre (London) Production Files, 1903–1957, Chelsea Palace Theatre program, September 1933. There were some all-servicewomen revues, such as *Girls Out of Uniform* (1945). See Steve Nicholson, *The Censorship of British Drama, 1900–1968, Volume Two: 1933–1952* (Exeter: University of Exeter Press, 2005), 321.

37. *Hull Daily Mail*, "Palace—'Which Is Which?,'" 6 June 1933.

38. V&A, LES ROUGES, *Daily Telegraph*, "Savoy Theatre 'Les Rouges et Noirs,'" 5 August 1919.

39. V&A, LES ROUGES, *Sussex Daily News*, 9 September 1919.

40. V&A, LES ROUGES, *Times*, "'Les Rouges Et Noirs' Army Entertainers at the Savoy," 5 August 1919.

41. *Sunderland Daily Echo and Shipping Gazette*, "'Splinters' in New Guise," 17 March 1934. The punctuation is from the original.

42. *Derby Evening Telegraph*, "Return Visit of 'Splinters' Melody and Mirth at the Grand," 23 January 1934.

43. Ana Carden-Coyne, *Reconstructing the Body: Classicism, Modernism, and the First World War* (Oxford: Oxford University Press, 2009), 83–84, 94.

44. Carden-Coyne, *Reconstructing the Body*, 83.

45. Carden-Coyne, *Reconstructing the Body*, 83.

46. For example, see Sigel, "Best Love," 108–13.

47. Boxwell, "The Follies of War," 6–8.

48. V&A, LES ROUGES, uncredited newspaper clipping, "Les Rouges Et Noirs," n.d.

49. Carden-Coyne, *Reconstructing the Body*, 86.

50. Carden-Coyne, *Reconstructing the Body*, 87.

51. Carden-Coyne, *Reconstructing the Body*, 86–87.

52. Quoted in D'Monté, ed., *British Theatre*, 118.

53. Quoted in Michael Hammond, "'So Essentially Human': The Appeal of Charles Chaplin's *Shoulder Arms* in Britain, 1918," *Early Popular Visual Culture* 8:3 (2010): 307, 310.

54. Hammond, "So Essentially Human," 309.

55. British Library Newsroom (BL NR), *Sketch*, Michael Orme, "At the Sign of the Cinema," 8 January 1930.

56. *Splinters* (1930). Another purpose for the scene, no doubt, was to show off the movie's technical achievements, as it was one of the first British films to feature sound in every scene. According to *Bioscope*, "[*Splinters*] surpasses in technical achievement anything of its kind ever made in Britain." See BFI RL, *Bioscope*, "Sound and Dialogue Subjects 'Splinters,'" 1 January 1930.

57. Light, *Forever England*, 66, 69.

58. Light, *Forever England*, 66–71.

59. Light, *Forever England*, 69.

60. Matt Houlbrook, "Soldier Heroes and Rent Boys: Homosex, Masculinities, and Britishness in the Brigade of Guards, circa 1900–1960," *Journal of British Studies* 42:3 (2003): 351–88.

61. Houlbrook, "Soldier Heroes and Rent Boys," 353.

62. Houlbrook, "Soldier Heroes and Rent Boys," 356, 357; Paul R. Deslandes, "The Male Body, Beauty and Aesthetics in Modern British Culture," *History Compass* 8:10 (2010): 1192.

63. Quoted in Houlbrook, "Soldier Heroes and Rent Boys," 374.

64. Houlbrook, "Soldier Heroes and Rent Boys," 375, 381.

65. Graham Dawson quoted in Houlbrook, "Soldier Heroes and Rent Boys," 352.

66. V&A, LES ROUGES, *Evening Standard*, M. W. D., "'Les Rouges et Noirs,'" 5 August 1919. Firsthand accounts of the revues from the performers themselves are scant. For a rare extended interview with Stone, see Peter Farrer, ed., *Cross-Dressing between the Wars: Selections from* London Life, 1923–1933 (Liverpool: Karn Publications Garston, 2000), 249–51.

67. V&A, LES ROUGES, *Evening Standard*, Corisande, "'Les Rouges et Noirs,'" 5 August 1919.

68. V&A, LES ROUGES, *Daily Express*, "Soldiers With Flaxen Tresses. Men of the First Army as Stage Beauties. 'Splinters,'" 5 August 1919.

69. V&A, LES ROUGES, *Brighton Standard*, "Brighton Palace Pier," 11 September 1919.

70. V&A, LES ROUGES, *London Opinion*, 16 August 1919.

71. Salita Solano and *American Magazine* quoted in Susan A. Glenn, *Female Spectacle: The Theatrical Roots of Modern Feminism* (Cambridge, MA: Harvard University Press, 2000), 170–71.

72. Carden-Coyne, *Reconstructing the Body*, 201–3.

73. Paul R. Deslandes, *The Culture of Male Beauty in Britain: From the First Photographs to David Beckham* (Chicago: University of Chicago Press, 2021), 153.

74. Carden-Coyne, *Reconstructing the Body*, 202–3; Deslandes, *The Culture of Male Beauty in Britain*, 119.

75. Deslandes, *The Culture of Male Beauty in Britain*, 134–35.

76. Joanna Bourke, *Dismembering the Male: Men's Bodies, Britain and the Great War* (London: Reaktion Books, 1996), 138–39, 198–209. For varied reactions to the Men's Dress Reform movement, see Farrer, ed., *Cross-Dressing between the Wars*.

77. For First World War servicemen being perceived as beautiful, see Deslandes, *The Culture of Male Beauty in Britain*, 123–62.

78. This information corresponds to a query posed by historian Paul Deslandes, who has probed the extent to which "the history of masculine aesthetics" should "privilege the body over the face." Deslandes, "The Male Body, Beauty and Aesthetics," 1203.

79. V&A, LES ROUGES, *London Opinion*, A Playful Stallite, "Plays & Players," 6 September 1919.

80. *Splinters* (1930).

81. *Splinters in the Navy* (1932).

82. BFI RL, *Bioscope*, "British Studios To-Day," 22 July 1931. One critic even mused, unprompted, that "[Stone] must be an extremely personable young man in private life by the way." V&A, LES ROUGES, uncredited newspaper clipping, "The National News, Splinters from France," 10 August 1919.

83. See also British Pathé, Film ID 1084.09, "The Rivals—Some Chippings from the New Splinters Dancing Troupe (1928)." For more on de-wigging, see Laurence Senelick, *The Changing Room: Sex, Drag and Theatre* (London: Routledge, 2000), 306. In a reversal of the de-wigging trope, the start of *Splinters* 1914–1933 sees Reg Stone putting on his wig, makeup, and frock. BL MC, LCP 1933/16, *Splinters* 1914–1933 by L. Arthur Rose, Licensed April 1933.

84. "Interested in Impersonating (Argentine)" quoted in Peter Farrer, ed., *Cross-Dressing between the Wars: Selections from* London Life *Part II, 1934–1941* (Liverpool: Karn Publications Garston, 2006), 204 (emphasis added).

85. "Interested in Impersonating (Argentine)" quoted in Farrer, ed., *Cross-Dressing between the Wars: Selections from* London Life *Part II*, 204.

86. BFI RL, *Picturegoer*, 13 February 1932.

87. V&A, LES ROUGES, *London Mail*, 23 August 1919.

88. V&A, LES ROUGES, *Bournemouth Graphic*, "Clever Company of Army Artistes," 27 June 1919. "Nancy" was a common colloquialism for same-sex desiring and/or effeminate men during this period. Variants of this usage date back to the seventeenth century. The term was used alongside similar slang terms such as "molly" in the eighteenth and nineteenth centuries. See "nan, n.1," *OED Online*, www.oed.com/view/Entry/237306 (accessed 17 October 2020); "nancy, n. and adj.," *OED Online*, www.oed.com/view/Entry/124950 (accessed 17 October 2020); "nancy boy, n.," *OED Online*, www.oed.com/view/Entry/245828 (accessed 17 October 2020); "Miss Nancy, n.," *OED Online*, www.oed.com/view/Entry/234183 (accessed 17 October 2020). See also Houlbrook, *Queer London*, 139.

89. Edith Thompson quoted in "Letters of Edith Thompson and Frederick Bywaters," in Edith Jessie Thompson, ed. René Weis (2019), https://edithjessiethompson.co.uk/primary-source-texts/letters-of-edith-thompson-and-frederick-bywaters/ (accessed 9 September 2022).

90. BL MC, LCP Corr 1933/12058, *Splinters* 1914–1933, Reader's Report, 19 April 1933.

91. BL MC, LCP Corr 1933/12058, *Splinters* 1914–1933, handwritten note on Reader's Report, 20 April 1933. When the play *The Gay Young Bride* (1923), a recent export from America, was refused a license over the Lord Chamberlain's Office's objection to its cross-dressing scenes, the show's star, London-born female impersonator Herbert Clifton, wrote to the censor asking why his play was unlicensed when the 1920 *Splinters* production was allowed. The Lord Chamberlain's Office pleaded ignorance by stating that they did not know that *Splinters* contained cross-dressing. The Office's response in this instance is odd but somewhat plausible. The 1920 *Splinters* script does not explicitly indicate that the women's parts are played by men and, as Les Rouges had only been formed somewhat recently, the Office could have been ignorant as to the nature of the revue. The censor's discomfort with female impersonation in the case of *The Gay Young Bride* had to do with context: Clifton's character plays a man posing as his friend's bride-to-be. Once Clifton cut some content involving displays of

(pretend) affection between the cross-dressed character and his "fiancé," the play was licensed and soon received rave reviews from critics. Papers remarked that the show had audiences "laughing and clapping unrestrainedly for an hour and three-quarters," and Clifton was singled out for his "marvellous array of fashionable dresses" and "really fine soprano [singing] voice." See Steve Nicholson, *The Censorship of British Drama, 1900-1968, Volume One: 1900-1932* (Exeter: University of Exeter Press, 2003), 219-20; BL MC, LCP 1920/17, *Splinters*, licensed 28 June 1920, Reader's Report, 26 June 1920; *Leeds Mercury*, "The Hippodrome," 12 August 1924; *Hastings and St Leonards Observer*, "'The Gay Young Bride' at the Gaiety Theatre," 14 June 1924; *Stage*, "The Gay Young Bride," 3 January 1924. See also *Portsmouth Evening News*, "Fun at the Hippodrome," 15 July 1924; *Sheffield Daily Telegraph*, "Laughter at the Hippodrome," 15 April 1924.

92. BL MC, LCP Corr 1933/12058, *Splinters* 1914-1933, Letter from S. W. Harris to the Lord Chamberlain's Office, 27 October 1933; BL MC, LCP Corr 1933/12058, *Splinters* 1914-1933, Letter from Samuel Rose to the Lord Chamberlain's Office, 7 November 1933.

93. BL MC, LCP Corr 1937/624, *Splinters*, Reader's Report, 1 September 1937.

94. Johnston, *The Lord Chamberlain's Blue Pencil*, 171-72. For information on the lifting of the ban, see Steve Nicholson, *The Censorship of British Drama 1900-1968, Volume Three: The Fifties* (Exeter: University of Exeter Press, 2011), 110-39.

95. Nicholas De Jongh, *Politics, Prudery and Perversions: The Censoring of the English Stage 1901-1968* (London: Methuen, 2001), 99.

96. For example, the censor explicitly clarified in the case of *We're No Ladies* (1958) that "[The Lord Chamberlain] has no apparent grounds for refusing to licence a play merely because it is to be performed by female impersonators, female impersonation in this country being as old as the stage." See BL MC, LCP Corr 1958/667, *We're No Ladies* by Phil Starr, Letter from the Lord Chamberlain's Office to the Clerk of the London County Council, 10 February 1958.

97. For further analysis on the Lord Chamberlain's Office's relationship with drag, see chapter 4.

98. Houlbrook, "Lady Austin's Camp Boys," 31-61. From the 1920s and for decades afterward, drag balls organized by African Americans in Harlem, such as the annual Hamilton Lodge Ball, were not only cultural touchstones of the drag scene but fixtures of New York City cultural life in their own right. In contrast to the vilification that the patrons of the Holland Park Avenue ball faced in the press and in court in 1930s Britain, Harlem drag balls in that same decade flourished with some support from the African American press in particular. See, for example, James F. Wilson, *Bulldaggers, Pansies, and Chocolate Babies: Performance, Race,*

and Sexuality in the Harlem Renaissance (Ann Arbor: University of Michigan Press, 2011), 82–89.

99. *Morning Advertiser* quoted in Houlbrook, "Lady Austin's Camp Boys," 32.

100. For more on Wild, see Laura Doan, *Disturbing Practices: History, Sexuality, and Women's Experience of Modern War* (Chicago: University of Chicago Press, 2013), 176–86.

101. Quoted in Houlbrook, "Lady Austin's Camp Boys," 32.

102. Anonymous quoted in Houlbrook, "Lady Austin's Camp Boys," 36.

103. Houlbrook, *Queer London*, 268. See also Colonel Victor Barker's court cases in the 1920s and 1930s. James Vernon, "'For Some Queer Reason': The Trials and Tribulations of Colonel Barker's Masquerade in Interwar Britain," *Signs* 26:1 (2000): 37–62. Historian Laura Doan has observed that media coverage of Barker was favorable, demonstrating that gender variance as media spectacle was not essentially a negative phenomenon. Laura Doan, *Fashioning Sapphism: The Origins of a Modern English Lesbian Culture* (New York: Columbia University Press, 2001), 92.

104. Although the newer ex-servicemen's drag revues featured some former Les Rouges performers, they were distinct from the Les Rouges/*Splinters* canon. For a more thorough study of the post–Second World War revues, see chapter 4.

105. The cast of the musical was the only integrated company in the American armed forces during the Second World War. See Laurence Bergreen, "Irving Berlin: *This Is the Army*," *Prologue* 28:2 (1996): 96–97.

106. See BL MC, LCP Corr 1943/5280, *Skirts* by A. G. Brest, Licensed 31 December 1943.

107. BL MC, LCP Corr 1944/5696, *We Were in the Forces* (Revised) by John D. Roberton, Reader's Report, 21 July 1944; University of East Anglia (UEA) Archives and Special Collections, Norwich, UK, Tinkler and Williams' Theatre Collection (T&W), Williams' Listing, press-cuttings books, Norwich, 1955, uncredited newspaper clipping, "All Male Show Is Better Than Ever," May 1955; *Stage*, James Hartley, "Lines from Lancs," 29 April 1954.

108. Chris Waters, "Disorders of the Mind, Disorders of the Body Social: Peter Wildeblood and the Making of the Modern Homosexual," in *Moments of Modernity: Reconstructing Britain, 1945–1964*, ed. Becky Conekin, Frank Mort, and Chris Waters (London: Rivers Oram Press, 1999), 136.

109. Waters, "Disorders of the Mind, Disorders of the Body Social," 145.

110. Quoted in Brian Lewis, *Wolfenden's Witnesses: Homosexuality in Postwar Britain* (Basingstoke: Palgrave Macmillan, 2016), 206.

111. Waters, "Disorders of the Mind, Disorders of the Body Social," 144.

112. Quoted in Waters, "Disorders of the Mind, Disorders of the Body Social," 147.

113. Quoted in Waters, "Disorders of the Mind, Disorders of the Body Social," 145.

114. Danny La Rue, *From Drags to Riches: My Autobiography* (London: Viking, 1987), 75.

115. *Stage*, Hartley, "Lines from Lancs," 29 April 1954.

116. *Stage* quoted in Frank Mort, *Capital Affairs: London and the Making of the Permissive Society* (London: Yale University Press, 2010), 266. For more on the decline of the variety theater, see Oliver Double, *Britain Had Talent: A History of Variety Theatre* (London: Bloomsbury, 2012), 82–87.

117. Quoted in Mort, *Capital Affairs*, 266.

118. Gillian A.M. Mitchell, *Adult Responses to Popular Music and Intergenerational Relations in Britain, c.* 1955-1975 (London: Anthem Press, 2019), 107–54. Historians such as Mitchell have argued that after the death of the traditional variety theater by the end of the 1950s, a "residual variety culture" lived on into the 1960s and 1970s. This was seen in phenomena like light entertainment programs on television and popular music artists such as Cliff Richard, Cilla Black, and Tommy Steele integrating variety-type tropes and performance styles into their acts. See Mitchell, *Adult Responses to Popular Music*, 135.

Chapter 3

1. Danny La Rue, *From Drags to Riches: My Autobiography* (London: Viking, 1987), 61.

2. La Rue, *From Drags to Riches*, 105.

3. La Rue's first major television appearance was on Jack Hylton's *Monday Show* (1957–58) in 1958. Unfortunately, footage of the episode appears to have been lost. In Britain, commercial television was established in 1955. In 1950, 4 percent of the British adult population owned a television. By 1955, television ownership had grown to 40 percent, and it reached 80 percent by 1960. See James Nott, *Going to the Palais: A Social and Cultural History of Dancing and Dance Halls in Britain,* 1918-1960 (Oxford: Oxford University Press, 2015), 107.

4. La Rue, *From Drags to Riches*, 116.

5. *Queen Passionella* ran from the 1968 Christmas season through June 1969. The show reportedly still held the record for longest-running pantomime in January 1997, though it is unclear whether it still holds the record today. See Mander & Mitchenson Theatre Collection, University of Bristol (M&M), Danny La Rue:

MM/REF/PE/VA/141, *Telegraph Magazine*, Andrew Martin, "Super Trouper," 4 January 1997.

6. Arguably the most notable drag act on British television prior to La Rue was ventriloquist and *Forces Showboat* (1947) performer Bobbie Kimber. Kimber's television career was hurt when a 1952 *Daily Mirror* article accused Kimber of being a "hoax" as the ventriloquist had never explicitly mentioned being a female impersonator while onscreen. Author Richard Anthony Baker has claimed, questionably, that Kimber was the first female impersonator to perform in the Royal Variety show. Kimber appeared in the show in 1947. See Richard Anthony Baker, *Old-Time Variety: An Illustrated History* (Barnsley: Pen & Sword Books, 2011), 178–81. Kimber was not the only notable female impersonator who integrated ventriloquism into their act. British painter Walter Hibbert Lambert, also known as Lydia Dreams, had a drag act in which he played a nurse tending to a patient represented by a dummy. See New York Public Library for the Performing Arts, Billy Rose Theatre Division, Robinson Locke Collection, series 2, vol. 31, p. 71.

7. Rexton S. Bunnett, "La Rue, Danny [*real name* Daniel Patrick Carroll]," *Oxford Dictionary of National Biography* (10 January 2013), https://doi.org/10.1093/ref:odnb/101923 (accessed 24 August 2022); *Guardian*, Dennis Barker, "Danny La Rue," 2 June 2009; Victoria & Albert Theatre and Performance Archives (V&A), Blythe House, Theatre and Performance Biographical Files: BIOG LA RUE BOX 199, *Daily Mirror*, Ronald Ricketts, "Danny Is Students' New 'Leader,'" 6 March 1971.

8. Laurence Senelick, *The Changing Room: Sex, Drag and Theatre* (London: Routledge, 2000), 247–48.

9. Roger Baker, *Drag: A History of Female Impersonation in the Performing Arts* (London: Cassell, 1994), 206.

10. Peter Underwood, *Danny La Rue: Life's a Drag!* (London: W.H. Allen, 1975), 19. See also La Rue, *From Drags to Riches*, 115–17. La Rue's conservatism was revealed in part by the validation he sought from establishment elites like royalty, many of whom visited his club. These included Princess Margaret, Princess Anne, Grace Kelly, and Prince Rainier. The husband of Princess Margaret, society photographer Lord Snowdon, photographed La Rue for *Vogue*.

11. See, for example, M&M, Danny La Rue, *Telegraph Magazine*, Martin, "Super Trouper," 4 January 1997.

12. Jeffrey Weeks, *Sex, Politics and Society: The Regulation of Sexuality since 1800* (New York: Longman Group, 1981), 249–52.

13. Frank Mort, *Capital Affairs: London and the Making of the Permissive Society* (London: Yale University Press, 2010), 4.

14. See the introduction in Marcus Collins, ed., *The Permissive Society and Its Enemies: Sixties British Culture* (London: Rivers Oram Press, 2007), esp. 15–25.

15. National Opinion Polls quoted in Sam Brewitt-Taylor, "Christianity and the Invention of the Sexual Revolution in Britain, 1963–1967," *Historical Journal* 60:2 (2017): 520.

16. For more on Whitehouse and her association, see Dominic Sandbrook, *White Heat: A History of Britain in the Swinging Sixties* (London: Abacus, 2007), 578–81.

17. Alison Light, *Forever England: Femininity, Literature and Conservatism between the Wars* (London: Routledge, 1991), 10.

18. Light, *Forever England*, 11.

19. E. H. H. Green, *Ideologies of Conservatism: Conservative Political Ideas in the Twentieth Century* (Oxford: Oxford University Press, 2002), 171, 173, 187.

20. Green, *Ideologies of Conservatism*, 171, 157–91.

21. Amy C. Whipple, "Speaking for Whom? The 1971 Festival of Light and the Search for the 'Silent Majority,'" *Contemporary British History* 24:3 (2010): 319–39, esp. 333–35.

22. On "Janus-faced" conservatism, see Light, *Forever England*, 10.

23. Danny La Rue's closed for good in March 1972 after the building was sold to a property developer. La Rue, who prided himself on being a workaholic, appeared at his club for almost every performance, even when he was doing other evening shows in the West End or further afield. See La Rue, *From Drags to Riches*, 134–37; M&M, Danny La Rue, P.H., *Stage and Television Today*, "Danny: The 'Drag Act' Who Became London's 'King of Clubs'—Now Abdicating (Temporarily) after a Reign of 8 Years," 23 March 1972.

24. La Rue, *From Drags to Riches*, 117.

25. See, for example, *Advocate*, Marti Gould Cummings, "Why Drag Queens Will Lead the Revolution," 13 August 2019; *Ebony*, Tracey Ross, "The King of Queens: Why RuPaul Matters," 28 January 2013; *Guardian*, Isabelle Kliger, "'For Queer Individuals, This Is Life or Death': The Drag Race Stars Getting Political," 28 October 2020; *Guardian*, Rebecca Nicholson, "'Drag Was Always a Protest, a Political Statement': RuPaul's Drag Race UK Finalists Open Up," 13 March 2021; *Yahoo! News*, Leigh Nordstrom, "'Drag Has Always Been a Form of Activism and Protest': Shangela Gets to Work," 15 June 2020.

26. For example, see Mark Edward and Stephen Farrier, eds., *Contemporary Drag Practices and Performers: Drag in a Changing Scene, Volume 1* (London: Bloomsbury, 2020). The *Journal of Homosexuality*'s special double issue on drag studies contains numerous examples of this trend. For instance, see Richard

Niles, "Wigs, Laughter, and Subversion: Charles Busch and Strategies of Drag Performance," *Journal of Homosexuality* 46:3–4 (2004): 35–53; Steven P. Schacht, "Beyond the Boundaries of the Classroom: Teaching about Gender and Sexuality at a Drag Show," *Journal of Homosexuality* 46:3–4 (2004): 225–40.

27. For example, see Judith Butler, "Imitation and Gender Insubordination," in *Inside/Out: Lesbian Theories, Gay Theories*, ed. Diana Fuss (London: Routledge, 1991), 13–31, esp. 21, 27–28; Simon Doonan, *Drag: The Complete Story* (London: Laurence King Publishing, 2020). The drag performer RuPaul Charles has argued that seemingly innocuous cross-dressing is somehow political, stating, "I've no patience for politics, but everytime [*sic*] I bat my false eyelashes, I'm making a political statement." See Twitter, RuPaul Charles, https://twitter.com/RuPaul /status/383017405045571584, 26 September 2013 (accessed 14 October 2021).

28. For more on reactionary drag, see Mark Edward and Stephen Farrier, eds., "Drag: Applying Foundation and Setting the Scene," in *Contemporary Drag Practices and Performers: Drag in a Changing Scene, Volume* 1, 5; Carole-Anne Tyler, "Boys Will Be Girls: The Politics of Gay Drag," in *Inside/Out*, 32–70; Mary Kirk, "Kind of a Drag: Gender, Race, and Ambivalence in *The Birdcage* and *To Wong Foo, Thanks for Everything! Julie Newmar*," *Journal of Homosexuality* 46:3–4 (2004): 169–80; Benny LeMaster, "Discontents of Being and Becoming Fabulous on *RuPaul's Drag U*: Queer Criticism in Neoliberal Times," *Women's Studies in Communication* 38:2 (2015): 167–86.

29. M&M, Danny La Rue, *Times*, Michael Billington, "Evening with Danny La Rue," 23 December 1968.

30. M&M, Danny La Rue, *Daily Express*, Herbert Kretzmer, "Close to the Panto Tradition," 23 December 1968.

31. V&A, Theatre and Performance Miscellaneous Files: Drag Artistes, *Cosmopolitan*, Nicholas de Jongh, "Women in Drag: Not a Fetish but a Turn On," April 1974.

32. For some examples, see *Independent*, "Danny La Rue: Female Impersonator Who Turned Drag into an Art Form," 1 June 2009; *Telegraph*, "Danny La Rue," 1 June 2009. There was controversy that some outlets such as the *New York Times* neglected to mention La Rue's long-term relationship with his manager, Jack Hanson, in their obituaries. Hanson died in 1984. See *Atlantic*, The Daily Dish, "The American Press and the Closet," 9 June 2009.

33. Quoted in M&M, Danny La Rue, *Independent Magazine*, David Usborne, "Danny La Rue," n.d.; M&M, Danny La Rue, *Guardian*, Catherine Stott, "Queen Passionella," 11 December 1968; M&M, Danny La Rue, *Sunday Express Magazine*, Tattler, "Out to Lunch: Danny La Rue," 13 December 1987; La Rue, *From Drags to*

Riches, 107 M&M, Danny La Rue, *Sunday Times*, John Carey, "The Man Who Took Sex Out of Glamour," 25 October 1987. La Rue's laments sometimes contradicted his own lifestyle. For example, despite his insistence that "my performance is never camp and I'm not a camp person's performer," he was good friends with famously camp pianist Liberace, whom La Rue consulted when designing the interior of his club. La Rue continued to deride gay culture even after he publicly acknowledged his longtime relationship with his manager Jack Hanson after Hanson's death in 1984. In one interview the entertainer described drag in gay venues as "dreadful" and said of the typical gay bar and club attendees, "I feel uncomfortable, because I think they all look like clones. They all have moustaches and I can't stand that." Still, he sometimes appeared at gay venues, almost always in menswear, for charity events. See M&M, Danny La Rue, *Independent Magazine*, Usborne, "Danny La Rue," n.d.; M&M, Danny La Rue, *Guardian*, Stott, "Queen Passionella," 11 December 1968.

34. M&M, Danny La Rue, *Sunday Times*, Carey, "The Man Who Took Sex Out of Glamour," 25 October 1987.

35. Dialogue transcribed from the 1972 recording of *Danny La Rue at the Palace*. The televised version of the show was the most-watched ITV program of the week it aired. See *Danny La Rue at the Palace* (dir. Steve Minchin, Thames Television, 1972); La Rue, *From Drags to Riches*, 160.

36. *Danny La Rue at the Palace*.

37. In reality, Powell voted in favor of the 1967 act. He also voted in favor of earlier attempts at homosexual law reform. See Alkarim Jivani, *It's Not Unusual: A History of Lesbian and Gay Britain in the Twentieth Century* (London: Michael O'Mara Books, 1997), 146; *Telegraph*, "There's Nowt So Queer as Folk," 21 December 1996.

38. La Rue poked fun at other doctrinaire conservatives such as Mary Whitehouse. One such gag involved La Rue playing *Gone with the Wind* (1939) character Scarlett O'Hara, declaring, "I'm part of the South. I can't tell you which part—Mary Whitehouse might be a-watchin'." See *Danny La Rue: The Ladies I Love* (dir. David Bell, London Weekend Television, 1974).

39. *Danny La Rue at the Palace*.

40. *Danny La Rue at the Palace*.

41. La Rue, *From Drags to Riches*, 33.

42. La Rue, *From Drags to Riches*, 108.

43. La Rue, *From Drags to Riches*, 34 (punctuation from the original). Though La Rue's reminiscences are romanticized, it is true that Soho went from having a mixed residential and commercial ambience to being a mostly commercial district by the 1950s. See Mort, *Capital Affairs*, 241.

44. Daniel Farson, *Soho in the Fifties* (London: Michael Joseph, 1988), 164.

45. Quoted in Farson, *Soho in the Fifties*, 164.

46. M&M, Danny La Rue, *Daily Express*, Kretzmer, "Close to the Panto Tradition," 23 December 1968.

47. British Library Manuscript Collections (BL MC), Lord Chamberlain's Plays Correspondence files (LCP Corr) 1966/766, *Come Spy with Me* by Bryan Blackburn, Reader's Report, 16 April 1966. The Lord Chamberlain's Office received a complaint from one member of the public about "Danny La Rue's actions" in *Come Spy with Me* but the Office brushed off the complainant's concerns. "No action on this—the evidence is far too slender to bother the theatre," decreed an Office memo. See BL MC, LCP Corr 1966/766, *Come Spy with Me*, Note to John Johnston from JK, 11 August 1966; BL MC, LCP Corr 1966/766, *Come Spy with Me*, Internal Lord Chamberlain's Office memo, 18 August 1966.

48. M&M, Danny La Rue, *Daily Mail*, Peter Lewis, "Not in Front of the Children, Danny," 23 December 1968.

49. M&M, Danny La Rue, *Financial Times*, B. A. Young, "Queen Passionella," 23 December 1968.

50. M&M, Danny La Rue, *Times*, Billington, "Evening with Danny La Rue," 23 December 1968. La Rue's performances regularly incorporated Jewish humor, perhaps to a surprising degree given that he was Irish Catholic. For instance, La Rue's parody of the 1875 opera *Carmen*, performed at his club, features a character named Lolita Goldberg (a.k.a. "The mixer for the shiksas," "The Jimmy Young of Golders Green") who is the source of much Jewish-related humor. See British Library Sound Archive (BL SA), 1LP0075093, *Danny La Rue in London*, recorded 1969. For more on pantomime and family audiences, see chapter 1.

51. V&A, BIOG LA RUE, *Evening Standard*, Sydney Edwards, "Cheeky Chappy in a Frock," 13 December 1968.

52. Underwood, *Danny La Rue*, 135. The *Oxford English Dictionary* defines "wotcher" as an "alteration of *what cheer?*," meaning "how do you feel?" or "how are you?" See "Wotcher, int.," *OED Online* (Oxford: Oxford University Press, September 2021), www.oed.com/view/Entry/230410?redirectedFrom=wotcher (accessed 12 October 2021).

53. Quoted in V&A, BIOG LA RUE, *Evening Standard*, Yvonne Thomas, "Aah, the Joy of Taking Off My Girdle and Eating Mum's Irish Stews," 11 February 1970.

54. Underwood, *Danny La Rue*, 20.

55. *New York Times*, Clive Barnes, "Is It a Male or Female? Danny La Rue Winning New Fans in London," 31 August 1970.

56. Quoted in Underwood, *Danny La Rue*, 75.

57. "Talk of drag and female impersonators anywhere in the British Isles," wrote biographer Peter Underwood in 1974, "and within a moment the name of Danny La Rue is mentioned, a distinction that applies to very few other entertainers alive today." See Underwood, *Danny La Rue*, 10.

58. La Rue, *From Drags to Riches*, 229; quoted in Underwood, *Danny La Rue*, 125.

59. Underwood, *Danny La Rue*, 106. See also Senelick, *The Changing Room*, 250. In 1973 La Rue announced his intention to retire from drag in favor of legitimate theater, declaring, "I'm hanging my tits up." When the planned retirement was reversed in 1975, it was proclaimed that "he is keeping his boobs in business," all synecdochically making a distinction between actor and theatrical construction. See M&M, Danny La Rue, uncredited newspaper clipping, James Green, "Danny La Rue Burns His Bra," 19 November 1973; V&A, BIOG LA RUE, *Evening Standard*, Michael Owen, "Danny La Rue to Carry on After All," 24 February 1975; V&A, BIOG LA RUE, *Telegraph*, "Drag," 20 November 1973.

60. *Our Miss Fred* (dir. Bob Kellett, Willis World Wide Productions, 1972).

61. M&M, Danny La Rue, uncredited newspaper clipping, David Wigg, "Lovely Rita . . . Lauren . . . Marlene, or is it Danny?," n.d.

62. See V&A, BIOG LA RUE, program for *Danny La Rue at the Palace*, 1970; La Rue, *From Drags to Riches*, 156. A 1973 article claimed that La Rue "has hundreds of gowns worth between £1,000 and £2,500 each. His wigs are worth up to £150." Conceivably, this could have made La Rue's wardrobe worth $1 million in the early 1970s, but this is not a certainty. See V&A, BIOG LA RUE, *Telegraph*, "Drag," 20 November 1973.

63. La Rue released a whole album featuring his renditions of music hall standards. See BL SA, 1LP0102835, Danny La Rue, *Music Hall*, 1970.

64. The show, in which even the audience attending the episode tapings wore period costumes, was noted for its sedate, family-friendly depiction of the music hall, which took liberties with historical accuracy. It was the longest-running television program in the world when it ended in 1983. See *BFI ScreenOnline*, David Sharp, "Good Old Days, The (1953–83)," www.screenonline.org.uk/tv/id/788925 /index.html, n.d. (accessed 14 October 2021).

65. Tracy Hargreaves, "'There's No Place Like Home': History and Tradition in *The Forsyte Saga* and the BBC," *Journal of British Cinema and Television* 6:1 (2009): 22. As the BBC1 re-airings took place on Sunday evenings, church and pub opening hours were altered to suit the series' programming schedule. Media scholar Iris Kleinecke has observed that *The Forsyte Saga*, and period dramas in general, have appealed to women audiences in particular. The same was true of

La Rue's act. See Iris Kleinecke, "Representations of the Victorian Age: Interior Spaces and the Detail of Domestic Life in Two Adaptations of Galsworthy's *The Forsyte Saga*," *Screen* 47:2 (2006): 160.

66. Hargreaves, "There's No Place Like Home," 21–40.

67. Hargreaves, "There's No Place Like Home," 25.

68. Hargreaves, "There's No Place Like Home," 28.

69. Kleinecke, "Representations of the Victorian Age," 145; Hargreaves, "There's No Place Like Home," 36.

70. Raphael Samuel quoted in Hargreaves, "There's No Place Like Home," 28, 35–36.

71. Daniel O'Brien, "A Vintage Year for Scoundrels: Shapes of Villainy in *Adam Adamant Lives!*," *Intensities: The Journal of Cult Media* 6 (2013): 76. Cultural scholar Peter Wright, who has also analyzed *Adam Adamant Lives!*, has observed a similarly ambivalent attitude toward the permissive society in the television program *The Prisoner* (1967–68). "At times, it seems to subscribe to the decade's antiestablishment, libertarian ethos," Wright has argued. "On other occasions [creator and star Patrick] McGoohan's political conservatism underpins an attack on such values and their representatives." See Peter Wright, "British Television Science Fiction," in *A Companion to Science Fiction*, ed. David Seed (Oxford: John Wiley & Sons, 2008), 294; see also 289–305.

72. O'Brien, "A Vintage Year for Scoundrels," 57–79; James Chapman, *Saints and Avengers: British Adventure Series of the 1960s* (London: I. B. Tauris, 2002), 148.

73. O'Brien, "A Vintage Year for Scoundrels," 70–71; Chapman, *Saints and Avengers*, 150–51.

74. O'Brien, "A Vintage Year for Scoundrels," esp. 62, 77. Viewing figures for *Adam Adamant Lives!* were good, but the program was canceled after two series. Cultural historian James Chapman has speculated that the show was canceled due to "hostility" and bemusement toward it within the BBC. See Chapman, *Saints and Avengers*, 154.

75. Show writer Brian Clemens recalled that the BBC of the 1960s was primarily focused on providing edifying television content and was thus uncomfortable with escapist entertainment. *The Cult of . . . "Adam Adamant Lives!"* (dir. Agnus McIntyre, BBC Four, 2006).

76. Mr. Boydell quoted in Sandbrook, *White Heat*, 446–47.

77. Miss D. Wilson quoted in Hargreaves, "There's No Place Like Home," 37.

78. Mort, *Capital Affairs*, 266.

79. Quoted in V&A, BIOG LA RUE, *Evening Standard*, Thomas, "Aah, the Joy," 11 February 1970. See also La Rue, *From Drags to Riches*, 187.

80. Collins, ed., *The Permissive Society and Its Enemies*, 20.

81. Collins, ed., *The Permissive Society and Its Enemies*, 20.

82. Matt Houlbrook, "Daring to Speak Whose Name? Queer Cultural Politics, 1920–1967," in *The Permissive Society and its Enemies*, ed. Marcus Collins, 56.

83. See Eric Lindsay, "The Casino de Paris Striptease Theatre Club Story," https://ericlindsay.wordpress.com/the-casino-de-paris-striptease-theatre-club/, n.d. (accessed 3 January 2023); M&M, Drag: MM/REF/TH/SU/SP/2, *Sun*, Henry Fielding, "How I Wouldn't Spend a Spare £50,000," 23 November 1966; M&M, Drag, *This Is London*, 9 December 1966; M&M, Drag, uncredited newspaper clipping, "Two-Way Portrait," 1966; *Pathé News*, "Quick Change Artist," 20 April 1967; Paul Willetts, *The Look of Love: The Life and Times of Paul Raymond, Soho's King of Clubs* (London: Serpent's Tail, 2013), 105, 175, 227–28. Ricky Renée's club was located at 24/26 Russell Street. The club was previously meant to be fronted by another female impersonator, Sonne Teal, who died in a plane crash before the venue opened. Other notable British glamour drag acts of the 1960s included Manchester-based Bunny Lewis and "Mr. Rhyl" Johnny Dallas. See *A Couple of Beauties* (dir. Francis Searle, Bayford Films, 1972); Bill Ellis, *Entertainment in Rhyl and North Wales* (Chalford: Chalford Publishing Company, 1997), 49; *What's a Girl Like You . . .* (dir. Charlie Squires, London Weekend Television, 1969). There is a good deal of archival material relating to Lewis housed at the Bishopsgate Institute, London.

84. *Goodbye Gemini* (dir. Alan Gibson, Inc. Cinerama, 1970). See also *What's a Girl Like You . . . .*

85. *New York Times*, Barnes, "Is It a Male or Female?," 31 August 1970.

86. Drag beauty pageants were taking place in similarly conspicuous locations in Britain in the late 1960s and 1970s. For example, the Porchester Hall in West London, the Theatre Royal Stratford, and the Hilton Hotel on Park Lane (which hosted the Miss Female Impersonator [International] competition) all hosted such events.

87. *New York Times*, Renata Adler, "Screen: 'Queen' of Drag is Crowned: Documentary Depicts a Camp Beauty Contest," 18 June 1968.

88. During the 1940s through the 1960s, many American cities boasted glamorous drag revue clubs that catered to a mainstream clientele. Such venues included Wonder Club in New Orleans, the Jewel Box Lounge in Kansas City, Missouri, and Glade Show Lounge in Honolulu.

89. Senelick, *The Changing Room*, 389–91. Le Carrousel also attracted an international cohort of performers, such as British model April Ashley and Canadian drag artist Sonne Teal. American female impersonator Ricky Renée, whom

Teal had worked with at Club 82, was performing in German clubs such as Cabaret "Pointe" in Hamburg when he inherited the role of emcee of Teal's as-of-yet-unopened Covent Garden nightclub after Teal died in a plane crash in 1966. This anecdote provides a glimpse into how globally interconnected the drag scene was in the mid-twentieth century. See Lindsay, "The Casino de Paris Striptease Theatre Club Story," https://ericlindsay.wordpress.com/the-casino-de-paris-striptease-theatre-club/, n.d. (accessed 3 January 2023).

90. Though *Funeral Parade of Roses* tries to sensationalize transvestites and other members of the demimonde—certainly more so than *The Queen*, for instance—the characters are still palatable for straight audiences. "The film shows us an underworld of male prostitutes, pimps and drug pushers that looks comfortably middle-class, not much more desperate than Saturday at a country club," one critic observed. See *New York Times*, Vincent Canby, "The Screen: Oedipus Myth is Theme of 'Parade of Roses,'" 8 June 1973.

91. When Madame Jojo, a.k.a. John Wright, left Madame Jojo's club in 1991, Paul Raymond obtained an injunction to prevent him from using the stage name "Madame Jojo," forcing Wright to perform as merely "Jojo." Jojo's act was described, in similar terms to La Rue's, as "the sort of show you could take your grandmother to." For a time Madame Jojo's had a policy whereby only the performers were allowed to be in drag. See V&A, DRAG ARTISTES, *Daily Telegraph*, Kim Fletcher, "Dame Fights to Keep His Good Name," 14 August 1991; V&A, DRAG ARTISTES, uncredited newspaper clipping, "Sequins Are a Boy's Best Friend," Imogen Edwards-Jones, n.d.; Senelick, *The Changing Room*, 399–402.

92. See Senelick, *The Changing Room*, 409–43.

93. Quoted in V&A, DRAG ARTISTES, *Evening Standard Magazine*, Imogen Edwards-Jones, "A Life in the Style of Winston," January 1992.

94. Quoted in V&A, DRAG ARTISTES, *Evening Standard Magazine*, Edwards-Jones, "A Life in the Style of Winston," January 1992. Austin can be seen in *The Gender Bender* (dir. Laurens C. Postma, YoYo Productions, 1992).

95. Marc Singer, *Grant Morrison: Combining the Worlds of Contemporary Comics* (Jackson: University Press of Mississippi, 2012), 78.

Chapter 4

1. John Johnston, *The Lord Chamberlain's Blue Pencil* (London: Hodder and Stoughton, 1990), 245–46.

2. Annotations in blue pencil have long been associated with various forms of censorship and were in use by the Lord Chamberlain's Office since at least the

early twentieth century in order to annotate playscripts. See Johnston, *The Lord Chamberlain's Blue Pencil*, 16–17.

3. Johnston, *The Lord Chamberlain's Blue Pencil*, 23–31, 237–46. The Lord Chamberlain's authority did not extend to the Republic of Ireland or post-partition Northern Ireland. Brad Kent, "Shaw, *The Bell*, and Irish Censorship in 1945," *SHAW: The Journal of Bernard Shaw Studies* 30 (2010): 161. See also Joan Fitz-Patrick Dean, *Riot and Great Anger: Stage Censorship in Twentieth-Century Ireland* (Madison: University of Wisconsin Press, 2004), esp. 7, 11.

4. Johnston, *The Lord Chamberlain's Blue Pencil*, 255. In referring to the institution of the Lord Chamberlain's Office, I will also use the terms "the Office," "St James's Palace" (where the Office was based), and "the censor." "The Lord Chamberlain" will be used to refer to the position, as well as individual Lords Chamberlain. This is in line with other writings on the Lord Chamberlain's Office. For example, see Nicholas De Jongh, *Politics, Prudery and Perversions: The Censoring of the English Stage* 1901–1968 (London: Methuen 2000), ix–xvi.

5. Rebecca D'Monté, ed., *British Theatre and Performance* 1900–1950 (London: Bloomsbury, 2015), 244–45.

6. Lord Cobbold, the Lord Chamberlain when the 1968 act was passed, still hoped in vain that a formal system of theater censorship would remain in place, but he was in favor of removing the responsibility for theater censorship from his Office. David Thomas, David Carlton, and Anne Etienne, *Theatre Censorship: From Walpole to Wilson* (Oxford: Oxford University Press, 2007), 197.

7. Johnston, *The Lord Chamberlain's Blue Pencil*, 236.

8. Johnston, *The Lord Chamberlain's Blue Pencil*, 23–29; Thomas, Carlton, and Etienne, *Theatre Censorship*, 42–59. See also chapter 1 of this book.

9. Katherine Newey, "Theatre," in *The Cambridge Companion to Victorian Culture*, ed. Francis O'Gorman (Cambridge: Cambridge University Press, 2010), 123; Dave Russell, "Popular Entertainment, 1776–1895," in *The Cambridge History of British Theatre. Volume 2: 1660 to 1895*, ed. Joseph Donahue (Cambridge: Cambridge University Press, 2015), 379. Once a play was licensed it could be viewed by audiences of all ages. The idea of an "adults only" license was considered by the Lord Chamberlain, but the proposed reform was rejected by the Home Office in June 1957. See Johnston, *The Lord Chamberlain's Blue Pencil*, 156–60.

10. Johnston, *The Lord Chamberlain's Blue Pencil*, 23–29; De Jongh, *Politics, Prudery and Perversions*, ix–xi. Unlicensed scripts could still be published in book form and performed in private theaters.

11. On the difficulty for scholars in pinning down the censor's rules, see Steve Nicholson, *The Censorship of British Drama 1900–1968, Volume Two: 1933–1952* (Exeter: Exeter University Press, 2005), 3.

12. Sometimes the Lord Chamberlain's Office obliged the submitters of the script if they wanted to meet to discuss disagreements over a case. These meetings were granted out of courtesy at St James's Palace's discretion, however, and were not forums for launching an appeal.

13. Johnston, *The Lord Chamberlain's Blue Pencil*, 250–51.

14. For example, see De Jongh, *Politics, Prudery and Perversions*, xi; Johnston, *The Lord Chamberlain's Blue Pencil*, 249; Frank Mort, *Capital Affairs: London and the Making of the Permissive Society* (London: Yale University Press, 2010), 255.

15. Steve Nicholson, *The Censorship of British Drama 1900–1968, Volume Four: The Sixties* (Exeter: University of Exeter Press, 2015), 125.

16. Nicholson, *The Censorship of British Drama, Volume Four*, 125.

17. See British Library Manuscript Collections (BL MC), Lord Chamberlain's Plays Correspondence files (LCP Corr) 1946/6791, *Soldiers in Skirts* (revised) by Mannie Jay, Internal Lord Chamberlain's Office memo, 12 January 1946. See De Jongh, *Politics, Prudery and Perversions*, xi; Steve Nicholson, "Staging Hitler, Not Staging Hitler," in *British Theatre and Performance* 1900–1950, ed. Rebecca D'Monté, 223; Nicholson, *The Censorship of British Drama, Volume Two*, 9–54.

18. BL MC, LCP Corr 1940/3355, *Strip Ahoy* by Mannie Jay and Sydney Myers, Reader's Report, 9 March 1940.

19. See, for example, BL MC, LCP Corr 1947/7870, *Forces Showboat* by Ralph Marshall, Internal Lord Chamberlain's Office memo, 15 April 1947; BL MC, LCP Corr 1958/667, *We're No Ladies* by Phil Starr, Letter from H. C. R. A. Bennett to the Lord Chamberlain's Office, 6 January 1958.

20. See, for example, De Jongh, *Politics, Prudery and Perversions*; Richard Findlater, *Banned! A Review of Theatrical Censorship in Britain* (London: Panther, 1968); Johnston, *The Lord Chamberlain's Blue Pencil*; Dominic Shellard, Steve Nicholson, and Miriam Handley, *The Lord Chamberlain Regrets . . . A History of British Theatre Censorship* (London: British Library, 2004).

21. Johnston, *The Lord Chamberlain's Blue Pencil*, 278.

22. There was no explicit legal basis for the private theater loophole. See Steve Nicholson, *The Censorship of British Drama 1900–1968, Volume Three: The Fifties* (Exeter: University of Exeter Press, 2011), 78.

23. BL MC, LCP Corr 1939/2978, *Cosmopolitan Merry-Go-Round* by Joe Seymour, Program from the Chelsea Palace Theatre, 31 July 1939.

24. BL MC, LCP Corr 1939/2978, *Cosmopolitan Merry-Go-Round*, George Titman, "Chelsea Palace Theatre Revue 'Cosmopolitan Merry-Go-Round,'" 3 August 1939; BL MC, LCP Corr 1939/2978, *Cosmopolitan Merry-Go-Round*, Program from the Chelsea Palace Theatre, 31 July 1939. According to the Metropolitan Police file on the case, De Vere's "correct name" was Geoffrey Hawkins. He was "aged 29 years, height 5′6″ or 7″, pale complexion, black hair, slim build, clean shaven." See the National Archives of the UK (TNA), Public Record Office (PRO), Records of the Metropolitan Police (MEPO) 3/943: "Gerald De Vere: presenting and acting a revue scene before obtaining Lord Chamberlain's approval (1939)," Summons for Gerald De Vere, 16 September 1939. "Lovely to Look At" is a standard popularized by the film adaptation of the 1933 musical *Roberta*.

25. "Within the Lord Chamberlain's Office, Titman was known as the 'expert' on 'the question of the brassieres and trunks,'" historian Steve Nicholson has noted. Nicholson, *The Censorship of British Drama, Volume Two*, 228.

26. BL MC, LCP Corr 1939/2978, *Cosmopolitan Merry-Go-Round*, George Titman, "Chelsea Palace Theatre Revue 'Cosmopolitan Merry-Go-Round,'" 3 August 1939. The scene reportedly lasted "a matter of minutes." BL MC, LCP Corr 1939/2978, *Cosmopolitan Merry-Go-Round*, *Chelsea News and General Advertiser*, "Disrobing Act Onstage," 29 September 1939. This description makes the scene appear more earnestly sensuous than it probably was. A later description of De Vere's act describes the scene as a comic burlesque, with the female impersonator disrobing and "with gestures indicating feminine embarrassment . . . partially cover[ing] [his] breasts with the hair from the wig which he was wearing." BL MC, LCP Corr 1939/2978, *Cosmopolitan Merry-Go-Round*, "Re Gerald De Vere, Endsleigh Productions Ltd., Joe Seymour, and Adney Walter Gibbons," 22 September 1939.

27. BL MC, LCP Corr 1939/2978, *Cosmopolitan Merry-Go-Round*, George Titman, "Chelsea Palace Theatre Revue 'Cosmopolitan Merry-Go-Round,'" 3 August 1939.

28. TNA PRO MEPO 3/943, "Gerald De Vere."

29. BL MC, LCP Corr 1939/2978, *Cosmopolitan Merry-Go-Round*, "Re Gerald De Vere, Endsleigh Productions Ltd., Joe Seymour, and Adney Walter Gibbons," 22 September 1939.

30. BL MC, LCP Corr 1939/2978, *Cosmopolitan Merry-Go-Round*, "Re Gerald De Vere, Endsleigh Productions Ltd., Joe Seymour, and Adney Walter Gibbons," 22 September 1939.

31. Quoted in Johnston, *The Lord Chamberlain's Blue Pencil*, 127. The Lord Chamberlain would occasionally hint at policies on male nudity but offered few concrete details on the subject. One rare piece of information came via a response to a "Mr

Billy Kaye" who enquired as to whether kilts could be worn onstage without underpants. "Any performer appearing in a stage play without underpants would . . . have
to do so with the knowledge that he would be held absolutely responsible for any act
of exposure whether inadvertent or deliberate," responded the Lord Chamberlain's
Office. See Nicholson, *The Censorship of British Drama, Volume Three*, 7.

32. Quoted in Johnston, *The Lord Chamberlain's Blue Pencil*, 134.

33. Frank Mort, "Striptease: The Erotic Female Body and Live Sexual Entertainment in Mid-Twentieth-Century London," *Social History* 32:1 (2007): 31. In
one of the many clarifications the Lord Chamberlain's Office made regarding its
stance on nudity, it was noted that tableaux poses needed to represent preexisting works of visual art or be of "sufficient artistic merit." See Nicholson, *The Censorship of British Drama, Volume Two*, 219.

34. Judith R. Walkowitz, "The 'Vision of Salome': Cosmopolitanism and
Erotic Dancing in Central London, 1908–1918," *American Historical Review* 108:2
(2003): 348; Nicholson, *The Censorship of British Drama, Volume Two*, 213.

35. D'Monté, ed., *British Theatre*, 86.

36. BL MC, LCP Corr 1939/2978, *Cosmopolitan Merry-Go-Round, Chelsea
News and General Advertiser*, "Disrobing Act Onstage," 29 September 1939. When
asked during the court proceedings if "Mr. De Vere is an eccentric dancer,"
Titman (misnamed as "Titmuss" in the article) responded, "Yes." In this context,
"eccentric" could be read as a euphemism for a same-sex-desiring man, or the
word could connote an unconventional gender presentation, but the precise
meaning here is unclear.

37. BL MC, LCP Corr 1939/2978, *Cosmopolitan Merry-Go-Round*, Letter from
the D.P.P. to the Lord Chamberlain's Office, 22 September 1939.

38. BL MC, LCP Corr 1939/2978, *Cosmopolitan Merry-Go-Round, Chelsea
News and General Advertiser*, "Disrobing Act Onstage," 29 September 1939.

39. BL MC, LCP Corr 1939/2978, *Cosmopolitan Merry-Go-Round*, Letter from
the Lord Chamberlain's Office to the D.P.P., 23 September 1939.

40. TNA PRO MEPO 3/941, "Alleged indecent dance act and Bottle Parties
at 'Paradise' 189, Regent Street (1937)," Letter from Metropolitan Police to the
Lord Chamberlain's Office, 20 May 1937. For more on the Windmill theater, in-
cluding the Office's relationship with the Windmill and its manager, Vivian Van
Damm, see Mort, *Capital Affairs*, 243–80; Mort, "Striptease," 27–53; Nicholson,
The Censorship of British Drama, Volume Two, 213, 222, 224.

41. TNA PRO MEPO 3/941, "Alleged indecent dance act," Letter from the
Lord Chamberlain's Office to the Metropolitan Police, 21 May 1937. "The Coronation troubles" mentioned here likely refer to the abdication crisis.

42. *Daily Telegraph*, "Move to Check Undesirable Stage Shows," 25 June 1937.

43. TNA PRO MEPO 3/942, "Request for police co-operation in London Council proceedings against nude performance at Grand Theatre, Clapham (1938)," Internal Metropolitan Police memo, 30 September 1938.

44. De Jongh, *Politics, Prudery and Perversions*, 71–72.

45. BL MC, LCP Corr 1945/6276, *Soldiers in Skirts*, Reader's Report, 3 May 1945.

46. BL MC, LCP Corr 1945/6276, *Soldiers in Skirts*, Internal Lord Chamberlain's Office memo, 5 May 1945. Interestingly, an alternative title for the 1950 show *Cinderella Goes to Town*, featuring female impersonator double act Vic Ford and Chris Sheen, was *Boys Will Be Girls*. In this case the title was approved without disparaging comment from the Lord Chamberlain. See BL MC, LCP Corr 1950/1520, *Boys Will Be Girls* by Will Collins, Licensed 21 April 1950.

47. BL MC, LCP Corr 1945/6276, *Soldiers in Skirts*, Reader's Report, 3 May 1945.

48. The revues were often referred to contemporarily as "all-male shows," or some variation on that phrase. Overall, I have identified over a dozen individual revues staged between 1918 and 1954 as ex-servicemen's drag revues. For the veracity of the performers' status as former servicemen, see Paul Buckland, *Chorus of Witches* (Richmond, VA: Valancourt Books, 2021), 226; Kris Kirk and Ed Heath, *Men in Frocks* (London: GMP Publishers, 1984), 18. For more on the genesis of the post–Second World War ex-servicemen's drag revues, see chapter 2.

49. Danny La Rue, *From Drags to Riches: My Autobiography* (London: Viking, 1987), 71.

50. *Forces Showboat* was also known by the alternative titles *Get In* and *Get In for Laughter*. The success of the 1940s and 1950s ex-servicemen's drag revues, unlike those of Les Rouges, did not spill over into motion pictures in a significant way. A slight exception to this is the 1949 comedy *Skimpy in the Navy*. The film sees Ford and Sheen, who starred in multiple ex-servicemen's drag revues, playing secondary roles. Ford and Sheen spend most of the film out of feminine garb as Spud and Joe, two bumbling antagonists who attempt to steal a treasure map from lead Skimpy Carter (Hal Monty). The duo gets to perform some turns in women's clothes, however, including a memorable rendition by Ford of the song "Nobody Loves a Fairy When She's Forty," a fairly explicit reference to "gay" culture when performed by a female impersonator. See *Skimpy in the Navy* (dir. Stafford Dickens, Advance Films, 1949). "Nobody Loves a Fairy" was popularized by (female) Welsh singer Tessie O'Shea and written by Arthur Le Clerq.

51. *Independent*, Anthony Hayward, "Danny La Rue: Female Impersonator Who Turned Drag into an Art Form," 2 June 2009; Lisa Z. Sigel, "'Best Love': Fe-

male Impersonation in the Great War," *Sexualities* 19:1–2 (2016): 111; Kirk and Heath, *Men in Frocks*, 16.

52. Victoria & Albert Theatre and Performance Archives (V&A), Theatre and Performance Biographical Files: BIOG LA RUE BOX 199, *Evening Standard*, Sydney Edwards, "Cheeky Chappie in a Frock," 13 December 1968. Remarking on his wage while touring in the revues, Danny La Rue told the *Evening Standard*, "I'd never ever earned more than £20 a week and for most of the time in the early days I earned around £7 a week and starved." See also Kirk and Heath, *Men in Frocks*, 15, 28.

53. *Hull Daily Mail*, "Showboat 'Girls,' " 30 May 1950. Female impersonators in the revues later recalled that chorus members tended to grow their own hair long so that they only needed to attach small additional tufts of synthetic hair to their heads for each show rather than donning full wigs. This method was easier than maintaining a wig, especially as quality wigs were reportedly hard to come by in 1940s and 1950s Britain. The male casts' unconventional long hair attracted bemused stares offstage. Kirk and Heath, *Men in Frocks*, 13, 20.

54. *Western Morning News*, "Musical Comedy Revived," 26 July 1949; *Aberdeen Press and Journal*, "All-Male Revue at the Tivoli," 8 July 1947.

55. *Stage*, "Round the Halls from Our Own Correspondents," 10 July 1952.

56. BL MC, LCP Corr 1953/5876, *Call Us Mister* by John Buckley Management, Reader's Report, 7 October 1953.

57. See chapter 2 of this volume; De Jongh, *Politics, Prudery and Perversions*, 99; Nicholson, *The Censorship of British Drama, Volume Three*, 113.

58. BL MC, LCP Corr 1944/5385, *We Were in the Forces* by John D. Roberton, Report by Sergeant S. Jenkins to Chief Constable of Oldham Borough Police W. E. Schofield, 31 March 1944; BL MC, LCP Corr 1944/5385, *We Were in the Forces*, Report by D.S. 58 Stokes to Chief Constable of Blackpool H. Barnes, 21 April 1944.

59. BL MC, LCP Corr 1944/5385, *We Were in the Forces*, Report by P.S. 130 L. Clough to Chief Constable of Oldham Borough Police W. E. Schofield, 28 March 1944.

60. BL MC, LCP Corr 1944/5385, *We Were in the Forces*, Report by D.S. 58 Stokes to Chief Constable of Blackpool H. Barnes, 21 April 1944. The spelling, grammar, and punctuation are reproduced from the original document.

61. BL MC, LCP Corr 1944/5385, *We Were in the Forces*, Letter from Chief Constable of Oldham Borough Police W. E. Schofield to the Lord Chamberlain's Office, 6 April 1944.

62. BL MC, LCP Corr 1944/5385, *We Were in the Forces*, Internal Lord Chamberlain's Office memo, 11 April 1944.

63. BL MC, LCP Corr 1944/5696, *We Were in the Forces* (Revised) by John D. Roberton, Reader's Report, 21 July 1944.

64. LCP Corr 1947/7870, *Forces Showboat*, Report by P. C. W. Tinker of the Barnsley County Borough Police, 5 April 1949.

65. LCP Corr 1947/7870, *Forces Showboat*, Report by P. C. W. Tinker, 5 April 1949.

66. LCP Corr 1947/7870, *Forces Showboat*, Letter from P. C. W. Tinker to Chief Constable G. Parfitt of Barnsley County Borough Police, 8 April 1949.

67. LCP Corr 1947/7870, *Forces Showboat*, Letter from P. C. W. Tinker to Chief Constable G. Parfitt, 8 April 1949.

68. LCP Corr 1947/7870, *Forces Showboat*, Letter from the Lord Chamberlain's Office to the D.P.P., 11 April 1949.

69. LCP Corr 1947/7870, *Forces Showboat*, Letter from the D.P.P. to the Lord Chamberlain's Office, 13 April 1949.

70. BL MC, LCP Corr 1945/6276, *Soldiers in Skirts*, Report by Inspector R. Strong of the L.C.C., 6 December 1945.

71. Send-ups of Brazilian entertainer Carmen Miranda were a fixture of contemporary American and British drag acts, and she was arguably the most ubiquitously parodied figure among female impersonators during the 1940s and 1950s. Commenting on the frequency of Miranda impersonations among GIs, a *Theatre Arts* reporter wrote in 1944 that "cries of anguish can still be heard from harried Special Services officers who were tired of 'impersonations of Carmen Miranda.'" Quoted in Shari Roberts, "'The Lady in the Tutti-Frutti Hat': Carmen Miranda, a Spectacle of Ethnicity," *Cinema Journal* 32:3 (1993): 16.

72. BL MC, LCP Corr 1945/6276, *Soldiers in Skirts*, Report by Inspector R. Strong of the L.C.C., 6 December 1945.

73. BL MC, LCP Corr 1945/6276, *Soldiers in Skirts*, Report by Inspector R. Strong of the L.C.C., 6 December 1945.

74. BL MC, LCP Corr 1945/6276, *Soldiers in Skirts*, Letter from the Mannie Jay & Sydney Myers agency to the Lord Chamberlain's Office, 10 November 1945.

75. BL MC, LCP Corr 1945/6276, *Soldiers in Skirts*, Letter from the Lord Chamberlain's Office to the Mannie Jay & Sydney Myers agency, 13 December 1945.

76. BL MC, LCP Corr 1945/6276, *Soldiers in Skirts*, Letter from the L.C.C. Public Control Department to the Lord Chamberlain's Office, 18 December 1945.

77. BL MC, LCP Corr 1946/6791, *Soldiers in Skirts* (revised), Report on Chesterfield Magistrates' Court proceedings by H. C. Game, 14 March 1946.

78. BL MC, LCP Corr 1946/6791, *Soldiers in Skirts* (revised), Internal Lord Chamberlain's Office memo, 24 July 1946.

79. BL MC, LCP Corr 1945/6276, *Soldiers in Skirts*, Letter from the D.P.P. to the Lord Chamberlain's Office, 23 March 1946; BL MC, LCP Corr 1945/6276, *Soldiers in Skirts*, Letter from the Lord Chamberlain's Office to the D.P.P., 25 March 1946.

80. BL MC, LCP Corr 1945/6276, *Soldiers in Skirts*, Report by P.C. William Marsden of the Blackpool Police, 3 August 1946.

81. BL MC, LCP Corr 1946/6791, *Soldiers in Skirts* (revised), Report by Sergeant Slack of the City of Sheffield Police, 16 March 1952; BL MC, LCP Corr 1946/6791, *Soldiers in Skirts* (revised), Letter from the Lord Chamberlain's Office to the Chief Constable of the City of Sheffield Police, 27 March 1952.

82. BL MC, LCP Corr 1946/6791, *Soldiers in Skirts* (revised), Letter from the Chief Constable of the City of Sheffield Police to the Lord Chamberlain's Office, 2 April 1952. Another police officer judged "Fan Fayre" to be "not objectionable." See BL MC, LCP Corr 1945/6276, *Soldiers in Skirts*, Report by P.C. William Marsden, 3 August 1946.

83. BL MC, LCP Corr 1946/6791, *Soldiers in Skirts* (revised), Letter from the D.P.P. to the Lord Chamberlain's Office, 15 April 1952. St James's Palace rather pathetically sent the producers of *Soldiers in Skirts* a stern letter claiming that it was the Lord Chamberlain who had personally decided to not pursue legal action out of magnanimity. See BL MC, LCP Corr 1946/6791, *Soldiers in Skirts* (revised), Letter from the Lord Chamberlain's Office to JMZ Productions, 17 April 1952.

84. *Gloucestershire Echo*, "Lively Show by Soldiers in Skirts," 30 May 1950.

85. *Luton News and Bedfordshire Chronicle*, V.J.R., "Novelty Is the Keynote," 18 February 1954.

86. *Star*, "Soldiers 'Skirting' Borderline," 11 March 1952.

87. BL MC, LCP Corr 1945/6276, *Soldiers in Skirts*, Report by P.C. William Marsden, 3 August 1946.

88. See, for example, *Yorkshire Post and Leeds Intelligencer*, "Alhambra, Bradford," 22 September 1953.

89. *Stage*, "Round the Halls from Our Own Correspondents," 2 July 1953.

90. Quoted in Brian Lewis, *Wolfenden's Witnesses: Homosexuality in Postwar Britain* (Basingstoke: Palgrave Macmillan, 2016), 206. This quote was later forwarded to the Lord Chamberlain's Office by a Home Office official. See Nicholson, *The Censorship of British Drama, Volume Three*, 57. Here Wildeblood was likely attempting to distance discreet, professional-class homosexuals, such as himself, from gender-variant men.

91. BL MC, LCP Corr 1945/6276, *Soldiers in Skirts*, Letter from S. Oakes to the Lord Chamberlain's Office, 5 January 1947. The punctuation is reproduced from the original document.

92. Quoted in Nicholson, *The Censorship of British Drama, Volume Two*, 320–21.

93. BL MC, LCP Corr 1947/7870, *Forces Showboat*, Letter from George Richardson to the Lord Chamberlain's Office, 9 April 1947. The punctuation is reproduced from the original document. "Cornock disclosures" was probably a reference to the case of Ann Cornock of Henleaze, who in December 1946 was charged with the murder of her husband, Cecil Cornock. During Ann's trial it was disclosed that Cecil had a predilection for masochistic sex and transvestism. Reportedly he regularly had Ann tie him up and beat him with a cane while he wore women's clothing. In 1947 Ann was found not guilty of murdering her husband. See Nicola Sly, *Bristol Murders* (Stroud: History Press, 2008), 115–22; Linda Stratmann, *Gloucestershire Murders* (Stroud: Sutton, 2005), 139–49.

94. BL MC, LCP Corr 1945/6276, *Soldiers in Skirts*, Letter from the Mannie Jay & Sydney Myers agency to the Lord Chamberlain's Office, 15 April 1947.

95. BL MC, LCP Corr 1947/7870, *Forces Showboat*, Internal Lord Chamberlain's Office memo, 15 April 1947.

96. BL MC, LCP Corr 1947/7870, *Forces Showboat*, Internal Lord Chamberlain's Office memo, 15 April 1947. Game expressed some reservations about a performer uttering the line "no balls for you." "No double meaning may have been intended," remarked the senior examiner thoughtfully, "but it certainly has one and I wonder whether we ought not to ask the producer to remove it?"

97. The records of the Public Morality Council contain documents that provide insights into the PMC's views, as well as a collection of contemporary erotica. See London Metropolitan Archives: City of London (LMA), Records of the Public Morality Council (PMC), 1899–1967.

98. LMA, PMC. Of course the Public Morality Council usually could not see theatrical performances unless they had already been licensed by the censor, but they believed that registering complaints against already licensed shows could influence the censor's policies in the future. See Nicholson, *The Censorship of British Drama, Volume Two*, 55–56.

99. Lindsay Gordon quoted in Nicholson, *The Censorship of British Drama, Volume Two*, 63.

100. For an example of this attitude, see Nicholson, *The Censorship of British Drama, Volume Two*, 56–57.

101. Even negative assessments of ex-servicemen's drag revues in newspapers tended to be restrained. See *Sunderland Daily Echo and Shipping Gazette*, "A Waste of Nylons?," 17 June 1952; *Sunderland Daily Echo and Shipping Gazette*, Carvalho, "Taken to Task," 20 June 1952.

102. BL MC, LCP Corr License Refused (LR) 1964/1, *A Patriot for Me*, Letter from the Lord Chamberlain's Office to Miss Christine Smith of The English Stage Company Ltd., 11 September 1964. Osborne's 1959 play, *The World of Paul Slickey*, garnered much criticism due to its "sex changing theme." See Nicholson, *The Censorship of British Drama, Volume Three*, 203–13. For another 1960s-era play that the Lord Chamberlain's Office disapproved of, partially owing to its depiction of male cross-dressing, see Nicholson on *Beyond the Fringe* (1961) in Nicholson, *The Censorship of British Drama, Volume Four*, 43–44.

103. BL MC, LCP Corr LR 1964/1, *A Patriot for Me*, Reader's Report, 30 August 1964. Much of the British public would have been aware of the phenomenon of drag balls, due in part to press coverage of court cases involving police infiltration of such gatherings. For example, see Matt Houlbrook, "'Lady Austin's Camp Boys': Constituting the Queer Subject in 1930s London," *Gender & History* 14:1 (2002): 31–61.

104. John Osborne, *A Patriot for Me* (London: Faber & Faber, 1971). For the drag ball scene, see 71–91.

105. Osborne, *A Patriot for Me*, 73–74.

106. Osborne, *A Patriot for Me*, 72–74.

107. Nicholson, *The Censorship of British Drama, Volume Three*, 110. For some examples of the censor's inconsistent pre-1958 approach to homosexual themes on the stage, see pages 62–64 and 111–15.

108. Quoted in Johnston, *The Lord Chamberlain's Blue Pencil*, 171–72. Representations of female same-sex desire onstage were approached in a somewhat similar manner, but there were notable differences. See Helen Freshwater, "Suppressed Desire: Inscriptions of Lesbianism in the British Theatre of the 1930s," *New Theatre Quarterly* 17:4 (2001): 310–18.

109. Quoted in Johnston, *The Lord Chamberlain's Blue Pencil*, 172. The Lord Chamberlain ruled that all plays that had previously been unlicensed due to their homosexual content could be reviewed again within the framework of the new rules and no new reading fee would be charged for this process. This meant that readers had to review old plays for no pay. See Nicholson, *The Censorship of British Drama, Volume Three*, 136. For further examples of plays written in the 1950s involving male cross-dressing, see a discussion of *The Wicked and the Weak* (1954) in Nicholson, *The Censorship of British Drama, Volume Three*, 66; *A Resounding Tinkle* (1958) on page 170; *Aunt Edwina* (1959), which depicts "a Colonel in the Coldstream who becomes a woman," on pages 190–92; *A Girl Called Harry* (n.d.) on page 191; and *The World of Paul Slickey* (1959) on pages 203–13.

110. BL MC, LCP Corr LR 1964/1, *A Patriot for Me*, Internal Lord Chamberlain's Office memo, 11 May 1966 (emphasis added).

111. Quoted in Nicholson, *The Censorship of British Drama, Volume Three*, 136–37.

112. Quoted in Nicholson, *The Censorship of British Drama, Volume Three*, 135.

113. *Stage*, "Enlightenment," 13 November 1958. See also *Stage*, "Censorship Reform: Information Wanted for Further Action," 23 July 1959.

114. Quoted in *Stage*, R.B. Marriott, "Leading Personalities Welcome the Change in Censorship," 13 November 1958.

115. BL MC, LCP Corr LR 1964/1, *A Patriot for Me*, Letter from the Lord Chamberlain's Office to the Royal Court Theatre, 11 September 1964.

116. BL MC, LCP Corr LR 1964/1, *A Patriot for Me*, Internal Lord Chamberlain's Office memo, 11 May 1966.

117. BL MC, LCP Corr LR 1964/1, *A Patriot for Me*, Internal Lord Chamberlain's Office memo marked "Comptroller," ca. August 1966.

118. BL MC, LCP Corr LR 1964/1, *A Patriot for Me*, Internal Lord Chamberlain's Office memo from Senior Examiner C.D. Heriot to Comptroller Eric Penn, 14 August 1965.

119. BL MC, LCP Corr LR 1964/1, *A Patriot for Me*, Internal Lord Chamberlain's Office memo, 11 May 1966. See also Internal Lord Chamberlain's Office memo from Comptroller Eric Penn to the Lord Chamberlain, 13 August 1965. This memo notes that the play was attended by the Lord Chancellor and his wife on the night Penn attended.

120. See also Nicholson, *The Censorship of British Drama, Volume Three*, 57.

121. BL MC, LCP Corr LR 1964/1, *A Patriot for Me*, Internal Lord Chamberlain's Office memo, 11 May 1966.

122. BL MC, LCP Corr LR 1964/1, *A Patriot for Me*, Internal Lord Chamberlain's Office memo, 11 May 1966. The punctuation is reproduced from original document.

123. Quoted in H. Montgomery Hyde, *A History of Pornography* (London: Four Square Books, 1966), 18. The 1857 act was part of a contemporary global trend of state regulation of sexual material and knowledge. See Lisa Z. Sigel, "Looking at Sex: Pornography and Erotica since 1750," in *The Routledge History of Sex and the Body: 1500 to the Present*, ed. Sarah Toulalan and Kate Fisher (Oxon: Routledge, 2016), 229. Judge Cockburn lived a colorful professional and private life. He presided over many high-profile cases—"it was his great desire to have a page of *The Times* devoted to him every day," a colleague recalled—and he was known for his ostentatious demeanor. He never married but fathered two illegitimate children.

See Michael Lobban, "Cockburn, Sir Alexander James Edmund, twelfth baronet," *Oxford Dictionary of National Biography* (23 September 2004), https://doi .org/10.1093/ref:odnb/5765 (accessed 15 October 2021).

124. H.G. Cocks, "Saucy Stories: Pornography, Sexology and the Marketing of Sexual Knowledge in Britain, c. 1918–70," *Social History* 29:4 (2004): 467.

125. Philip Roberts, *The Royal Court Theatre and the Modern Stage* (Cambridge: Cambridge University Press, 1999), 103.

126. BL MC, LCP Corr LR 1964/1, *A Patriot for Me*, Report by John Johnston of the Lord Chamberlain's Office, 12 July 1965.

127. BL MC, LCP Corr LR 1964/1, *A Patriot for Me*, Internal Lord Chamberlain's Office memo, 12 July 1965.

128. BL MC, LCP Corr LR 1964/1, *A Patriot for Me*, Letter from the Attorney General's Office to the Lord Chamberlain's Office, 27 July 1965.

129. BL MC, LCP Corr LR 1964/1, *A Patriot for Me*, Internal Lord Chamberlain's Office memo marked "Asst Comptroller," n.d.; quoted in Nicholson, *The Censorship of British Drama, Volume Four*, 146.

130. Quoted in Nicholson, *The Censorship of British Drama, Volume Four*, 161.

131. BL MC, LCP Corr LR 1964/1, *A Patriot for Me*, *Sunday Times*, Howard Hobson, "The Casting Out of Lieutenant Redl," 4 July 1965.

132. BL MC, LCP Corr LR 1964/1, *A Patriot for Me*, *Western Mail (Cardiff)*, Graham Samuel, "Spies and Treachery in Old Vienna," 3 July 1965.

133. BL MC, LCP Corr LR 1964/1, *A Patriot for Me*, *Tribune*, Melvyn Jones, "An Open Letter to the Lord Chamberlain," 9 July 1965.

134. Quoted in Johnston, *The Lord Chamberlain's Blue Pencil*, 207–8.

135. BL MC, LCP Corr LR 1964/1, *A Patriot for Me*, Letter from Anthony Page to the Lord Chamberlain's Office, 10 August 1966, *Times Educational Supplement*, "The London Theatre: Masterpieces to Come," 6 August 1965.

136. See De Jongh, *Politics, Prudery and Perversions*, 198–99; Johnston, *The Lord Chamberlain's Blue Pencil*, 160; Nicholson, *The Censorship of British Drama, Volume Four*, 2.

137. For more on the 1968 act and an earlier attempt to amend theater censorship laws proposed by MP Dingle Foot, see Johnston, *The Lord Chamberlain's Blue Pencil*, 187, 225, 242, 252; Nicholson, *The Censorship of British Drama, Volume Four*, 64–65. Resistance to the abolition of censorship came from a few quarters, including the Society of West End Theatre Managers and the Association of Municipal Corporations. Outspoken traditionalists, such as the chairman of the Marylebone Young Conservatives, also voiced concerns. *Marylebone Mercury*,

"Young Tories Say 'No' to Censorship," 20 March 1970; *Marylebone Mercury*, "'Oh! Calcutta! Rubbish'—by Tory Who Hasn't Seen Show," 23 October 1970.

138. Mort, *Capital Affairs*, 141, 393n11.

139. This narrative was reflected in contemporary press reports on the shows. See *New York Times*, Anthony Lewis, "Londoners Cool to 'Hair's' Nudity: Four-Letter Words Shock Few at Musical's Debut," 29 September 1968; *Stage*, R.B. Marriott, "After the Censor: 'Hair,' Love-Rock Musical Opens Gloriously to Cheers and Boos and Makes History," 3 October 1968; *Daily Mirror*, Margaret Hall, "Stage Is Set for the Nude Bonanza," 12 June 1968; *Daily Mirror*, "Oh! Calcutta! Muck—or Freedom?," 29 July 1970.

Epilogue

Epigraph: Quoted in *Time Out London*, Rupert Smith, "Bette Bourne: Interview," 27 May 2008.

1. Alkarim Jivani, "It's Not Unusual: Gay and Lesbian History in Britain," in *Global Feminisms since 1945*, ed. Bonnie G. Smith (London: Routledge, 2000), 176. For more on radical drag actions, see Shaun Cole, "Gay Liberation Front and Radical Drag," *QED: A Journal in GLBTQ Worldmaking* 4:3 (2017): 165–69.

2. Michael James quoted in Alkarim Jivani, *It's Not Unusual: A History of Lesbian and Gay Britain in the Twentieth Century* (London: Michael O'Mara Books, 1997), 165.

3. Jivani, "It's Not Unusual," 178. A detailed account of these fissures can be found in Libcom.org, Stuart Feather, "A Brief History of the Gay Liberation Front," 21 November 2007.

4. Stuart Feather quoted in Lavinia Co-op, Crystal, and Stuart Feather, "Drag: Power & Politics," panel discussion, Newington Green Meeting House, London, 25 October 2021; Jivani, "It's Not Unusual," 174.

5. Jivani, "It's Not Unusual," 174; *Time Out London*, Smith, "Bette Bourne: Interview," 27 May 2008.

6. See, for example, Chris D'Bray, "Camp and Drag in the Mainstream: A Critical Study of the Phenomenon of Drag Performance in the Northern British Fun Pubs, 1973–1993," in *Drag Histories, Herstories & Hairstories: Drag in a Changing Scene, Volume 2*, ed. Mark Edward and Stephen Farrier (London: Bloomsbury, 2021), 29–40.

7. Esther Newton, *Mother Camp: Female Impersonators in America* (Chicago: University of Chicago Press, 1979), xi.

8. Newton, *Mother Camp*, 3. Newton briefly entertains the notion of straight drag artists on pages 6–7.

9. Peter Ackroyd, *Dressing Up: Transvestism and Drag: The History of an Obsession* (London: Thames and Hudson, 1979), 14. This definition is not consistent throughout Ackroyd's book. See, for example, pages 107 and 130.

10. See, for example, *Journal of Homosexuality* 46:3–4 (2004).

11. Further, some straight audiences saw drag performance as a way to engage with the subculture of gender-variant and same-sex desiring men. See the introduction to this book.

12. See, for example, Neil McKenna, *Fanny & Stella: The Young Men Who Shocked Victorian England* (London: Faber and Faber, 2013); Charles Upchurch, "Forgetting the Unthinkable: Cross-Dressers and British Society in the Case of the Queen vs. Boulton and Others," *Gender & History* 12:1 (2000): 127–57.

13. See, for example, Kris Kirk and Ed Heath, *Men in Frocks* (London: GMP Publishers, 1984), 15–16.

14. Kirk and Heath, *Men in Frocks*, 16, 20, 24.

15. See Paul Buckland, *Chorus of Witches* (Richmond, VA: Valancourt Books, 2021). Biographical details on Buckland are scant.

16. *Herald* (Scotland), "Tantrums and Tiaras," 21 July 2001; Mander & Mitchenson Theatre Collection, University of Bristol (M&M), Danny La Rue: MM/REF/PE/VA/141, *Independent Magazine*, David Usborne, "Danny La Rue," n.d. The reason the Church initially refused La Rue's request for Hanson to be buried in the plot appears to be because Hanson was not Catholic, not because Hanson and La Rue were a same-sex couple.

17. Ackroyd, *Dressing Up*, 14; *Guardian*, Rebecca Nicholson, "'Drag Was Always a Protest, a Political Statement': RuPaul's Drag Race UK Finalists Open Up," 13 March 2021; *Yahoo! News*, Leigh Nordstrom, "'Drag Has Always Been a Form of Activism and Protest': Shangela Gets to Work," 15 June 2020.

Bibliography

Archival Collections

British Film Institute National Archives, BFI Reuben Library, London
British Film Institute National Archives, BFI Stephen Street, London
British Library Manuscript Collections, London
British Library, Newsroom, London
British Library Sound Archive, Rare Books & Music Collections, London
London Metropolitan Archives: City of London, Clerkenwell
Mander & Mitchenson Collection, University of Bristol Theatre Collection, Bristol
National Archives of the UK, Records of the Metropolitan Police Office, Kew
New York Public Library for the Performing Arts, Billy Rose Theatre Division, New York City
ONE National Gay & Lesbian Archives, University of Southern California Libraries, Los Angeles
University of East Anglia Archives and Special Collections, Norwich
Victoria & Albert Theatre and Performance Archives, Blythe House, London

Published Sources

Newspapers, Magazines, Periodicals, and Other News Sources

Advocate
Atlantic
Axios
Bath Chronicle and Weekly Gazette

Belfast News-Letter

Berkeley Beacon

Bioscope

Bournemouth Graphic

Brighton Standard

British Pathé

BuzzFeed

Call Boy

CBC Radio

Chelsea News and General Advertiser

Cosmopolitan (United Kingdom)

Daily Express (United Kingdom)

Daily Film Renter (United Kingdom)

Daily Herald (United Kingdom)

Daily Mail (United Kingdom)

Daily Mirror (United Kingdom)

Daily News (United Kingdom)

Daily Telegraph (United Kingdom)

Dare

Derby Daily Telegraph

Derby Evening Telegraph

Dundee Courier

Dundee Evening Telegraph

Ebony

Eastern Daily Press

Empire News (United Kingdom)

Era (United Kingdom)

Evening Standard (United Kingdom)

Financial Times (United Kingdom)

Gay & Lesbian Review Worldwide

Globe and Mail (Canada)

Gloucestershire Echo

Grantham Journal

Guardian (United Kingdom)

Guardian (United States)

Hastings and St Leonards Observer

Hull Daily Mail

Hull Times

Independent (United Kingdom)

Irish Times

Kinematograph Weekly

Leamington Spa Courier

Leeds Mercury

LGBTQ Nation

Libcom.org

London Mail

London Opinion

Luton News and Bedfordshire Chronicle

Magnet

Marylebone Mercury

Monthly Film Bulletin (United Kingdom)

Morning Advertiser (United Kingdom)

Motherwell Times

New Scientist (United Kingdom)

New York Amsterdam News

New York Times

Northern Echo (United Kingdom)

Nottingham Evening Post

NPR.org

Observer (United Kingdom)

Observer Magazine (United Kingdom)

Pall Mall Gazette

People Today (United States)

Photo Bits (United Kingdom)

Picturegoer (United Kingdom)

Portsmouth Evening News

Quartz

Sheffield Daily Telegraph

Sketch (United Kingdom)

Sporting Times (United Kingdom)

Stage (United Kingdom)

Stage and Television Today (United Kingdom)

Star (United Kingdom)

Sun (United Kingdom)

Sunday Express Magazine (United Kingdom)

Sunday Mirror (United Kingdom)

Sunday People (United Kingdom)

Sunday Times (United Kingdom)

Sunday Times Magazine (United Kingdom)

Sunderland Daily Echo and Shipping Gazette

Sussex Daily News

Tatler (United Kingdom)

Telegraph (United Kingdom)

Telegraph Magazine (United Kingdom)

This Is London

Time Out London

Times (United Kingdom)

Times Educational Supplement (United Kingdom)

Tribune (United Kingdom)

Uncensored (United States)

Western Daily Press (United Kingdom)

Western Mail (Cardiff)

Western Morning News (United Kingdom)

Whisper (United States)

Yahoo! News

Yorkshire Evening Post

Yorkshire Post and Leeds Intelligencer

Books and Articles

Ackroyd, Peter. *Dressing Up: Transvestism and Drag: The History of an Obsession.* London: Thames and Hudson, 1979.

Anthony, Barry. *The King's Jester: The Life of Dan Leno, Victorian Comic Genius.* London: I.B. Tauris, 2010.

Aston, Elaine. "Male Impersonation in the Music Hall: The Case of Vesta Tilley." *New Theatre Quarterly* 4:15 (1988): 247–57.

Auerbach, Nina. "Before the Curtain." In *The Cambridge Companion to Victorian and Edwardian Theatre*, edited by Kerry Powell. Cambridge: Cambridge University Press, 2004.

Baker, Paul. *Polari—The Lost Language of Gay Men.* London: Routledge, 2002.

Baker, Paul, and Jo Stanley. *Hello Sailor! The Hidden History of Gay Life at Sea.* London: Routledge, 2003.

Baker, Richard Anthony. *Old-Time Variety: An Illustrated History.* Barnsley: Pen & Sword Books, 2011.

Baker, Roger. *Drag: A History of Female Impersonation in the Performing Arts.* London: Cassell, 1994.

Bakshi, Sandeep. "A Comparative Analysis of Hijras and Drag Queens." *Journal of Homosexuality* 46:3–4 (2004): 211–23.

Baldwin, Stanley. *On England and Other Addresses.* London: P. Allan, 1926.

Balzer, Carsten. "The Beauty and the Beast: Reflections about the Socio-Historical and Subcultural Context of Drag Queens and 'Tunten' in Berlin," *Journal of Homosexuality* 46:3–4 (2004): 55–71.

Bauer, Heike. *English Literary Sexology: Translations of Inversion, 1860–1930.* Basingstoke: Palgrave Macmillan, 2009.

Benyon, John. *Masculinities and Culture.* Buckingham: Open University Press, 2002.

Bergman, David, ed. *Camp Grounds: Style and Homosexuality.* Amherst: University of Massachusetts Press, 1993.

Bergreen, Laurence. "Irving Berlin: *This Is the Army.*" *Prologue* 28:2 (1996): 95–105.

Berlanstein, Lenard R. "Breeches and Breaches: Cross-Dress Theatre and the Culture of Gender Ambiguity in Modern France." *Comparative Studies in Society and History* 38:2 (1996): 338–69.

Berlant, Lauren, and Sianne Ngai. "Comedy Has Issues." *Critical Inquiry* 43 (2017): 233–49.

Bland, Lucy. *Modern Women on Trial: Sexual Transgression in the Age of the Flapper.* Manchester: Manchester University Press, 2013.

Bland, Lucy, and Laura Doan, eds. *Sexology in Culture: Labelling Bodies and Desires.* Chicago: University of Chicago Press, 1998.

Bolich, G. G. *Transgender History & Geography: Crossdressing in Context, Vol. 3.* Raleigh, NC: Psyche's Press, 2007.

Bornstein, Kate. *Gender Outlaw: On Men, Women, and the Rest of Us.* New York: Vintage Books, 1995.

Bourke, Joanna. *Dismembering the Male: Men's Bodies, Britain and the Great War.* London: Reaktion Books, 1996.

Boxwell, David A. "The Follies of War: Cross-Dressing and Popular Theatre on the British Front Lines, 1914–1918." *Modernism/Modernity* 9:1 (2002): 1–20.

Boyes, Georgina, ed. *Step Change: New Views on Traditional Dance.* London: Francis Boutle, 2001.

Brady, Sean. *Masculinity and Male Homosexuality in Britain, 1861–1913.* Basingstoke: Palgrave Macmillan, 2005.

Bray, Alan. *Homosexuality in Renaissance England.* London: Gay Men's Press, 1982.

Brennan, Nial, and David Gudelunas, eds. *RuPaul's Drag Race and the Shifting Visibility of Drag Culture: The Boundaries of Reality TV*. Basingstoke: Palgrave Macmillan, 2018.

Brewitt-Taylor, Sam. "Christianity and the Invention of the Sexual Revolution in Britain, 1963–1967." *Historical Journal* 60:2 (2017): 519–46.

Brown, Geoff, and Tony Aldgate. *The Common Touch: The Films of John Baxter*. London: BFI Publishing, 1989.

Buckland, Paul. *Chorus of Witches*. Richmond, VA: Valancourt Books, 2021.

Bullough, Vern L., and Bonnie Bullough. *Cross Dressing, Sex, and Gender*. Philadelphia: University of Pennsylvania Press, 1993.

Burnett, John. *A History of the Cost of Living*. Harmondsworth: Penguin Books, 1969.

Butler, Jeremy G., ed. *Star Texts: Image and Performance in Film and Television*. Detroit, MI: Wayne State University Press, 1991.

Butler, Judith. *Gender Trouble: Feminism and the Subversion of Identity*. New York: Routledge, 1989.

———. "Imitation and Gender Insubordination." In *Inside/Out: Lesbian Theories, Gay Theories*, edited by Diana Fuss. London: Routledge, 1991.

Carden-Coyne, Ana. *Reconstructing the Body: Classicism, Modernism, and the First World War*. Oxford: Oxford University Press, 2009.

Carriger, Michelle Liu. "'The Unnatural History and the Petticoat Mystery of Boulton and Park': A Victorian Sex Scandal and the Theatre Defense." *TDR: The Drama Review* 57:4 (2013): 135–56.

Chapman, James. *Saints and Avengers: British Adventure Series of the 1960s*. London: I.B. Tauris, 2002.

Chauncey, George. *Gay New York: Gender, Urban Culture, and the Makings of the Gay Male World, 1890–1940*. New York: Basic Books, 2019.

Cherryman, Nick. "The Tranimal: Throwing Gender Out of Drag?" In *Contemporary Drag Practices and Performers: Drag in a Changing Scene, Volume 1*, edited by Mark Edward and Stephen Farrier. London: Bloomsbury, 2020.

Chibnall, Steve, and Brian McFarlane. *The British "B" Film*. Basingstoke: Palgrave Macmillan, 2009.

Cocks, H.G. *Nameless Offences: Homosexual Desire in the Nineteenth Century*. London: I.B. Tauris, 2003.

———. "Saucy Stories: Pornography, Sexology and the Marketing of Sexual Knowledge in Britain, c. 1918–70." *Social History* 29:4 (2004): 465–84.

———. "Secrets, Crimes and Diseases, 1800–1914." In *A Gay History of Britain: Love and Sex between Men Since the Middle Ages,* edited by Matt Cook, H. G. Cocks, Robert Mills, and Randolph Trumbach. Oxford: Greenwood World Publishing, 2007.

Cocks, H. G., and Matt Houlbrook, eds. *Palgrave Advances in the Modern History of Sexuality.* New York: Palgrave, 2006.

Cohen, Ed. *Talk on the Wilde Side: Toward a Genealogy of a Discourse on Male Sexualities.* London: Routledge, 1993.

Cole, Shaun. *Don We Now Our Gay Apparel: Gay Men's Dress in the 20th Century.* New York: Berg Publishers, 2000.

———. "Gay Liberation Front and Radical Drag." *QED: A Journal in GLBTQ Worldmaking* 4:3 (2017): 165–69.

Collins, Marcus, ed. *The Permissive Society and Its Enemies: Sixties British Culture.* London: Rivers Oram Press, 2007.

Conekin, Becky, Frank Mort, and Chris Waters, eds. *Moments of Modernity: Reconstructing Britain, 1945–1964.* London: Rivers Oram Press, 1999.

Conlin, Jonathan. "The Strange Case of the Chevalier d'Éon." *History Today* 60:4 (2010): 45–51.

Cook, Matt. "Queer Conflicts: Love, Sex and War, 1914–1967." In *A Gay History of Britain: Love and Sex between Men Since the Middle Ages,* edited by Matt Cook, H. G. Cocks, Robert Mills, and Randolph Trumbach. Oxford: Greenwood World Publishing, 2007.

Cook, Matt, H. G. Cocks, Robert Mills, and Randolph Trumbach, eds. *A Gay History of Britain: Love and Sex between Men Since the Middle Ages.* Oxford: Greenwood World Publishing, 2007.

Costello, John. *Love, Sex, and War: Changing Values, 1939–45.* London: William Collins, Sons, 1985.

Crick, Martin. *The History of the Social-Democratic Federation.* Staffordshire: Keele University Press, 1994.

Critchley, Simon. *On Humour (Thinking in Action).* New York: Routledge, 2001.

Crozier, Ivan. "Nineteenth-Century British Psychiatric Writing about Homosexuality before Havelock Ellis: The Missing Story." *Journal of the History of Medicine and Allied Sciences* 63:1 (2008): 65–102.

David, Ronald L. *The Glamour Factory: Inside Hollywood's Big Studio System.* Dallas, TX: Southern Methodist University Press, 1993.

Davis, Jim. "'Slap On! Slap Ever!': Victorian Pantomime, Gender Variance, and Cross-Dressing." *New Theatre Quarterly* 30:3 (2014): 218–30.

Davis, Jim, ed. *Victorian Pantomime: A Collection of Critical Essays*. Basingstoke: Palgrave Macmillan, 2010.

D'Bray, Chris. "Camp and Drag in the Mainstream: A Critical Study of the Phenomenon of Drag Performance in the Northern British Fun Pubs, 1973-1993." In *Drag Histories, Herstories & Hairstories: Drag in a Changing Scene, Volume 2*, edited by Mark Edward and Stephen Farrier. London: Bloomsbury, 2021.

Dean, Joan FitzPatrick. *Riot and Great Anger: Stage Censorship in Twentieth-Century Ireland*. Madison: University of Wisconsin Press, 2004.

De Jongh, Nicholas. *Politics, Prudery and Perversions: The Censoring of the English Stage, 1901-1968*. London: Methuen, 2001.

Dello Stritto, Frank J., and Andi Brooks. *Vampire Over London: Bela Lugosi in Britain*. Houston: Cult Movies Press, 2015.

Denisoff, Dennis. "Popular Culture." In *The Cambridge Companion to Victorian Culture*, edited by Francis O'Gorman. Cambridge: Cambridge University Press, 2010.

Deslandes, Paul R. *The Culture of Male Beauty in Britain: From the First Photographs to David Beckham*. Chicago: University of Chicago Press, 2021.

———. "The Male Body, Beauty and Aesthetics in Modern British Culture." *History Compass* 8:10 (2010): 1191-208.

Dickinson, Tommy. *"Curing Queers": Mental Nurses and Their Patients, 1935-74*. Manchester: Manchester University Press, 2015.

Dixon, Wheeler Winston, and Gwendolyn Audrey Foster. *A Short History of Film*. New Brunswick, NJ: Rutgers University Press, 2013.

D'Monté, Rebecca, ed. *British Theatre and Performance 1900-1950*. London: Bloomsbury, 2015.

Doan, Laura. *Disturbing Practices: History, Sexuality, and Women's Experience of Modern War*. Chicago: University of Chicago Press, 2013.

———. *Fashioning Sapphism: The Origins of a Modern English Lesbian Culture*. New York: Columbia University Press, 2001.

Donahue, Joseph, ed. *The Cambridge History of British Theatre. Volume 2: 1660 to 1895*. Cambridge: Cambridge University Press, 2015.

Doonan, Simon. *Drag: The Complete Story*. London: Laurence King Publishing, 2020.

Double, Oliver. *Britain Had Talent: A History of Variety Theatre*. London: Bloomsbury, 2012.

Drushel, Bruce E. and Brian M. Peters, eds. *Sontag and the Camp Aesthetic: Advancing New Perspectives*. London: Lexington Books, 2017.

Dyer, Joyce, Jennifer Cognard-Black, and Elizabeth MacLeod Walls, eds. *From Curlers to Chainsaws: Women and Their Machines*. East Lansing: Michigan State University Press, 2016.

Dyer, Richard. *The Culture of Queers*. London: Routledge, 2002.

———. *Heavenly Bodies: Film Stars and Society*. London: Macmillan Education, 1987.

———. *Stars*. London: BFI Publishing, 1979.

Edward, Mark, and Stephen Farrier, eds. *Contemporary Drag Practices and Performers: Drag in a Changing Scene, Volume* 1. London: Bloomsbury, 2020.

———. "Drag: Applying Foundation and Setting the Scene." In *Contemporary Drag Practices and Performers: Drag in a Changing Scene, Volume* 1, edited by Mark Edward and Stephen Farrier. London: Bloomsbury, 2020.

———. *Drag Histories, Herstories and Hairstories: Drag in a Changing Scene, Volume* 2. London: Bloomsbury, 2021.

Ellis, Bill. *Entertainment in Rhyl and North Wales*. Chalford: Chalford Publishing Company, 1997.

Epstein, Julia, ed. *Body Guards: Cultural Politics of Gender Ambiguity*. London: Routledge, 1994.

Eskridge, William N., Jr. "Privacy Jurisprudence and the Apartheid of the Closet, 1946–1961." *Florida State University Law Review* 24:4 (1997): 703–840.

Farmer, Richard. *Cinemas and Cinemagoing in Wartime Britain, 1939–45: The Utility Dream Palace*. Manchester: Manchester University Press, 2016.

Farrer, Peter, ed. *Borrowed Plumes: Letters from Edwardian Newspapers on Male Cross Dressing*. Liverpool: Karn Publications Garston, 1994.

———. *Confidential Correspondence on Cross Dressing, 1911–1915*. Liverpool: Karn Publications Garston, 1997.

———. *Confidential Correspondence on Cross Dressing, Pt. II, 1916–1920*. Liverpool: Karn Publications Garston, 1998.

———. *Cross-Dressing between the Wars: Selections from* London Life, *1923–1933*. Liverpool: Karn Publications Garston, 2000.

———. *Cross Dressing between the Wars: Selections from* London Life *Part II, 1934–1941*. Liverpool: Karn Publications Garston, 2006.

———. *Cross Dressing since the War: Selections from* Justice Weekly *1955–1972*. Liverpool: Karn Publications Garston, 2011.

———. *In Female Disguise: An Anthology of English and American Short Stories and Literary Passages*. Liverpool: Karn Publications Garston, 1992.

———. *Men in Petticoats: A Selection of Letters from Victorian Newspapers*. Liverpool: Karn Publications Garston, 1987.

Farson, Daniel. *Soho in the Fifties*. London: Michael Joseph, 1988.

Faulk, Barry J. *Music Hall and Modernity: The Late-Victorian Discovery of Popular Culture*. Athens: Ohio University Press, 2014.

Ferris, Lesley, ed. *Crossing the Stage: Controversies on Cross-Dressing*. London: Routledge, 1993.

Fielding, Steven. *A State of Play: British Politics on Screen, Stage and Page, from Anthony Trollope to* The Thick of It. London: Bloomsbury, 2014.

Findlater, Richard. *Banned! A Review of Theatrical Censorship in Britain*. London: Panther, 1968.

Fischer, Lucy, and Marcia Landy, eds. *Stars, The Film Reader*. London: Routledge, 2004.

Fletcher, Cyril. *Nice One Cyril*. London: Barrie & Jenkins, 1978.

Foucault, Michel. *The History of Sexuality, Volume 1: An Introduction*. London: Allen Lane, 1979.

Freshwater, Helen. "Suppressed Desire: Inscriptions of Lesbianism in the British Theatre of the 1930s." *New Theatre Quarterly* 17:4 (2001): 310–18.

Fuller, J. G. *Troop Morale and Popular Culture in the British and Dominion Armies 1914–1918*. Oxford: Clarendon Press, 1991.

Fuss, Diana, ed. *Inside/Out: Lesbian Theories, Gay Theories*. London: Routledge, 1991.

Garber, Marjorie. *Vested Interests: Cross-Dressing and Cultural Anxiety*. New York: Routledge, 1992.

Geffen, Sasha. *Glitter Up the Dark: How Pop Music Broke the Binary*. Austin: University of Texas Press, 2020.

Gerstner, David A, ed. *Routledge International Encyclopedia of Queer Culture*. London: Routledge, 2006.

Gledhill, Christine, ed. *Stardom: Industry of Desire*. London: Routledge, 1991.

Glenn, Susan A. *Female Spectacle: The Theatrical Roots of Modern Feminism*. Cambridge, MA: Harvard University Press, 2000.

Gomery, Douglas. *The Hollywood Studio System*. London: Macmillan, 1986.

Goodman, Lizbeth, and Jane de Gay, eds. *The Routledge Reader in Gender and Performance*. London: Routledge, 1998.

Gow, Gordon. *Hollywood in the Fifties*. London: International Film Guide Series, 1971.

Green, E. H. H. *Ideologies of Conservatism: Conservative Political Ideas in the Twentieth Century*. Oxford: Oxford University Press, 2002.

Greenhalgh, Charlotte. *Aging in Twentieth-Century Britain*. Oakland: University of California Press, 2018.

Gundle, Stephen. *Glamour: A History*. Oxford: Oxford University Press, 2008.

Halberstam, J. Jack. *The Queer Art of Failure*. Durham, NC: Duke University Press, 2011.

Hall, Lesley. *Sex, Gender and Social Change in Britain Since 1880*. Basingstoke: Palgrave Macmillan, 2000.

Halladay, Laurel. "A Lovely War: Male to Female Cross-Dressing and Canadian Military Entertainment in World War II." *Journal of Homosexuality* 46:3–4 (2004): 19–34.

Halperin, David M. *How to Do the History of Homosexuality*. Chicago: University of Chicago Press, 2002.

Hammond, Michael. "'So Essentially Human': The Appeal of Charles Chaplin's *Shoulder Arms* in Britain, 1918." *Early Popular Visual Culture* 8:3 (2010): 297–313.

Hargreaves, Tracy. "'There's No Place Like Home': History and Tradition in *The Forsyte Saga* and the BBC." *Journal of British Cinema and Television* 6:1 (2009): 21–40.

Harris, Joseph. "What Butler Saw: Cross-Dressing and Spectatorship in Seventeenth-Century France." *Paragraph* 29:1 (2006): 67–79.

Hayton, David. "From Barbarian to Burlesque: English Images of the Irish c. 1660–1750." *Irish Economic and Social History* 15 (1988): 5–31.

Hekma, Gert, ed. *A Cultural History of Sexuality, Volume 6: In the Modern Age*. New York: Berg, 2011.

Hinds, Hillary, and Jackie Stacey. "Imagining Feminism, Imaging Femininity: The Bra-Burner, Diana, and the Woman Who Kills." *Feminist Media Studies* 1:2 (2001): 153–77.

Hirschfeld, Magnus. *Transvestites: The Erotic Drive to Cross-Dress*. Translated by Michael A. Lombardi-Nash. Buffalo, NY: Prometheus Books, 1991.

Holland, Peter. "The Play of Eros: Paradoxes of Gender in English Pantomime." *New Theatre Quarterly* 13:51 (1997): 195–204.

———, ed. *Shakespeare Survey Volume 58. Writing about Shakespeare*. Cambridge: Cambridge University Press, 2005.

Hollinger, Karen. *The Actresses: Hollywood Acting and the Female Star*. London: Routledge, 2006.

Hopkins, Steven J. "'Let the Drag Race Begin': The Rewards of Becoming a Queen." *Journal of Homosexuality* 46:3–4 (2004): 135–49.

Houlbrook, Matt. "Daring to Speak Whose Name? Queer Cultural Politics, 1920–1967." In *The Permissive Society and its Enemies: Sixties British Culture*, edited by Marcus Collins. London: Rivers Oram Press, 2007.

———. "'Lady Austin's Camp Boys': Constituting the Queer Subject in 1930s London." *Gender & History* 14:1 (2002): 31–61.

———. "'The Man with The Powder Puff' in Interwar London." *Historical Journal* 50:1 (2007): 145–71.

———. "The Private World of Public Urinals: London 1918–57." *London Journal* 25:1 (2000): 52–70.

———. *Queer London: Perils and Pleasures in the Sexual Metropolis, 1918–1957.* London: University of Chicago Press, 2005.

———. "Soldier Heroes and Rent Boys: Homosex, Masculinities, and Britishness in the Brigade of Guards, circa 1900–1960." *Journal of British Studies* 42:3 (2003): 351–88.

Hyde, H. Montgomery. *A History of Pornography.* London: Four Square Books, 1966.

James, Robert. *Popular Culture and Working-Class Taste in Britain, 1930–39: A Round of Cheap Diversions?* Manchester: Manchester University Press, 2010.

Janes, Dominic. "The 'Curious Effects' of Acting: Homosexuality, Theatre and Female Impersonation at the University of Cambridge, 1900–39." *Twentieth Century British History* 33:2 (2022): 169–202.

———. *Oscar Wilde Prefigured: Queer Fashioning and British Caricature, 1750–1900.* Chicago: University of Chicago Press, 2016.

———. "The Varsity Drag: Gender, Sexuality and Cross-Dressing at the University of Cambridge, 1850–1950." *Journal of Social History* 55:3 (2022): 695–723.

Jarret, Lucinda. *Stripping in Time: A History of Erotic Dancing.* London: Pandora, 1997.

Jivani, Alkarim. *It's Not Unusual: A History of Gay and Lesbian Britain in the Twentieth Century.* London: Michael O'Mara Books, 1997.

———. "It's Not Unusual: Gay and Lesbian History in Britain." In *Global Feminisms since 1945*, edited by Bonnie G. Smith. London: Routledge, 2000.

Johnston, John. *The Lord Chamberlain's Blue Pencil.* London: Hodder & Stoughton, 1990.

Joseph, Channing Gerard. "Swann, William Dorsey." *Oxford African American Studies Center*, 20 May 2021.

Kathman, David. "How Old Were Shakespeare's Boy Actors?" In *Shakespeare Survey Volume 58. Writing about Shakespeare*, edited by Peter Holland. Cambridge: Cambridge University Press, 2005.

Kenny, Robert V. *The Man Who Was Old Mother Riley: The Lives and Films of Arthur Lucan and Kitty McShane*. Albany, GA: BearManor Media, 2014.

Kent, Brad. "Shaw, *The Bell*, and Irish Censorship in 1945." *SHAW: The Journal of Bernard Shaw Studies* 30 (2010): 161–74.

Kent, Susan Kingsley. *Aftershocks: Politics and Trauma in Britain, 1918–1931*. Basingstoke: Palgrave Macmillan, 2009.

———. *Making Peace: The Reconstruction of Gender in Interwar Britain*. Princeton, NJ: Princeton University Press, 1993.

Kibler, M. Alison. "The Stage Irishwoman." *Journal of American Ethnic History* 24:3 (2005): 5–30.

King, Barry. "Articulating Stardom." *Screen* 26:5 (1985): 27–50.

———. "The Star and the Commodity: Notes Towards a Performance Theory of Stardom." *Cultural Studies* 1:2 (1987): 145–61.

King, Thomas A. *The Gendering of Men, 1600–1750: Volume 1, The English Phallus*. London: University of Wisconsin Press, 2004.

———. *The Gendering of Men, 1600–1750: Volume 2, Queer Articulations*. London: University of Wisconsin Press, 2008.

———. "Performing 'Akimbo': Queer Pride and Epistemological Prejudice." In *The Politics and Poetics of Camp*, edited by Moe Meyer. London: Routledge, 1994.

Kirk, Kris, and Ed Heath. *Men in Frocks*. London: GMP Publishers, 1984.

Kirk, Mary. "Kind of a Drag: Gender, Race, and Ambivalence in *The Birdcage* and *To Wong Foo, Thanks for Everything! Julie Newmar*." *Journal of Homosexuality* 46:3–4 (2004): 169–80.

Kleinecke, Iris. "Representations of the Victorian Age: Interior Spaces and the Detail of Domestic Life in Two Adaptations of Galsworthy's *The Forsyte Saga*." *Screen* 47:2 (2006): 139–62.

Kohn, Marek. *Dope Girls: The Birth of the British Drug Underground*. London: Granta Books, 2003.

Krämer, Peter. *The New Hollywood: From Bonnie and Clyde to Star Wars*. London: Wallflower Press, 2005.

Landy, Marcia. *British Genres: Cinema and Society, 1930–1960*. Princeton, NJ: Princeton University Press, 1991.

Langer, Susanne K. *Feeling and Form: A Theory of Art*. New York: Charles Scribner's Sons, 1953.

Langkjær, Michael A. "A Case of Misconstrued Rock Military Style: Mick Jagger and his Evzone 'Little Girl's Party Frock' *Fustanella*, Hyde Park, July 5, 1969."

Endymatologika: Endyesthai (To Dress): Historical, Sociological and Methodological Approaches, Conference Proceedings, Athens, Greece, 9–11 April 2010, Nafplion: Peloponnesiako Laografiko Hidryma / Peloponnesian Folklore Foundation, vol. 4 (2012): 111–19.

Lant, Antonia. *Blackout: Reinventing Women for Wartime British Cinema.* Princeton, NJ: Princeton University Press, 1991.

Laqueur, Thomas. *Making Sex: Body and Gender from the Greeks to Freud.* Cambridge, MA: Harvard University Press, 1992.

La Rue, Danny. *From Drags to Riches: My Autobiography.* London: Viking, 1987.

Leck, Ralph M. *Vita Sexualis: Karl Ulrichs and the Origins of Sexual Science.* Urbana: University of Illinois Press, 2016.

LeMaster, Benny. "Discontents of Being and Becoming Fabulous on *RuPaul's Drag U*: Queer Criticism in Neoliberal Times." *Women's Studies in Communication* 38:2 (2015): 167–86.

Lewis, Brian. *Wolfenden's Witnesses: Homosexuality in Postwar Britain.* Basingstoke: Palgrave Macmillan, 2016.

Lewis, Jon, and Eric Smoodin, eds. *Looking Past the Screen: Case Studies in American Film History and Method.* London: Duke University Press, 2007.

Light, Alison. *Forever England: Femininity, Literature and Conservatism between the Wars.* London: Routledge, 1991.

Lott, Eric. *Love & Theft: Blackface Minstrelsy and the American Working Class.* New York: Oxford University Press, 2013.

Lyle, Timothy. "'Check with Yo' Man First; Check with Yo' Man': Tyler Perry Appropriates Drag as a Tool to Re-Circulate Patriarchal Ideology." *Callaloo* 34:3 (2011): 943–58.

Makepeace, Clare. "'Pinky Smith Looks Gorgeous!' Female Impersonators and Male Bonding in Prisoner of War Camps for British Servicemen in Europe." In *Men, Masculinities and Male Culture in the Second World War*, edited by Linsey Robb and Juliette Pattinson. London: Palgrave Macmillan, 2017.

Maschio, Geraldine. "Ethnic Humour and the Demise of the Russell Brothers." *Journal of Popular Culture* 26:1 (1992): 81–91.

McCormack, Mark, and Liam Wignall. "Drag Performers' Perspectives on the Mainstreaming of British Drag: Towards a Sociology of Contemporary Drag." *Sociology* 56:1 (2022): 3–20.

McKenna, Neil. *Fanny & Stella: The Young Men Who Shocked Victorian England.* London: Faber and Faber, 2013.

McLaren, Angus. *The Trials of Masculinity: Policing Sexual Boundaries, 1870–1930.* Chicago: University of Chicago Press, 1997.

Meecham, Pam. "Reconfiguring the Shipping News: Maritime's Hidden Histories and the Politics of Gender Display." *Sex Education: Sexuality, Society and Learning* 8:3 (2008): 371–80.

Mitchell, Gillian A. M. *Adult Responses to Popular Music and Intergenerational Relations in Britain, c.* 1955–1975. London: Anthem Press, 2019.

Morrison, Grant. *Doom Patrol* 2:35. New York: DC Comics, 1990.

Mort, Frank. *Capital Affairs: London and the Making of the Permissive Society.* London: Yale University Press, 2010.

———. "Mapping Sexual London: The Wolfenden Committee on Homosexual Offences and Prostitution: 1954–7." *New Formations: Sexual Geographies* 37 (1999): 92–113.

———. "Striptease: The Erotic Female Body and Live Sexual Entertainment in Mid-Twentieth-Century London." *Social History* 32:1 (2007): 28–53.

Mumford, Kevin J. *Interzones: Black/White Sex Districts in Chicago and New York in the Early Twentieth Century.* New York: Columbia University Press, 1997.

Naremore, James. *Acting in the Cinema.* Berkeley: University of California Press, 1990.

Nead, Lynda. "Strip: Moving Bodies in the 1890s." *Early Popular Visual Culture* 3:2 (2005): 135–50.

Newey, Katherine. "Theatre." In *The Cambridge Companion to Victorian Culture,* edited by Francis O'Gorman. Cambridge: Cambridge University Press, 2010.

Newly, Patrick. *The Amazing Mrs Shufflewick: The Life of Rex Jameson.* London: Third Age Press, 2007.

———. *Bawdy But British! The Life of Douglas Byng.* London: Third Age Press, 2009.

Newton, Esther. *Mother Camp: Female Impersonators in America.* Chicago: University of Chicago Press, 1979.

Nicholson, Steve. *The Censorship of British Drama 1900–1968, Volume One: 1900–1932.* Exeter: University of Exeter Press, 2003.

———. *The Censorship of British Drama 1900–1968, Volume Two: 1933–1952.* Exeter: University of Exeter Press, 2005.

———. *The Censorship of British Drama 1900–1968, Volume Three: The Fifties.* Exeter: University of Exeter Press, 2011.

———. *The Censorship of British Drama 1900–1968, Volume Four: The Sixties.* Exeter: University of Exeter Press, 2015.

———. "Staging Hitler, Not Staging Hitler." In *British Theatre and Performance 1900–1950,* edited by Rebecca D'Monté. London: Bloomsbury, 2015.

Niles, Richard. "Wigs, Laughter, and Subversion: Charles Busch and Strategies of Drag Performance." *Journal of Homosexuality* 46:3–4 (2004): 35–53.

Norton, Rictor. *Mother Clap's Molly House: The Gay Subculture in England 1700–1830*. London: GMP Publishers, 1992.

Nott, James. *Going to the Palais: A Social and Cultural History of Dancing and Dance Halls in Britain, 1918–1960*. Oxford: Oxford University Press, 2015.

Oakley, Gilbert. *Sex Change and Dress Deviation*. London: Morntide, 1970.

O'Brien, Daniel. "A Vintage Year for Scoundrels: Shapes of Villainy in *Adam Adamant Lives!*" *Intensities: The Journal of Cult Media* 6 (2013): 57–79.

O'Gorman, Francis, ed. *The Cambridge Companion to Victorian Culture*. Cambridge: Cambridge University Press, 2010.O'Rourke, Chris. "Exploiting Ambiguity: *Murder!* and the Meanings of Cross-Dressing in Interwar British Cinema." *Journal of British Cinema and Television* 17:3 (2020): 289–312.

Oram, Alison. *Her Husband Was a Woman! Women's Gender-Crossing in Modern British Popular Culture*. London: Routledge, 2007.

Osborne, John. *A Patriot for Me*. London: Faber & Faber, 1971.

Parker, Derek, and Julia Parker. *The Natural History of the Chorus Girl*. Newton Abbot, UK: David & Charles, 1975.

Parr, Joy. "What Makes a Washday Less Blue? Gender, Nation, and Technology Choice in Postwar Canada." *Technology and Culture* 38:1 (1997): 153–86.

Parslow, Joe. "Dragging the Mainstream: *RuPaul's Drag Race* and Moving Drag Practices between the USA and the UK." In *Contemporary Drag Practices and Performers: Drag in a Changing Scene, Volume 1*, edited by Mark Edward and Stephen Farrier. London: Bloomsbury, 2020.

Peacock, Louise. *Slapstick and Comic Performance: Comedy and Pain*. New York: Palgrave Macmillan, 2014.

Peniston-Bird, Corinna, and Emma Vickers, eds. *Gender and the Second World War: The Lessons of War*. London: Palgrave, 2017.

Peraino, Judith A. "Mick Jagger as Mother." *Social Text* 33:3 (2015): 75–113.

Phellas, Constantinos, ed. *Researching Non-Heterosexual Sexualities*. Surrey: Ashgate Publishing, 2012.

Poore, Benjamin. "Reclaiming the Dame: Cross-Dressing as Queen Victoria in British Theatre and Television Comedy." *Comedy Studies* 3:2 (2012): 177–89.

Powell, Kerry, ed. *The Cambridge Companion to Victorian and Edwardian Theatre*. Cambridge: Cambridge University Press, 2004.

Prosser, Jay. "Transsexuals and the Transsexologists: Inversion and the Emergence of Transsexual Subjectivity." In *Sexology in Culture: Labelling Bodies and Desires*, edited by Lucy Bland and Laura Doan. Chicago: University of Chicago Press, 1998.

Pugh, Martin. *We Danced All Night: A Social History of Britain between the Wars*. London: Vintage, 2009.

Quinion, Michael. *Port Out, Starboard Home: The Fascinating Stories We Tell about the Words We Use*. London: Penguin, 2005.

Rachamimov, Alon. "The Disruptive Comforts of Drag: (Trans)Gender Performances among Prisoners of War in Russia, 1914–1920." *American Historical Review* 111:2 (2006): 362–82.

Radcliffe, Caroline. "Dan Leno: Dame of Drury Lane." In *Victorian Pantomime: A Collection of Critical Essays*, edited by Jim Davis. Basingstoke: Palgrave Macmillan, 2010.

———. "The Ladies' Clog Dancing Contest of 1898." In *Step Change: New Views on Traditional Dance*, ed. Georgina Boyes. London: Francis Boutle, 2001.

Rebellato, Dan. *1956 and All That: The Making of Modern British Drama*. London: Routledge, 1999.

Redmond, Sean, and Su Holmes, eds. *Stardom and Celebrity: A Reader*. London: Sage, 2007.

Rhyne, Ragan. "Racializing White Drag." *Journal of Homosexuality* 46:3–4 (2004): 181–94.

Richards, Jeffrey. *The Golden Age of Pantomime: Slapstick, Spectacle and Subversion in Victorian England*. London: I. B. Tauris, 2014.

Robb, Linsey, and Juliette Pattinson, eds. *Men, Masculinities and Male Culture in the Second World War*. London: Palgrave Macmillan, 2017.

Roberts, Phillip. *The Royal Court Theatre and the Modern Stage*. Cambridge: Cambridge University Press, 1999.

Roberts, Shari. "'The Lady in the Tutti-Frutti Hat': Carmen Miranda, a Spectacle of Ethnicity." *Cinema Journal* 32:3 (1993): 3–23.

Rodger, Gillian M. *Just One of the Boys: Female-to-Male Cross-Dressing on the American Variety Stage*. Urbana: University of Illinois Press, 2018.

Rogin, Michael. "Blackface, White Noise: The Jewish Jazz Singer Finds His Voice." *Critical Inquiry* 18:3 (1992): 417–53.

Rose, Kenneth. *King George V*. London: Weidenfeld and Nicolson, 1984.

Ross, Andrew. *No Respect: Intellectuals and Popular Culture*. London: Routledge, 1989.

Rowbotham, Judith. "A Deception on the Public: The Real Scandal of Boulton and Park." *Liverpool Law Review* 36 (2015): 123–45.

Rowe, Kathleen K. "Roseanne: Unruly Woman as Domestic Goddess." *Screen* 31:4 (1990): 408–19.

Russell, Dave. "Popular Entertainment, 1776–1895." In *The Cambridge History of British Theatre. Volume 2: 1660 to 1895*, edited by Joseph Donahue. Cambridge: Cambridge University Press, 2015.

Sandbrook, Dominic. *White Heat: A History of Britain in the Swinging Sixties*. London: Abacus, 2007.

Schacht, Steven P. "Beyond the Boundaries of the Classroom: Teaching about Gender and Sexuality at a Drag Show." *Journal of Homosexuality* 46:3–4 (2004): 225–40.

Schacht, Steven P., and Lisa Underwood. "The Absolutely Fabulous but Flawlessly Customary World of Female Impersonators." *Journal of Homosexuality* 46:3–4 (2004): 1–17.

Schaffner, Anna Katharina. *Modernism and Perversion: Sexual Deviance in Sexology and Literature, 1850–1930*. Basingstoke: Palgrave Macmillan, 2012.

Sculthorpe, Derek. *Malcolm Scott: The Woman Who Knows*. Orlando, FL: BearManor Media, 2022.

Sears, Clare. *Arresting Dress: Cross-Dressing, Law, and Fascination in Nineteenth-Century San Francisco*. London: Duke University Press, 2015.

Sedgwick, Eve Kosofsky. *Epistemology of the Closet*. Berkeley: University of California Press, 1990.

Senelick, Laurence. "Boys and Girls Together: Subcultural Origins of Glamour Drag and Male Impersonation on the Nineteenth-Century Stage." In *Crossing the Stage: Controversies on Cross-Dressing*, edited by Lesley Ferris. London: Routledge, 1993.

———. *The Changing Room: Sex, Drag and Theatre*. London: Routledge, 2000.

Serlin, David Harley. "Christine Jorgensen and the Cold War Closet." *Radical History Review* 62 (1995): 136–65.

Shade, Ruth. "Take My Mother-in-Law: 'Old Bags,' Comedy and the Sociocultural Construction of the Older Woman." *Comedy Studies* 1:1 (2010): 71–83.

Shellard, Dominic, ed. *British Theatre in the 1950s*. Sheffield: Sheffield Academic Press, 2000.

Shellard, Dominic, Steve Nicholson, and Miriam Handley. *The Lord Chamberlain Regrets . . . A History of British Theatre Censorship*. London: British Library, 2004.

Sigel, Lisa Z. "'Best Love': Female Impersonation in the Great War." *Sexualities* 19:1–2 (2016): 98–118.

———. "Looking at Sex: Pornography and Erotica since 1750." In *The Routledge History of Sex and the Body: 1500 to the Present*, edited by Sarah Toulalan and Kate Fisher. Oxon: Routledge, 2016.

———. *Making Modern Love: Sexual Narratives and Identities in Interwar Britain.* Philadelphia: Temple University Press, 2012.

Singer, Marc. *Grant Morrison: Combining the Worlds of Contemporary Comics.* Jackson: University Press of Mississippi, 2012.

Sladen, Simon. "Wicked Queens of Pantoland." In *Drag Histories, Herstories and Hairstories: Drag in a Changing Scene, Volume 2,* edited by Mark Edward and Stephen Farrier. London: Bloomsbury, 2021.

Slide, Anthony. *Great Pretenders: A History of Female and Male Impersonation in the Performing Arts.* Lombard, IL: Wallace-Homestead, 1986.

Sly, Nicola. *Bristol Murders.* Stroud: History Press, 2008.

Smith, Bonnie G., ed. *Global Feminisms since 1945.* London: Routledge, 2000.

Sontag, Susan. *Against Interpretation and Other Essays.* New York: Delta Books, 1966.

Stempel, Tom. *American Audiences on Movies and Moviegoing.* Lexington: University Press of Kentucky, 2001.

Stokoe, Kayte. *Reframing Drag: Beyond Subversion and the Status Quo.* Abingdon, Oxon: Routledge, 2020.

St. Pierre, Paul Matthew. *Music Hall Mimesis in British Film, 1895–1960: On the Halls on the Screen.* Madison, NJ: Farleigh Dickinson University Press, 2009.

Stratmann, Linda. *Gloucestershire Murders.* Sutton: Stroud, 2005.

Stryker, Susan. *Transgender History.* Berkeley: Seal Press, 2008.

Stryker, Susan, and Stephen Whittle, eds. *The Transgender Studies Reader.* New York: Routledge, 2006.

Summers, Claude J., ed. *The Queer Encyclopedia of Music, Dance, & Musical Theater.* San Francisco: Cleis Press, 2004.

Sutton, David. *A Chorus of Raspberries: British Film Comedy 1929–1939.* Exeter: University of Exeter Press, 2000.

Szczelkun, Stefan. *The Conspiracy of Good Taste: William Morris, Cecil Sharp, Clough Williams-Ellis and the Repression of Working Class Culture in the 20th Century.* London: Working Press, 1993.

Taylor, Millie. *British Pantomime Performance.* Bristol: Intellect, 2007.

———. "Continuity and Transformation in Twentieth-Century Pantomime." In *Victorian Pantomime: A Collection of Critical Essays,* edited by Jim Davis. Basingstoke: Palgrave Macmillan, 2010.

Taylor, Verta, and Leila J. Rupp. "Chicks with Dicks, Men in Dresses." *Journal of Homosexuality* 46:3–4 (2004): 13–133.

Thomas, Bob. *Joan Crawford.* New York: Simon and Schuster, 1962.

Thomas, David, David Carlton, and Anne Etienne. *Theatre Censorship: From Walpole to Wilson*. Oxford: Oxford University Press, 2007.

Tilden, Norma. "Maytag Washer, 1939." In *From Curlers to Chainsaws: Women and Their Machines*, edited by Joyce Dyer, Jennifer Cognard-Black, and Elizabeth MacLeod Walls. East Lansing: Michigan State University Press, 2016.

Tobin, Robert Deam. *Peripheral Desires: The German Discovery of Sex*. Philadelphia: University of Pennsylvania Press, 2015.

Toulalan, Sarah, and Kate Fisher, ed. *The Routledge History of Sex and the Body: 1500 to the Present*. Oxon: Routledge, 2016.

Trumbach, Randolph. "Modern Sodomy: The Origins of Homosexuality, 1700–1800." In *A Gay History of Britain: Love and Sex between Men Since the Middle Ages*, edited by Matt Cook, H.G. Cocks, Robert Mills, and Randolph Trumbach. Oxford: Greenwood World Publishing, 2007.

Tyler, Carole-Anne. "Boys Will Be Girls: The Politics of Gay Drag," in *Inside/Out: Lesbian Theories, Gay Theories*, edited by Diana Fuss. London: Routledge, 1991.

Underwood, Peter. *Danny La Rue: Life's a Drag!* London: W.H. Allen, 1975.

Upchurch, Charles. *Before Wilde: Sex between Men in Britain's Age of Reform*. London: University of California Press, 2009.

———. "Forgetting the Unthinkable: Cross-Dressers and British Society in the Case of the Queen vs. Boulton and Others." *Gender & History* 12:1 (2000): 127–57.

Varty, Anne. "Pantomime Transformations: Genre, Gender and *Charley's Aunt*." *Nineteenth Century Theatre and Film* 39:2 (2012): 39–53.

Vernon, James. "'For Some Queer Reason': The Trials and Tribulations of Colonel Barker's Masquerade in Interwar Britain." *Signs* 26:1 (2000): 37–62.

Vickers, Emma. *Queen and Country: Same-Sex Desire in the British Armed Forces, 1939–45*. Manchester: Manchester University Press, 2013.

Vickers, Emma, and Emma Jackson. "Sanctuary or Sissy? Female Impersonation as Entertainment in the British Armed Forces, 1939–1945." In *Gender and the Second World War: The Lessons of War*, edited by Corinna Peniston-Bird and Emma Vickers. London: Palgrave, 2017.

Vincendeau, Ginette. *Brigitte Bardot*. London: Palgrave Macmillan, 2013.

Walkowitz, Judith R. "Cosmopolitanism, Feminism, and the Moving Body." *Victorian Literature and Culture* 38 (2010): 427–49.

———. "The 'Vision of Salome': Cosmopolitanism and Erotic Dancing in Central London, 1908–1918." *American Historical Review* 108:2 (2003): 337–76.

Waters, Chris. "Disorders of the Mind, Disorders of the Body Social: Peter Wildeblood and the Making of the Modern Homosexual." In *Moments of Modernity: Reconstructing Britain, 1945-1964*, edited by Becky Conekin, Frank Mort, and Chris Waters. London: Rivers Oram Press, 1999.

———. *"Talk on the Wilde Side: Toward a Genealogy of a Discourse on Male Sexualities* by Ed Cohen Review." *Victorian Studies* 38:1 (1994): 109-10.

Weeks, Jeffrey. *Sex, Politics and Society: The Regulation of Sexuality since* 1800. New York: Longman Group, 1981.

Werther, Ralph. *Autobiography of an Androgyne*, edited by Scott Herring. New Brunswick, NJ: Rutgers University Press, 2008.

Wexman, Virginia White. *Creating the Couple: Love, Marriage, and Hollywood Performance*. Princeton, NJ: Princeton University Press, 1993.

Whipple, Amy C. "Speaking for Whom? The 1971 Festival of Light and the Search for the 'Silent Majority.'" *Contemporary British History* 24:3 (2010): 319-39.

Whyman, Rose. *Stanislavski: The Basics*. London: Routledge, 2013.

Wilchins, Riki Anne. *Queer Theory, Gender Theory: An Instant Primer*. Los Angeles: Alyson Books, 2004.

———. *Read My Lips: Sexual Subversion and the End of Gender*. Ithaca, NY: Firebrand Books, 1997.

Willetts, Paul. *The Look of Love: The Life and Times of Paul Raymond, Soho's King of Clubs*. London: Serpent's Tail, 2013.

Wilson, James F. *Bulldaggers, Pansies, and Chocolate Babies: Performance, Race, and Sexuality in the Harlem Renaissance*. Ann Arbor: University of Michigan Press, 2011.

Wilson, Jason. *Soldiers of Song: The Dumbells and Other Canadian Concert Parties of the First World War*. Waterloo, Ontario: Wilfrid Laurier University Press, 2012.

Woodson, C. G. "The Negro Washerwoman, a Vanishing Figure." *Journal of Negro History* 15:3 (1930): 269-77.

Wright, Peter. "British Television Science Fiction." In *A Companion to Science Fiction*, edited by David Seed. Oxford: John Wiley & Sons, 2008.

Films, Television Programs, and Commercial Recordings

A Couple of Beauties (dir. Francis Searle, Bayford Films, 1972)
A Drop of the Hard Shuff . . . For Adults Only: Mrs. Shufflewick Live! At the New Black Cap (Decca, SKL 5155, 1973)

The Cult of . . . "Adam Adamant Lives!" (dir. Agnus McIntyre, BBC Four, 2006)

Danny La Rue at the Palace (dir. Steve Minchin, Thames Television, 1972)

Danny La Rue in London (DJM Silverline, DJSL 003, 1969)

Danny La Rue: Music Hall (Columbia, SCX 6428, 1970)

Danny La Rue: The Ladies I Love (dir. David Bell, London Weekend Television, 1974)

The Gender Bender (dir. Laurens C. Postma, YoYo Productions, 1992)

Goodbye Gemini (dir. Alan Gibson, Inc. Cinerama, 1970)

Kathleen Mavourneen (dir. Norman Lee, Argyle British Productions, 1937)

Mother Riley Meets the Vampire (dir. John Gilling, Renown Pictures Corporation, 1952)

Old Mother Riley's Budget/Old Mother Riley Takes Her Medicine (Columbia, FB 2702, 1941)

Old Mother Riley's Ghosts (dir. John Baxter, British National Films, 1941)

Old Mother Riley in Business (dir. John Baxter, British National Films, 1940)

Old Mother Riley, MP (dir. Oswald Mitchell, Butcher's Film Service, 1939)

Old Mother Riley's Past (Columbia, FB 2663, 1941)

On Your Way, Riley (dir. John Glenister, Yorkshire Television, 1985)

Our Miss Fred (dir. Bob Kellett, Willis World Wide Productions, 1972)

Skimpy in the Navy (dir. Stafford Dickens, Advance Films, 1949)

Splinters (dir. Jack Raymond, British and Dominions Films Corporation, 1930)

Splinters in the Air (dir. Alfred Goulding, Herbert Wilcox Productions, 1937)

Splinters in the Navy (dir. Walter Forde, Twickenham Film Studios Productions, 1932)

Stars on Parade (dir. Oswald Mitchell, Butcher's Film Service, 1936)

What's a Girl Like You . . . (dir. Charlie Squires, London Weekend Television [LWT], 1969)

Online Resources

BFI ScreenOnline (www.screenonline.org.uk/)

Black Jazz Artists (19–20th Century) (http://blackjazzartists.blogspot.com/)

British Newspaper Archive (www.britishnewspaperarchive.co.uk/)

British Pathé (www.britishpathe.com/)

Edith Jessie Thompson (https://edithjessiethompson.co.uk/)

ericlindsay: "From A to Zee" The Transition of an Actor to an International Stage Illusionist with Many Stops and Hiccups on the Way (https://ericlindsay.wordpress.com/)

Gale Primary Sources (www.gale.com/primary-sources)

The Gay Subculture in Georgian England, by Rictor Norton (https://
rictornorton.co.uk/subcult.htm)

History.com (www.history.com/)

Homosexuality in Nineteenth-Century England: A Sourcebook, ed. Rictor
Norton (https://rictornorton.co.uk/eighteen/nineteen.htm)

Oxford African American Studies Center (https://oxfordaasc.com/)

Oxford Dictionary of National Biography (www.oxforddnb.com/)

Oxford English Dictionary Online (www.oxforddnb.com/)

ProQuest Historical Newspapers (https://proquest.com/pq-hist-news/)

Rusholme & Victoria Park Archive (https://rusholmearchive.org)

Twitter (https://twitter.com)

Unpublished Source

Co-op, Lavinia, Crystal, and Stuart Feather. "Drag: Power & Politics," panel
discussion, Newington Green Meeting House, London, 25 October 2021.

Index

dame; drag revues; entertainment; parody; satire

Come Spy with Me (1966), 85, 94, 189n47

commercial recordings, 4, 32, 38, 49, 165n41, 169n73, 190n63

consumer culture, 86, 100

Cornock, Ann, 202n93

cosmopolitanism, 100

Cosmopolitan Merry-Go-Round (1939), 112–20

County Councils' Association, 118

Covent Garden Theatre, 162n12

Coward, Noël, 78

crime fiction, 71

Criminal Investigation Department, 80

cross-dressing: as antiestablishment practice, 7, 150n26; as daily routine of activists, 143; definition of, 5; legal and law enforcement responses to, 7–10, 79–80, 127, 150n27; in private as transvestism, 15. *See also* drag; female impersonators; transvestism

Daily Express, 73

Daily Film Renter, 50

Daily Mail, 50, 94–95

Daily Mirror, 185n6

Daily Telegraph, 67

Dallas, Johnny, 192n83

dame, 20–23, 32–58; definition of, 11; dress of the interwar and postwar, 167n62; modernization of the, 32–33, 51–58; origins of the, 20, 36–37, 57; in pantomime, 20, 21, 23, 34–47, 55–58, 161n2, 162n9, 163n21, 168n65; Victorian, 16–17, 20–22, 36–38, 47. *See also* comedy; pantomime

dandies, 8–9; as subjects of mockery, 8

Danny La Rue at the Palace (1970–72), 90–92, 93*fig.*, 97, 188n35

Davies, Ray, 166n49

Davis, Jim, 6

Dawkes, Sonny, 81*fig.*

DC Comics, 105

death penalty, 139

De Jongh, Nicholas, 78, 90

Demobbed (1944), 44

Dennis, Terry, 4

Department of Public Prosecutions (D.P.P.), 114, 123, 125–26, 130, 137–38

Derkas, 23

Deslandes, Paul, 180n78

De Vere, Gerald, 113–16, 196n26, 197n36

Dietrich, Marlene, 92, 159n105

D'Monté, Rebecca, 174n1, 177n27

Doan, Laura, 183n103

Donaldson-Hudson, Dorothy, 94

drag: active servicemen in, 80; avant-garde, 104; in beauty pageants, 90, 102, 192n86; concert party, 59–60, 62–63, 69–71, 84, 97, 174n2, 177n26; conservative, 84–105, 187n28; definition of, 4–5; demonstrations against, 30; emergence of the terminology of, 19–20; ex-servicemen in, 57–83, 120–30, 144–45, 177n27, 183n104, 198n48, 198n50, 202n101; female, 5–6, 14, 104, 153n49; and gay culture, 29, 58, 90, 102, 105, 142–45, 187n33, 198n50; glamour, 20–23, 102, 104, 162n19, 192n83; as globally interconnected, 21–23, 29, 37–38, 96, 102, 104, 192n89; legal and law enforcement responses to, 7, 108, 117–20, 122–23, 126–27, 130,

drag *(continued)*
    198n43, 201n82; meanings of, 4–6,
    30–31, 145–46; as progressive,
    liberal, or leftist art form, 7, 29, 89,
    142–43, 145, 187n27; as queer art
    form, 5, 145; radical, 142–43; and
    sexual immorality, 16, 47, 107–8,
    119, 139–41; as sexually charged
    experience, 16–19, 76; studies of,
    85–86, 89, 143–44, 150n21, 150n25,
    159n109, 186n26; as subcultural art
    form, 30, 144; transgender, 105,
    144. *See also* cross-dressing; drag
    balls; drag revues; female imper-
    sonators; homosexuality; subcul-
    ture; theater; transvestism
drag balls, 9, 29, 61, 79, 130, 152n40,
    182n98; depicted in theatrical
    performance, 130, 131*fig.*, 134–35,
    137–39; press coverage of, 79,
    182n98, 203n103. *See also* drag;
    homosexuality; subculture
drag revues: ex-servicemen's, 57–83,
    120–30, 144–45, 177n27, 183n104,
    198n48, 198n50, 202n101; as genre
    of revue, 59, 149n19. *See also*
    comedy; drag; entertainment;
    female impersonators; Les Rouges
    et Noirs; theater
Drag: Self-Portraits and Body Politics
    (2018), 29–30
Drag SOS (2019), 29
Dreams, Lydia, 185n6. *See also*
    Lambert, Walter Hibbert
Drury Lane Theatre, 11, 37–39, 162n12,
    163n21
Dumbells, The, 176n22
Dundee Evening Telegraph, 22

Eastern Daily Press, 22
Edinburgh Fringe, 57

Edward VII, King, 22
Edwardian era, 38, 99, 168n64
Electrophone, 38, 163n24
Ellis, Bill, 158n103
Ellis, Havelock: *Eonism*, 14
Ellisia, George, 122
Eltinge, Julian, 22, 27*fig.*
entertainment: commercialized
    sexual, 92; erotic, 115–16; escapist,
    191n75; light, 113, 184n118;
    racialized, 158n100; for service-
    men, 176n18; working-class, 50–54,
    167n62, 170n84. *See also* children;
    clubs; comedy; dame; drag revues;
    music halls; pantomime; theater
eonism, 14, 154n61. *See also* transves-
    tism
Errol, Bert, 22, 24*fig.*
Ervine, St. John Greer, 69
Evans, Norman, 44–45, 166n47
Evening Standard, 73
Everage, Dame Edna, 85
Everybody's Talking about Jamie
    (2017–present), 29
Everybody's Talking about Jamie (2021),
    29
extravaganza, 36, 157n91. *See also*
    theater

fashion magazines, 21, 48, 49*fig.*, 85
female impersonators, 5, 15–17, 22–23,
    30, 33, 84–109; and Carmen
    Miranda, 200n71; definitions and
    etymology of, 5, 148n5, 156n87;
    ex-servicemen as, 57–83, 111,
    120–30, 144–45, 177n27, 183n104,
    198n48, 198n50, 202n101; as
    "genuine" women, 22, 45, 114,
    148n2, 166n49; as homosexuals, 82,
    127, 141, 144–45; and male
    impersonators, 104; misogyny of,

143; negative views of, 77, 127–28, 142–43; nonwhite, 22, 25*fig.*, 158n99; partially undressed, 76, 113–16; "second-rate," 51; ventriloquism and, 185n6. *See also* beauty; cross-dressing; drag; drag revues; male impersonators

femininity: beauty that reflects, 21, 48, 74; congenial British, 65; fashions of, 48, 74; mature, 48; shattering of the vision of, 75–76, 95–96, 113–14, 121, 180n83, 196n26; of women, 22, 48, 73–74, 91; youthful, 48, 74. *See also* gender; women

feminist philosophy, 143

fetishism: 14–18, 76; and sadomaso-chism, 156n75; violent, 202n93

Fields, Gracie, 51–53

film, 23, 29, 32–33, 37–38, 44–58, 80, 84–85, 97, 102, 104, 143; "blue," 92; documentary, 102; Les Rouges et Noirs in, 65–71, 75–77, 177n26; Old Mother Riley in, 49–54, 56, 161n2, 165n40, 167n55, 169n72, 173n109; Roll of Honour in, 69; silent short, 38–39, 161n5

Financial Times, 95

Findlater, Richard, 41, 83

First World War, 59, 62–65, 68, 74, 115, 158n103, 180n77

Fisher, John, 34

Fletcher, Cyril, 111, 170n77

flip-books, 38

Fong, Regina, 105. *See also* Bundy, Reg

Foot, Dingle, 205n137

Forces in Petticoats (1952), 62, 80, 121

Forces Showboat (1947), 80, 120–23, 128–29, 185n6, 198n50

Ford, Vic, 198n46, 198n50

Formby, George, 51–52

Forsyte Saga, The (1967), 99–100, 190n65

Foucault, Michel, 13, 16; *The History of Sexuality*, 154n55

Freud, Sigmund, 14–15

Fuller, J. G., 63

Funeral, The; Or Grief A-La-Mode (1701), 36

Funeral Parade of Roses (1969), 104, 193n90

Galsworthy, John, 99

Game, H. C., 129, 202n96

Garber, Marjorie, 5; *Vested Interests: Cross-Dressing and Cultural Anxiety*, 6, 144

Gauze, Mystery, 22, 25*fig.*, 158n100

gay liberation movement, 142. *See also* homosexuality; British Gay Liberation Front (GLF)

Gay Young Bride, The (1923), 181n91

gender: commentary on, 4; expression of, 31; feminine presentation of, 8; regressive politics of, 55; and sexuality, 5, 7, 79; traditional conceptions of audiences regarding, 89, 148n2. *See also* cisgender; femininity; male gender variance; masculinity; women

George V, King, 42, 63, 164n39

Gibney, Jennifer, 58

"girlie" shows, 74. *See also* chorus line shows

"God Save the Queen" (song), 3–4

Going Gay (1952), 45, 172n100

Goodbye Gemini (1970), 102

Good Housekeeping, 48

Good Old Days, The (1953–83), 85, 97

gramophone records. *See* commercial recordings

Grand Order of Water Rats, 85

Greater London Council, 50
Grimaldi, Joseph, 41, 170n85
Gutheil, Emil, 15
Gwatkin, N. W., 117

Hair: The American Tribal Love-Rock Musical (1967), 140, 206n139
Halperin, David, 16
Hammond, Michael, 70
Hanson, Jack, 145, 187n32, 188n33, 207n16
harlequinade: protopantomime, 41, 157n91; Regency-period, 36. *See also* theater
Harmer, Juliet, 100
Harper, Gerald, 99
Harward, Timothy, 111
Haymarket Theatre, 162n12
Hefner, Hugh, 95
Heriot, C. D., 94, 135
heteronormativity, 7
heterosexuality, 6
Hill, Ronald John, 1–4, 7, 134–35, 137
Hindle, Annie, 6
Hinge and Bracket, 57
Hirschfeld, Magnus: *Transvestites: The Erotic Drive to Cross-Dress*, 14–15
history: of aesthetics of masculinity, 180n78; of culture and sexuality, 5, 84–105; of female drag, 6; of gender and sexuality, 6, 62, 160n115; queer, 5
Hives, Jack, 66, 178n35
Hollywood, 21; glamorous leading ladies of, 52–53, 92; La Rue's impersonations of stars of, 92, 93*fig.*
Home Office, 118, 139, 194n9
homosexuality: as bourgeois affectation, 135; conceptual birth of, 13, 154n55; drag claimed as art form for, 5, 29, 143–44; partial decrimi-

nalization of, 91, 139; prosecution by law enforcement for, 9, 10, 79, 82; subculture of, 2, 8, 19, 207n11; Viennese underworld of, 130, 132. *See also* drag; drag balls; gay liberation movement; homosexual law reform; sexuality; sodomy; subculture; theater; transvestism
homosexual law reform, 16, 82, 91, 101, 127, 132, 188n37. *See also* homosexuality
Hope, Bob, 104
Horne, General Sir Henry, 177n24
Hotels and Restaurants Association of Great Britain, 118
Howard, Sydney, 75, 177n26
Hoyle, David, 141
Hull Daily Mail, 121
Hylton, Jack: *Monday Show* (1957–58), 184n3

"I'll Marry Him" (popular song), 38
Impersonator, The (1961), 168n65
Instagram, 30

Jagger, Mick, 23, 91, 159n107
Jameson, Rex, 57–58. *See also* Shuff
John Bull, 61
Johnston, John, 112, 137
Jojo, Madame, 104, 193n91. *See also* Wright, John
Jones, Hal, 63, 66, 70, 122
Jorgenson, Christine, 15
Journey's End (1929), 68

Kama Sutra, 95
Kathleen Mavourneen (1937), 55
Kemp, Lindsay, 104
Kenny, Robert V., 161, 168n64
Keynes, John Maynard, 88
Kimber, Bobbie, 185n6

Kinematograph Weekly, 50
King, Thomas A., 151n30
Kinky Gerlinky, 104
Kinora viewers, 38
Kleinecke, Iris, 190n65
Krafft-Ebing, Richard von: *Psycho-pathia Sexualis*, 13

Labour Party, 88
Lady Chatterley's Lover (1928), 137
Lamarr, Hedy, 84
Lambert, Walter Hibbert, 185n6. *See also* Dreams, Lydia
Lancashire, 52
Landy, Marcia, 45
La Rue, Danny, 23, 82–105, 93*fig.*, 98*fig.*, 120, 145, 168n65, 186n23, 187n32, 199n52, 207n16; announce-ment of the retirement of, 190n59; awards of, 85; Catholicism of, 90, 145, 189n50; conservatism of, 87–89, 105, 185n10; death of, 90, 145; on doctrinaire conservatives, 188n38; first major television appearance of, 184n3; *From Drags to Riches*, 96; on gay culture, 90, 188n33; Jewish humor of, 189n50; "On Mother Kelly's Doorstep" (single), 85–86, 97, 105; value of the wardrobe of, 190n62
Le Carrousel, 104, 192n89
Leeds Mercury, 22
Lennon, John, 91, 101
Leno, Dan, 11, 34, 35*fig.*, 36–39, 40*fig.*, 41, 45–46, 163n21, 163n32
Les Rouges et Noirs, 59–80, 101, 120–22, 126, 175n4, 176n17; films that feature, 65–71, 75–77, 177n26; institutional support for, 177n24. *See also* drag revues
Lewis, Bunny, 192n83

Liberace, 188n33
Light, Alison, 71, 87
Lind, John, 22, 26*fig.*
Liverpool, 39
Lloyd, Eric, 126
Loesser, Frank, 80
London: Churchill's nightclub in, 84; Danny La Rue's nightclub in, 23, 85, 186n23, 187n33; moral degradation in interwar, 61; permissive cultural and political attitudes in, 86, 100–101; Ricky Renée's nightclub in, 102, 192n83; Soho scene of, 94, 117, 188n43; theatrical perform-ances in, 10–11, 32–34, 36–38, 41–51, 53–58, 83, 105–41, 162n12, 177n24, 177n27, 178n36, 181n91, 182n96, 184n116, 184n118, 198n43, 201n83; Winston's nightclub in, 84. *See also* clubs; West End
London County Council (L.C.C.), 118, 124–25
London Life, 16, 18, 76
London Mail, 77
London Opinion, 73, 75
London Palladium, 170n77
Lord Chamberlain's Office, 1–4, 61–62, 77–78, 94, 106–41, 147n1, 181n91, 182n96, 189n47, 194n4, 195n12, 201n83; annotations in blue pencil in use by the, 106, 193n2; conservative critics of the, 110–11, 129–30, 133, 202n98; extent of the authority of the, 162n12, 194n3; liberal critics of the, 110, 134; policies on nudity of the, 114–19, 196n31, 197n33; press critics of the, 134, 138–39. *See also* censorship
"Lovely to Look At" (song), 113–14, 196n24
Love on the Dole (1941), 53

Lucan, Arthur, 20, 32–38, 33*fig.*, 41–58, 49*fig.*, 101–2, 161n1, 166n48, 169n76, 172n100; as children's entertainer, 56–57, 173n109; death of, 32, 56–57, 160, 167n54, 172n98, 173n110; praise in the media for, 32–34, 37, 41, 45, 50, 53, 57, 164n39. *See also* Old Mother Riley

Lugosi, Bela, 50–51, 169n76

Lumley, Roger (Lord Scarbrough), 132–33, 139

macaronis, 8–9

Macmillan, Prime Minister Harold, 88

Maharishi Mahesh Yogi, 91

male gender variance: of audience members, 144; definition of, 5; displays of, 78, 120, 151n36; as male effeminacy, 8, 176n15; as media spectacle, 183n103; of "Nancies," 77, 181n88; of "painted boy menace," 61; of pansies, 16, 19; positive responses to interwar, 62, 176n15; professional-class homosexuality and, 201n90; and same-sex desire, 13–14, 16; and sexual immorality, 79. *See also* gender; masculinity

male impersonators, 5–6, 14, 104, 153n49; female impersonators and, 104. *See also* female impersonators

Manders, Billie, 22–23, 158n103

Mannie Jay, 120

Mary, Queen, 42, 63

masculinity: and female impersonators, 71, 75–76, 95–97; history of the aesthetics of, 180n78; and homosexuality, 14, 16, 143, 154n54; and nationhood, 72. *See also* gender; male gender variance

Mathews, Charles James: "The Maid of All Work," 49*fig.*

McNally, Edward, 82

McShane, Kitty, 32–34, 33*fig.*, 42, 46, 49, 54–58, 161n2, 167n55, 168n65; estrangement from Lucan of, 173n110; praise in the media for, 164n39; violent attacks on Lucan of, 172n100

Men's Dress Reform movement, 74, 180n76

Metropolitan Police, 117–18

Miranda, Carmen, 121, 124; send-ups of, 200n71

Miwa, Akihiro, 104

modernity, 36; conservative, 87–88

molly culture, 8–9, 151n30, 152n38, 181n88. *See also* subculture

Montagu-Scott, Edward (Lord Montagu), 82

Montagu trial (1953–54), 132

Morrison, Grant, 105

Mother Clap's molly house, 9, 151n36

Mother Goose (1903), 38–39, 40*fig.*

Mother Riley Meets the Vampire (1952), 50–51, 161n2, 169n76

Motion Picture Herald, 33

Mrs. Brown's Boys (2011–present), 58

music halls, 11, 57; dame element in, 23, 34; family-friendly depiction of the, 190n64; references to, 84, 97; performances in, 125, 127; short films in, 38. *See also* entertainment; theater; vaudeville

Mutoscopes, 38

nationalization: of British finance, 88; of British industry, 88

National Viewers' and Listeners' Association, 87

striptease: censorship of, 115–17, 125; as fan dancing sequences, 124; of male in drag, 113, 168n63; mock, 47. *See also* nudity

subculture: of gender-variant and same-sex desiring men, 207n11; homosexual, 2, 8, 19, 207n11; pansy, 19, 119. *See also* drag: as subcultural art form; drag balls; homosexuality; molly culture; *Paris Is Burning* (1990)

Summers, Claude J., 162n19

Sunday Dispatch, 158n103

Sunday Times, 138

Super Splinters (1927), 175n4

Surrey Theatre, 37

Sussex Daily News, 67

Sutton, David, 52

Swann, William Dorsey, 152n40

Sydney Myers, 120

Teal, Sonne, 192n83, 192n89

television, 29, 82, 84; British ownership of a, 184n3; drag acts on British, 185n6; edifying content of the BBC in the 1960s for, 191n75; light entertainment programs on, 85, 184n118

theater: censorship of homosexual themes in the, 121–22, 132–39; dame element in, 20, 34, 36–54, 173n106; definition of drag in, 19; drag performance in, 3, 7, 10–11, 13–14, 20–22, 32–34, 105, 113–30, 134, 140–41; Elizabethan, 20; Jacobean, 20; male impersonation in the, 14; portrayal of homosexuality in the, 132–39; as postwar industry, 106–7; realist, 105; regulation of nude performance in the public, 112–19; representations of female same-sex desire onstage in

the, 203n108; "stage Irishman" in, 55–56; staging of unlicensed plays in private, 112, 137, 194n10, 195n22; variety, 57, 82–83, 97, 100, 184n116, 184n118. *See also* burlesque; censorship; clubs; drag; drag revues; entertainment; extravaganza; harlequinade; homosexuality; music halls; pantomime

Theatre Notebook (journal), 111

Theatres Act (1843), 36, 106, 109–10, 162n12

Theatres Act (1968), 107, 113, 119, 123, 125, 139–40, 205n137

This Is the Army (1942), 80

This Was the Army (1946), 80, 81*fig.*, 121

Thompson, Edith, 77

TikTok, 30

Tilley, Vesta, 6

Times, 19, 41, 67, 95, 102, 177n24, 204n123

Times Educational Supplement, 139

Titman, George, 113–14, 196n25, 197n36

Tobin, Robert Deam, 154n55

Tory Party, 88

Towle, Donald, 161n2

Towle, Lucy Ann, 46

tranimals, 31

transgender people, 15, 90, 105

transvestism, 13–15, 18, 90, 95–96, 102, 105, 134, 138, 156n75, 202n93; definition of, 5; female, 13; as fetish, 14–15, 18, 96, 156n75, 202n93; and homosexuality, 14–15, 139; as obsessive-compulsive disorder, 15; scientific study of, 13–15; sensationalization of, 15, 193n90. *See also* cross-dressing; drag; eonism; homosexuality

Tribune, 138

Troubridge, Lieutenant-Colonel Sir Thomas St Vincent Wallace, 111
Trumbach, Randolph, 152n38
Tucker, Sophie, 121
Twentieth Century Theatre, 1–3

Ulrichs, Karl Heinrich, 13, 154n54
Underwood, Peter, 96, 190n57
United States: legal prohibitions of cross-dressing in the, 150n27; nineteenth-century drag balls in the, 152n40; theatrical heritage of the, 37. *See also* New York City
Usher, Archie, 124

vagrancy, 10
Variety Club of Great Britain, 85
vaudeville, 57. *See also* music halls
Venezuela, Ruby, 104
Victoria, Queen, 38
Victorian era, 6–7, 11, 38; ethos of the, 87; valorization of the, 99
Victoria Theatre, 56
violence: masochistic, 202n93; slapstick comedy involves injury and, 39, 167n56
Vogue (American), 85
Vogue (British), 48, 49*fig.*

W.A.A.C. (Women's Army Auxiliary Corps), 66
War Office, 72
Wednesday Play, The (1964–70), 100
We're No Ladies (1958), 1–4, 19, 149n19, 182n96
Werther, Ralph, 153n52
West, Con, 165n40, 166n48
West, Mae, 92
West End, 50, 84–86; evening shows of the, 186n23; provincial audiences

in the, 170n77; stage shows of the, 85. *See also* London
Western Mail (Cardiff), 138
Western Morning News, 121
Westminster Central Hall, 142
Westphal, Carl Friedrich Otto, 13
We Were in the Forces (1944), 80, 122
Which Is Which (1933), 175n4. *See also* Splinters 1914–1933 (1933)
White Cargo (1942), 84
Whitehouse, Mary, 87, 188n38
Wild, Sir Ernest, 79, 183n100
Wildeblood, Peter, 82, 127, 201n90; *Against the Law*, 16, 132
Williams, Tennessee, 104
Windmill Theatre, 58, 117, 124, 197n40
Windsor Castle, 60, 177n24
Woman's Weekly, 48
women: chaperones for single, 57; continental European, 65; fashionable older, 48; freedom and aesthetic individualism for, 74; passing as men, 176n15; regressive representation of, 54; standards of beauty of, 48, 74; trans, 144; working class, 55. *See also* femininity; gender
Wood, Jay Hickory, 39
Wood Green Empire, 129
working classes, 20–21, 34, 36, 39; audiences of the, 50–54; entertainment of the, 51; gender nonconforming people of the, 29; tastes of the, 56
Wright, John, 193n91. *See also* Jojo, Madame
Wright, Peter, 191n71

Yokel's Preceptor (ca. 1855), 8

Berkeley Series in British Studies

EDITED BY JAMES VERNON

Founded in 1893,
UNIVERSITY OF CALIFORNIA PRESS
publishes bold, progressive books and journals
on topics in the arts, humanities, social sciences,
and natural sciences—with a focus on social
justice issues—that inspire thought and action
among readers worldwide.

The UC PRESS FOUNDATION
raises funds to uphold the press's vital role
as an independent, nonprofit publisher, and
receives philanthropic support from a wide
range of individuals and institutions—and from
committed readers like you. To learn more, visit
ucpress.edu/supportus.